*Living Faithfully
in an Unjust World*

The publisher gratefully acknowledges the generous support of the Ahmanson Foundation Humanities Endowment Fund of the University of California Press Foundation.

Living Faithfully
in an Unjust World

COMPASSIONATE CARE IN RUSSIA

Melissa L. Caldwell

UNIVERSITY OF CALIFORNIA PRESS

University of California Press, one of the most distinguished university presses in the United States, enriches lives around the world by advancing scholarship in the humanities, social sciences, and natural sciences. Its activities are supported by the UC Press Foundation and by philanthropic contributions from individuals and institutions. For more information, visit www.ucpress.edu.

University of California Press
Oakland, California

Cataloguing-in-Publication Data is on file at the Library of Congress

ISBN (cloth): 978-0-520-28583-5
ISBN (paper): 978-0-520-28584-2
ISBN (epub): 978-0-520-96121-0

25   24   23   22   21   20   19   18   17
10   9   8   7   6   5   4   3   2   1

For Mikaela,
whose empathy knows no bounds

Contents

Illustrations

Preface

To most outside observers, today's Russia would probably not appear to be the likeliest candidate as a country where kindness, compassion, and even social justice are promoted as important cultural values. Over the past decade, Russia has consistently been described as one of the most dangerous places in the world for journalists and human rights activists, with numerous murders and attacks. The high-profile killings of journalist Anna Politkovskaya in 2006 and, in early 2015, of former prime minister Boris Nemtsov, and the death threats made against ordinary citizens, including members of the community described in this book, are just a few of many instances of violence against individuals who have attempted to make the world around them a better place.

Less visible, however, are acts of care and concern that happen in daily life, both spontaneously and formally through organized projects. Over many years of doing research in Moscow, I have seen belligerent, intoxicated young men gently and tenderly purchase food for the frail, elderly woman who tentatively approached them with a request for help, and have heard stories about heroic public servants such as a trolley bus driver who stopped while on a busy route and forced angry passengers to the curb to wait for another bus so that he could drive a Sudanese woman who had been robbed and beaten to a police station where she could file a police report and get medical assistance. I have seen elderly pensioners who are dependent on food from a soup kitchen share their meager rations with the stray cats that live around their apartments. And I have sat with friends active in human rights work who have received death threats by SMS and then listened to them vow that they were not afraid and would continue to speak out against injustices. Although these small acts of kindness and care do not usually make it into public accountings of daily life in Russia, they are nonetheless everywhere, if one only pays attention. When I have asked people about these acts of kindness and care and why they do them, my interlocutors have most typically shrugged them away as too ordinary and inconsequential to note. Such acts are, in other words, simply the normal things—the right things—one does if one is a true human being.

Over the past twenty years of doing fieldwork in Russia, and also at home in the United States, I have been fascinated by the many, many acts and professions of kindness that I have encountered, and I have been intrigued by how and why people engage in acts of care and attempt to respond to the injustices they see around them. Every day on my campus and in my classes, I see this commitment to doing good and social action among my students, who are passionately firm in their convictions that they can make a difference for others. And more personally, by virtue of adopting our beloved dog through a rescue group, I have watched as a spirit of care for animals has turned one small group of volunteers into a community of approximately five thousand kindred spirits of foster families, transporters, adopters, donors, and supporters who are dedicated to rescuing abandoned, abused, and homeless animals—more than six hundred dogs per year by this one rescue group alone.

Clearly, caring matters. And at the same time, caring is clearly a profoundly social experience. Experiences such as these lie behind my motivation to pursue this project and to think deeply about how and why caring can be a force for good in the world.

Because this is a book about care, it is also the product of many acts of care from many different people at many different stages. I am deeply humbled by the many people who shared their lives and work with me, in some cases at potential personal risk, and often in conversations that revealed that we saw the world in very different ways but nonetheless shared a belief in a universal human experience. Unfortunately, because of the size of this project over the years and because of safety concerns, especially for those who work on the front lines of critical human rights issues, I cannot identify and thank publicly every person and organization that provided assistance along the way. I hope that you recognize yourselves in this book and know how very grateful I am and how much I respect the work that you do.

Fortunately there are others I can thank publicly for their support, insights, and access to organizations and communities. Although they may not remember, Twila Schock and Bill Swanson started me on this research journey many years ago, first in Russia and then later in Germany, where I recall a particularly delightful meeting over coffee and a delicious hot *pflaumküchen*. More recently, Bob Bronkema has been an endless source of information, contacts, and critical insights. Despite some "philosophical differences" over our favorite sports teams (Go Vols, Bob!), I have greatly enjoyed the friendship that has emerged from our professional interactions. Sharon Cohen, who has been one of my dearest friends since a fateful high school summer program, has always been a voice of reason and example of the caring work of faith in action in a pluralist world. Sydney Ocran, Daniel Ekat, and Kifle Solomon graciously and generously answered numerous questions and gave me access to many different constituencies, often while engaged in numerous other tasks of coordinating volunteers and distributing aid. Lydia Troncale Bowen, Laura Stagl Clinton, and Alexandra Tyson-Beer were delightfully fun comrades-in-arms who incorporated me into their work and social networks and provided access to many organizations and communities that I would not otherwise have been able to enter. Claire and Mike Muraoka generously hosted me on several short visits to Russia. Sofia Alekseevna Komarova, Mark Teeter, Valentina Uspenskaia, and Dima Borodin continually introduced me to unexpected situations and challenged me to rethink my ideas and conclusions. Anna Borodina has been the dearest of friends and colleagues. Not only did she introduce me to helpful colleagues, but she also introduced me to her parents and her aunt, who have become my surrogate family in Russia. I can never repay the enormous debts of hospitality I owe them all.

Numerous colleagues have provided feedback on pieces of this work. Preliminary research was presented at two workshops at the Kennan

Institute for Russian Studies at the Woodrow Wilson Center in Washington, DC. I am grateful to Cathy Wanner, Mark Steinberg, Ruth Mandel, Blair Wilson, Maggie Paxson, William Pomerantz, and Renata Kosc-Harmatiy for organizing those workshops and the delightfully collegial and intellectual conversations that took place. At different moments, Ruth, Mark, and Cathy have assisted me in plowing through difficult sections of this work and share the credit for helping it see the light of day. Thank you to my fellow participants in those workshops for their ideas and provocations, especially Sascha Goluboff, Julie Hemment, Scott Kenworthy, Zoe Knox, Katherine Metzo, and Doug Rogers. Noor Borbieva provided terrific feedback on a preliminary version of what is now chapter 3. Jarrett Zigon deserves special recognition for trading ideas and chapters, both at the Kennan Institute and at the Max Planck Institute for Social Anthropology.

In addition to Moscow, I have had two "homes away from home" while I have worked on this project. Chris Hann first invited me to the Max Planck Institute for Social Anthropology in 2005, and then repeatedly rolled out the welcome mat for me so that I could research, write, and present work-in-progress among smart colleagues. The librarians at the MPI are the best I have ever met, and their collections are unparalleled. At the MPI, I was fortunate to work through materials in this book with Agata Ładykowska, Deema Kaneff, Frances Pine, Friederike Fleischer, Tobias Köllner, Tünde Komáromi, Markus Schlecker, and Detelina Tocheva.

In 2015, I was blessed beyond belief to spend my sabbatical in the anthropology department at the University of Manchester, where I had the incredible good fortune to be surrounded by smart, thoughtful, and delightfully provocative colleagues. They welcomed me in as one of their own and helped me work through many of the ideas contained here as I completed the first full draft of this book. A huge thank you to all of the faculty and students in the department, but especially to Jeanette Edwards, Penny Harvey, Madeleine Reeves, Karen Sykes, and Tony Simpson. I am particularly grateful to Gillian Evans, Katy Smith, and Chika Watanabe, who were incredibly generous with their time, suggestions, and friendship, and to Olga Ulturgasheva and her husband, who combined terrific collegiality with the best Siberian dumplings I have ever eaten. Above all, Maia Green deserves special recognition as the person who made it all happen and made me feel like I was at home, whether in her office or in her dining room. I can never say thank you enough to Maia and Thea for their warm welcome. Elsewhere in Manchester, I am grateful to my husband's colleagues who helped us make this a family sabbatical and to the extraordinary staff at Monkey Puzzle who helped our daughter fit in as a local.

At UC Santa Cruz, I have been lucky to have brilliant and caring colleagues who have patiently listened to and read my messy first drafts and shared their own work with me. Among many people, I would like to single out Don Brenneis, Jim Clifford, Julie Guthman, Donna Haraway, Susan Harding, Dan Linger, Mark Massoud, Carolyn Martin-Shaw, Megan Moodie, Lisa Rofel, Danilyn Rutherford, Anna Tsing, and Mike Urban for their contributions. Judith Habicht-Mauche and Chris Mauche have been the perfect combination of colleagues, neighbors, and toddler wranglers. The graduate and undergraduate students in my classes encouraged me to pursue these ideas, partly through their questions and partly through the models of social action that they practice every day. Lastly, I can easily claim to have won the graduate student jackpot with my advisees. Through their own work, their questions, and their encouragement, they have challenged me to improve my thoughts and introduced me to literatures and ideas I would not have otherwise encountered. Thank you to Sarah Bakker Kellogg, Sarah Chee, Rebecca Feinberg, Stephanie McCallum, Katy Overstreet, Carla Takaki Richardson, and Samantha Turner. Sarah Bakker Kellogg and Carla Takaki Richardson served as research assistants at different stages of the research, and Carla, Rebecca, and Stephanie have held down the fort at *Gastronomica* over the past several years.

Other people who have contributed at different stages include Vincanne Adams, Erica Bornstein, Robin Bush, Manduhai Buyandelger, Michael Feener, Philip Fountain, Patty Gray, Tracey Heatherington, Michael Herzfeld, Yuson Jung, Jakob Klein, Liisa Malkki, Rubie Watson, and Woody Watson. Elizabeth Dunn, Heath Cabot, and Cathy Wanner read complete drafts of this manuscript and offered substantial comments that have greatly improved it. I am especially indebted to Heath for her friendship and critical acumen that have helped shape this project in many, many ways over the years, but also most importantly at the final stages when I needed just the right nudge and insights.

At the University of California Press I have once again been the fortunate recipient of the best editorial support possible. A big thank you to

Reed Malcolm for his unflagging patience and support and to Stacy Eisenstark, Zuha Khan, and Dore Brown for their work to get this book into and through the production process. Many, many thanks to Paul Tyler, copy editor extraordinaire, who generously helped me make this book better on top of his work for *Gastronomica*.

Funding for the various phases of this project was provided by numerous organizations. Earlier stages were supported by the US Department of Education (Title VI); the Mellon Foundation; and the Kathryn W. and Shelby Cullom Davis Center for Eurasian Studies, the Department of Anthropology, and the Committee on Degrees in Social Studies at Harvard University. Later stages were supported by the Division of Social Sciences and the Committee on Research at the University of California, Santa Cruz, the National Council for Eurasian and East European Research, and the International Research and Exchanges Board (IREX). The University of Manchester supported the writing phase of a full draft of the manuscript with a Simon Visiting Professor Fellowship. An earlier version of chapter 4 appeared as "Placing Faith in Development: How Moscow's Religious Communities Contribute to a More Civil Society" in *Slavic Review* 71, no. 2 (2012): 261–87, published by the Association for Slavic, East European, and Eurasian Studies, and is reprinted in the book with the permission of the publisher. Additionally, parts of chapter 2 appeared in "The Politics of Rightness: Social Justice among Russia's Christian Communities," *Problems of Post-Communism* 56, no. 4 (2009): 29–40. All translations in the book are mine, and I am responsible for any errors.

Lastly, with a project like this, I am grateful for the care and suggestions of many friends and relatives, beginning with my compatriots in American Black and Tan Coonhound Rescue, who not only brought us our perfectly imperfect dog, but also introduced us to the amazing work done by thousands of animal rescue volunteers every day. An extra special thank you to Tine and John Kellogg for what has turned into a very close friendship. Thank you to my favorite in-laws Pat and Cliff Baker, and to Kathy and Ray Gaynor, Kristin, Joe, and Arwen Peto, Fran Teeter, Kara and Ben Tierney-Trevor, Danny Thomas, Stephanie Thomas, Jan and Bob Trevor, Leorah Zangwill, and Stacy Margolin and Howard Zangwill. My parents Bill and Sandy Caldwell have always encouraged my interests and curiosities, pushing me forward and occasionally sideways in new directions.

Otis and Helix, possessors of the softest ears and tummies in the animal kingdom, have provided much-needed comic relief.

As always, my husband, Andy Baker, has been my life support in this research, especially as the two decades of this research have coincided with the length of our marriage. From "holding down the fort" while I have been away for research and writing to negotiating with his company to secure a secondment to England so that I could spend my sabbatical hiding and writing at the University of Manchester, he provided the comforting "home" that made this project possible. By reading many, many chapters and discussing ideas with me, he has helped me flesh out and complicate this work. He is as much a part of this project as I am, and I am grateful in more ways than I can express. Finally, although our daughter, Mikaela, came into this project in the last stages, she is a vivid reminder of why the efforts of people to care matter in the world. Mikaela's arrival in our family was an act of true faith and love, and it is with profound joy that I watch as she lives out the potentialities that faith brings. This book is for her.

Note on Transliteration

I have followed the U.S. Library of Congress system of transliteration in this book, except in cases where spellings for certain proper names and other words have become more familiar to North American readers (for instance, Valya instead of Valia).

1 Compassion

"Compassion" is dedicated to humane relationships with homeless animals.

This simple inscription graces the elegant bronze sculpture of a dog, foot raised in the air to scratch his neck, that rests in the entrance to Moscow's Mendeleevskaia metro station. The dog commemorated in the sculpture was a stray, or more specifically, one of Moscow's metro dogs, a uniquely Russian breed of canine that travels the city on public transportation, often snoozing undisturbed on subway and bus seats, and surviving on the food and makeshift shelters left by fellow commuters and station workers.[1] He had lived in the passageway leading to the metro and was a familiar presence to countless commuters, many of whom provided him with food, bedding, and affection. In 2007, the dog was brutally killed, allegedly by hooligans.[2] In anguish over the senseless killing, local residents pooled their funds to commission the sculpture and then lobbied authorities to allow it to be placed in the metro station.

Much like what is done at other grave sites and public monuments throughout Russia, Moscow's commuters adorn the bronze dog with lit candles, store-bought bouquets of flowers wrapped in plastic, and hand-cut flowers placed in water in mayonnaise jars–turned-vases. In a city of

Figure 1. Titled "Compassion" and dedicated to a stray dog that lived in Moscow's Mendeleevskaia metro station, this sculpture promotes compassion for all homeless animals. Copyright Melissa L. Caldwell.

fifteen million people, where residents often complain about the rudeness and selfishness of their fellow citizens and worry about how easily one could be swallowed up in the anonymity of such a sprawling megacity, the highly personalized and deeply intimate touches bestowed on a sculpture commemorating a stray dog are moving.

The community efforts to erect this memorial came at a particular moment when people across Russia were actively and publicly discussing their relationships and responsibilities to one another, their communities, the nation, and the state. Central to these discussions have been concerns with addressing injustices and ensuring that care, kindness, and generosity remain at the forefront of daily life despite the increasing neoliberalization of society and the state's deliberate divestment from social welfare following the dissolution of the Soviet Union in 1991. Over the past twenty years that I have been conducting fieldwork in Russia, primarily in

Moscow and the Moscow region, a seeming constant has been the frequency with which friends, acquaintances, colleagues, and strangers alike have complained about the consequences of Russia's economic and political transformation. While enjoying the benefits of neoliberal capitalism in terms of improved consumer experiences at home and in public, the freedom to travel, and greater independence in their daily lives, Russians have also been critical of what they perceive as growing social problems caused by the values and practices that constitute their new political economy. Citing such diverse issues as socioeconomic stratification, joblessness, homelessness, poverty, criminality, abandonment of children and the elderly, prostitution, drug use and alcoholism, the desecration and destruction of parks, forests, and other environmentally fragile sites, worsening traffic congestion and emissions-caused pollution, and political and economic corruption, among many others, concerned Russians articulate broader anxieties about social instability and moral decline.

Offering striking evidence of the prevalence of these worries, my field notes from the 1990s and early 2000s are filled with stories from friends and acquaintances who were frustrated by what seemed to them to be a dramatic rupture of the social compact that they believed had previously knitted their society together. Russian friends in Moscow and elsewhere drew my attention to everyday sights of elderly pensioners and small children standing along city sidewalks, tearfully begging for a few coins to buy a loaf of bread, and to severely disabled veterans struggling to navigate steep metro steps on makeshift scooters that carried their legless and armless bodies. One friend, a doctor who worked closely with victims of domestic abuse, confided that she was deeply troubled by what seemed to her to be skyrocketing rates of homelessness and the medical and hygiene problems caused by life on the streets.

Alongside such concerns over socioeconomic disparities were complaints about disruptions of general civility in public and private spaces. Moscow's mounting traffic problems were a favorite topic, especially the prevalence of rude and dangerous drivers, as well as the publicly visible displays of alcoholism that accompanied the growing occupation of public spaces by young people at night and on weekends. Other acquaintances noted the apparent escalation of physical violence, especially acts of domestic violence between family members, including between parents and children. One friend, an English-language teacher whose clients included professionals from Moscow's leading businesses, was proud when her own professional successes were marked by her ability to become a home owner. Yet her initial excitement over her newly purchased apartment was quickly replaced by despair when she was forced to endure the constant fighting and screaming that emanated from the apartment next door. Still others complained about the graffiti, rubbish, and human excrement that littered both public walkways and vestibules of private buildings. Elderly friends specifically mentioned the fading away of public norms such as giving up one's seat on the metro for elderly, disabled, or pregnant passengers.

Within this context of mounting frustration and even resentment about social problems, the senseless killing of one of Moscow's metro dogs crystallized in a very public and visceral way the more widespread feelings of sadness and anger over the seeming disappearance of basic human decency and a loss of community cohesion. By investing considerable effort into mobilizing their neighborhood and working through Moscow's bureaucracy, local residents directly challenged hate and violence and sent a forceful message that shared values and practices of care and kindness remained at the core of daily Russian life. In this way, a simple statue of a stray dog turned the intimacies of compassion into a publicly performed act of civic responsibility.

For me, the installation of the Compassion statue beautifully exemplified the private and public acts of care and kindness that I have witnessed over my many years of doing research in Russia. I have witnessed countless people dig into their tote bags and pass on their own lunches to beggars and watched as elderly pensioners who depend on a food aid program dish some of their small daily portion of kasha onto paper plates for the stray cats that share their neighborhood. In the dead of winter, neighbors have propped open the doors to apartment building vestibules so that homeless people and animals might have a place to keep dry and warm. I have met and accompanied high school and university students who spend their evenings walking city streets to deliver sandwiches to homeless persons with whom they have developed deep and genuinely affectionate relationships. Middle-aged workers with tight paychecks and even tighter schedules conscientiously checked on their elderly and disabled neighbors by "dropping by" with the "too much" produce that they "accidentally" purchased at the market. Attorneys, social workers, and clergy whom I knew dismissed the hate mail and death threats they received in order to continue serving and publicly advocating for Russia's most disenfranchised populations: the homeless, ethnic and racial minorities, and undocumented migrants. Through such acts, ordinary citizens and public servants alike link personal acts of genuine kindness with larger political and ethical issues and values. They are not simply caring for others, but caring for others in ways that have the potential to intervene in some of the most pressing civic issues in today's Russia: poverty, crime, immigration, and intolerance.

The ordinariness with which people engage in such activities invites intriguing questions not just about why care, kindness, and compassion matter in today's Russia, but also about the kinds of social and political work that care does. How and why do people engage with social problems and injustices? What does it mean to care for or to love another person, especially a complete stranger? How do acts of care shift between spontaneous acts to deliberate and organized forms of societal or even political improvement? What constitutes "doing good" in a world in which there are many problems and few easy answers? How might instances of "doing good"—helping, caring for, and loving another person—be a necessary part of being an active citizen in the world? And are these forms of civic engagement modes of resisting Russia's newly neoliberal world, or are they modes of supporting, nurturing, and even reinventing this new society? Or are they both simultaneously?

In Moscow, concerns with addressing injustices and righting wrongs have been front and center for the communities and individuals that I have been following for the past two decades. From spontaneous, individual acts of kindness and compassion performed by individuals or small groups of persons to organized projects funded by national and international organizations and administered through formal groups, Russians like my friends and acquaintances have worked hard to channel their personal inclinations to help others into practical action. Clearly, these activities matter to people. Yet intriguingly, when queried about their personal motivations for helping and why these activities matter, respondents have brushed off their actions as simply things one does because they are the right things to do. Above all, despite the seemingly never-ending injustices and constantly worsening problems they describe around them, friends have articulated a compelling sense of optimism and hope that their efforts, no matter how small and inconsequential, will contribute to something larger that might in turn bring about significant changes in the world around them.

These are the issues and puzzles that animate this book.

At the center of this book is a Moscow-based assistance community that has emerged and coalesced over the past twenty years into a thriving network of charitable service providers with extensive reach across Moscow and Russia more generally. Caring for a broad and diverse range of Russia's population, both in Moscow and beyond, these charitable groups offer and support a broad array of programs that range from basic health services to public lobbying of Russian and international governments on urgent human rights matters. Positioning themselves as caretakers of their fellow human beings, as well as of the greater world around them, members of this community actively promote human decency and kindness in order to "do the right thing" and make the world a better place.

As the experiences and perspectives of the assistance workers, government officials, recipients, and supporters documented here reveal, their work and beliefs are shaped by a practical philosophy of goodness and kindness. In the face of the hardships, injustices, and despair these individuals witness on a regular basis, and confronted by problems they are too often helpless to prevent or alleviate, they nonetheless hold to an optimism that human kindness will ultimately prevail over poverty, injury, and injustice. Ultimately, what connects members of this diverse group of individuals and organizations is a shared concern that caring for others is not simply a practical matter or an idealistic, even utopian vision, but rather a project of faith and hope.

It is not insignificant that the individuals and organizations that comprise this network and subscribe to these views are enmeshed in what might conventionally be called "faith-based communities." At the heart of these communities is a core group of religiously affiliated organizations: Christian churches (Russian Orthodox, Catholic, Anglican, and Protestant), denominationally affiliated national and international development organizations (e.g., Caritas, Catholic Charities, Lutheran World Relief, the development department of the Russian Orthodox Church, among others), and small charities supported with funding and materials from religious communities. These organizations are linked into a broader network of development and humanitarian organizations with religious backgrounds (e.g., Habitat for Humanity, Human Rights Watch, Oxfam, and the Aga Khan Foundation), national and international development and humanitarian organizations (Russian state agencies and funding bodies, USAID, International Organization for Migration, United Nations High Commissioner for Refugees, the Russian Red Cross, and the International Red Cross), and numerous governmental social welfare agencies and secular nongovernmental social services organizations.

Yet as will become clear, the moniker of "faith-based community" obscures more than it reveals, as these individuals and communities defy easy classification and their practices of faith are oriented to a civic-minded social action that is explicitly pluralistic, and even resolutely secular in many instances. Although "faith-based" is a standard term in scholarly accounts describing such diverse organizations elsewhere in the world (e.g., Adams 2013; Dionne Jr. and Chen 2001; Elisha 2008), and was considered a reasonable generic gloss by the many different people I encountered in Moscow assistance organizations that were both religious and nonreligious, this term risks provoking assumptions that these organizations were explicitly and primarily focused on conversion, embedding religious doctrines and traditions into an ostensibly secular political and economic system, or even interpolating citizens and their lives into a religiously oriented political and economic framework (cf. Adams 2013; Elisha 2008: 211–12; Engelke 2007; Rudnyckyj 2010; Wanner 2007; Wanner and Steinberg 2008).

Within the network of assistance providers documented here, even as faith and hope are guiding ethics, religiosity and spirituality are often less important than a clear sense of a civic commitment to social justice. At the same time that the practical philosophies of goodness and kindness guiding people's activities may be grounded in and realized through religious communities and their particular denominational histories and doctrines, they are not uniquely religious per se. These were not conservative, evangelical Christians, but liberal, progressive Christian communities that positioned themselves outside proselytization efforts (cf. Elisha 2011; Engelke 2007; Wanner 2007). Church attendance, belief in or adherence to religious precepts, knowledge of church histories, and even self-identification as a believer were largely superseded by shared commitments to what many described as more fundamental and universal humanist qualities of human kindness and love. In fact, many people I interviewed and followed denied having any particular religious identity or affiliation or even any interest in religion beyond curiosity or a desire for feeling part of a community.[3] By contrast, what most of my interlocutors found compelling about religiously affiliated communities was the extent to which they provided logistical and ethical frameworks for modes of social action that were deeply enmeshed in secular, civic, and even state affairs.

Ultimately, in very tangible ways, this is a community in which faith matters, but where everyone wrestles with what "faith" means and how it can be mobilized into compassionate action that benefits the greater social good, whether for the nation, the state, or a larger human community. In so doing, these individuals and organizations collectively challenge what is understood by "faith" and its effects. Consequently, one of the explicit goals of this book is to unsettle expectations of what "faith-based" means by examining critically what faith is and what it does.

By documenting the efforts of these individuals and the organizations with which they are affiliated as they strive to serve and help others in Moscow, this book takes up the question of what constitutes faith-based compassion in Russian life today. Specifically, I am concerned with what it means to live faithfully when striving to correct injustices. A key piece to this discussion is a consideration of the issue of faith as a spiritual, philosophical, economic, and even civic quality that makes compassion possible and actionable. As such, this is not so much a book about religion, religious charities, or religious perspectives on poverty, injustice, or suffering more generally, as it is an ethnographic account of how members of this particular assistance community in Moscow have mobilized faith-driven ideals about compassion, service, and social action to create an alternative system of social welfare and social justice that is contributing meaningfully to Russian society.

PERFORMING CARE BETWEEN THE CIVIL AND THE CIVIC

In her ethnography of the Italian state's neoliberal projects to outsource and privatize the responsibility for providing care by conscripting the voluntary labor of ordinary citizens, Andrea Muehlebach (2012) has argued that these moves have reconfigured not just the organization of civic life, most notably divisions between public and private spheres, but also the nature of the citizen in this new world. Identifying this new citizen as a "moral neoliberal" who is motivated by affect to do the work of supporting and improving society, Muehlebach (2012: 11) asks, "what are we to make of the public production of citizens as heartfelt subjects?" This question is critically pertinent to the issues animating the cultures of compassion at play in Moscow and in Russia more generally. The events and issues that I discuss here come at a particular historical moment in Russia, as the state, its citizens, and other residents debate fundamental questions about their relationships to one another and specifically whether service to others is a civic responsibility (Malkki 2015; Muehlebach 2012).

Prior to the creation of the Soviet Union, acts of benevolence and compassion were carried out primarily through and by religious institutions. During the Soviet era of the twentieth century, benevolence and compassion lost their official connection to religious traditions and were transformed into state-sponsored activities rather than privately held ethics and activities. As such, the state recalibrated need into entitlements and charity into a social welfare system of rights and protections guaranteed to all citizens.[4] To provide labor for this collective social welfare system, the state encouraged—and even coerced—citizens into practicing compassion as part of a form of moral citizenship. Schools, workplaces, and neighborhood associations organized compulsory voluntary activities that mobilized citizens to provide caretaking for others: children, the disabled, the elderly, and other less fortunate individuals, as well as the environment, the state, and a more abstract notion of society.

Such official and mandatory forms of compassion often backfired, as citizens may have grudgingly participated in voluntary activities while distancing themselves from any sense of compassion or empathy for the beneficiaries of their actions. Instead, it was private and individual acts of mutual support and caretaking among family members, friends, and neighbors that were more often associated with feelings such as empathy or even friendship (Caldwell 2004). Consequently, caring activities were often bifurcated between what Jodi Halpern (2001) has described as empathic encounters—those in which care providers and recipients are emotionally connected—and encounters marked by "detached concern." As for the case of Russia, acquaintances have suggested that emotional disconnection between care providers and beneficiaries was characterized not simply by disinterest but by apathy or even active hostility (Caldwell 2007). Toward the end of the Soviet period, during a period of ongoing political, social, and environmental crises (including the Chernobyl disaster), community ethics of compassion shifted as grassroots citizens' groups began challenging not just the state's monopoly on controlling and directing compassionate activity, but more importantly its ability to provide adequate social services, by setting up independent charities.

These grassroots efforts by private citizens have been the backbone of charitable and philanthropic activity in Russia since the early 1990s, following the dissolution of the Soviet Union. The first decade of the post-Soviet transition was notable for extensive infusions of cash, supplies, and personnel from foreign governments and development organizations that were interested in ridding Russia and the other former Soviet Bloc countries of their state socialist pasts and transforming them into modern, neoliberal capitalist democracies. One of the most immediate responses by the Russian state was to reduce social welfare services, under the rationale that welfare was no longer an entitlement but was, in fact, an impediment to cultivating the new ethos of autonomy and independence required of post-Soviet citizens (Kornai 1997, 2001). By withdrawing from social welfare—or "social protection" (*sotsial'naia zashchita*) as social services are also termed in Russia—the Russian state left a gap in service provision that was filled by charitable and benevolent organizations and private citizens. More importantly, according to social services providers and recipients, this withdrawal was also an affective one, with the state acquiring a new neoliberal identity of impartiality and nonsentimentality, thereby leaving the affective work of "compassion" to private citizens and organizations. In the second and now third decades of Russia's post-Soviet period, nonprofit social services providers continue to supplement the limited efforts and abilities of state agencies.

Within this larger landscape of nonprofit social services provision in the 1990s, faith communities focused primarily on poverty relief. At the beginning of the post-Soviet period, when socioeconomic disparities were in greatest focus, programs that provided basic sustenance to the poorest Russians were the most common and popular: food relief programs, orphanage support, and material support for the disabled, elderly, and homeless.[5] Although some larger charitable groups, including those sponsored by faith communities, have been engaged in multiple projects and issues simultaneously, the field of social services as a whole has been marked by niches, as most programs have specialized in a small subset of related programs: children, immigrants, health care, education, or housing, among others. For instance, Russian Protestant minister Pastor Ivan's description of his congregation in the early 1990s—"we were like a distribution center here"—was due to their role as a hub for receiving and dispensing medicine and food, often from foreign donors.

Following that initial focus on immediate material needs, faith communities expanded their efforts to reach constituencies beyond the most impoverished. During the height of Russia's financial crisis in the mid-2000s, when rates of personal credit defaults were increasing, the Russian Orthodox Church (ROC) was a leader in creating programs focusing on financial management, debt counseling, and safe investing for middle-class professionals and recent retirees. A number of Christian congregations and faith-based NGOs created an alternative medical system with high-quality treatment programs and care for Muscovites from all socioeconomic levels. Nina, the director of the ROC's development department, stated that medical care at the ROC's charitable hospital in Moscow was so good that wealthy Russians attempted to buy their way into the wards, only to be turned down on the grounds that the ROC needed to keep the program accessible to all.

Another group of closely affiliated denominations cooperated on several distinct projects ranging from heritage preservation of historic religious buildings in Russia and immigration reform to creating materials for multiculturalism and tolerance initiatives in Russian school curricula. Yet other faith-based groups have tackled issues such as substance abuse, HIV/AIDS, prison reform, refugee and asylum processing, and entrepreneurialism and small business development, among others.[6] Clergy and staff have also received invitations to provide expert advising services on service provision, legal matters, management, and fund-raising to groups as diverse as the International Red Cross, professional labor unions, and the city of Moscow's philanthropy department.

Pastor Ivan reflected that in Moscow, there were many people who had realized that there was more to life than simply making money and they wanted to find ways to live meaningfully by helping others. He noted that without an organizational structure such as that offered by churches, people want to help but cannot; consequently, churches have important roles to play in providing specific and structured ways to help. Nina, the ROC development director, expressed a similar sentiment when she described the church's efforts to educate people to be responsible to and for their neighbors. She commented that in today's society, the church can help people do something for one another: "There are many ways to help others."

Consequently, acts of care and compassion have been associated, in both public sentiment and practical expression, with the work of private citizens, largely as simultaneously shoring up the needs of the state and offering powerful critiques of the shortcomings of the state. In the late 2000s, a popular form of public action occurred via social media, as "flash mobs" of civic-minded young adults organized spontaneously through internet communities to perform random acts of voluntarism and activism benefiting communities in need. Thus, much like in the Italian case described by Muehlebach, Russians' care work, whether rendered privately or through charitable organizations, is fundamentally embedded in the country's civic life (see also Hemment 2015).

Over the past ten years, the Russian state has increasingly recognized in public ways the value of kindness and compassion as part of an ethical citizenship. In 2009, Moscow's social defense agency launched a campaign to promote tolerance and compassion with a series of advertisements featuring young girls wearing blindfolds, accompanied by the simple caption "I see with my heart." By summer 2014, it was impossible to ignore Moscow's compassion campaign, as a "social media" advertising blitz had blanketed the city's streets with billboards encouraging residents to support and get involved in a diverse array of charitable initiatives ranging from children's cancer research and elder care to animal welfare. This is the ethos of compassion that is already alive and well among Moscow's faith-based communities and that has guided their work and allowed their activities to grow and become successful.

Figure 2. The caption to this billboard reads "I see with my heart." It appeared on busy Moscow streets in 2009 as part of the city's promotion of compassion as a civic virtue and activity. Copyright Melissa L. Caldwell.

FAITH AND THE POWER OF POTENTIAL

In Moscow, as in other parts of Russia, local responses to the outsourcing of social assistance have been diverse in terms of both organizational structure and ideological focus. The field has at different moments been composed of governmental social welfare agencies, Russian and foreign nongovernmental organizations (NGOs), informal operations run out of private citizens' apartments, and international relief agencies such as the International Red Cross, Doctors Without Borders, and the Peace Corps. At different moments, assistance programs have worked together, at cross-purposes, and in isolation from one another. Determinations of "success" or "effectiveness" are thus difficult to ascertain. Certainly for many aid seekers I have met, there is a persistent sense that there has been far too little assistance. As Ruth Mandel (2012: 224) has noted in an account of the rise and fall of post-Soviet assistance programs, "something has gone remarkably, profoundly wrong . . . . This period witnessed the highest per capita amount of international development assistance ever invested in a region, yet despite this deluge, many of the countries appear not to be better off."

Curiously, Moscow's faith-based social services programs have earned a reputation for being relatively more successful than their nonreligious counterparts in addressing need, a perspective documented for faith-based organizations operating elsewhere in the world (e.g., Adams 2013; Bornstein 2005; Elisha 2011; Fountain, Bush, and Feener, eds., 2015; Muehlebach 2012). Moscow aid seekers whom I interviewed expressed preferences for faith-based programs, citing what they believed to be the greater degree of personal care and greater amount of material support that these projects provided. A common response from interlocutors was the assertion that churches are simply more accustomed to helping others.

Perhaps the most common example of this alleged greater success that I heard during my research was the purported difference between faith-based and secular programs in addressing addiction problems in Russia. When describing relative success rates of different treatment programs, as measured in terms of continuing sobriety and lack of recidivism and return to rehabilitation, clergy, Russian social workers, and nonaffiliated health professionals alike were consistent in their assertions: as numerous individuals told me, while secular rehabilitation programs typically had success rates of about five to ten percent, Christian rehabilitation programs boasted success rates of around sixty to seventy percent.[7] I was never able to verify those figures, but whether or not they were accurate was not nearly as significant as the prevalent view that Christian programs were more effective.

Another set of success stories focused on the impact of faith-based organizations on human rights problems in Russia. International human rights organizations such as the United Nations High Commissioner for Refugees, the International Organization for Migration, Amnesty International, and Human Rights Watch have all partnered with Moscow-based religious organizations to work with Russian and international governmental agencies to provide unbiased, fair services to asylum seekers and other migrants with tenuous legal status. Perhaps more importantly, these organizations tend to rely on research data about asylum seekers, racial discrimination, and human rights violations generated by these faith-based organizations. Al Jazeera, the British Broadcasting Corporation, and the Economist are just a few of the international media organizations that have cited research data gathered by faith-based organizations. Even Russian media have drawn on their research to push Russian officials to respond to social problems.[8]

Other potential markers of the perceived successes of faith-based organizations include their recognition by the Russian government and official invitations to meetings with officials from welfare services, the police, migration services, and human rights projects. Staff and volunteers with several of the larger congregations and their social services programs received invitations to advise regional and federal departments about best practices for service provision, including fund-raising. Still other programs received grant funding from city and federal authorities. During summer 2009, when the city of Moscow's public campaign to promote compassion and charity was emerging in a "soft launch," two staff members from a church-sponsored NGO that I knew well received an invitation to meet with the director of the city's newly created agency to support philanthropic activities. During the meeting, the director explained that although city officials had allocated money to fund philanthropic groups, their office was having trouble identifying eligible groups with legitimate, and viable, projects. Because this particular church had a strong track record in providing critical social welfare services over an almost twenty-year period, the director strongly encouraged the staff members to apply for a grant from the city.

Even in the current period, during which the Russian government has enacted laws restricting the efforts of "foreign" organizations—most notably the so-called Foreign Agents Law, which requires nonprofit organizations that receive foreign funding to register themselves as "foreign agents," thereby effectively curbing their ability to organize and provide services—the faith-based groups described here have so far not suffered the same fate as many of their counterparts. In fact, faith-based groups such as the ones in this network continue to operate cautiously but openly, oftentimes in full view of the state. In one case, two faith-based groups provide services in a facility immediately adjacent to the Lubyanka, the headquarters of the KGB and its successor the FSB (Federal Security Service). Over the course of the past twenty years that I have been following this network of faith-based social services groups, they have outlasted the Peace Corps, Doctors Without Borders, USAID, the Ford Foundation, and the MacArthur Foundation, among many others. It is important to note, however, that although the overall network of faith-based social services groups has generally outlasted these organizations, some of the particular groups within that network have closed, moved, redefined themselves, or even completely reinvented and renamed themselves (including with new official legal registration from the Russian government). [9]

What accounts for the accomplishments of Moscow's faith-based organizations in maintaining and expanding their work, and even in some cases leveraging those achievements to inform and influence Russian legal and political attitudes and policy? There are, I suspect, several interrelated reasons. In many respects, faith-based organizations are better positioned to weather crises because their institutional structure as spiritual ministries can easily be adapted for social ministry work.[10] In addition, religious communities are more likely to respond to changing needs on the ground, not to expectations and priorities set by bureaucrats or external funders, which may or may not have a basis in reality. Several of the programs I have been following have shifted their projects dramatically over the years as local needs have shifted. One program that was created with the initial purpose of providing material, legal, and social support to single Russian mothers who were raising biracial children had gradually changed its focus over the past twenty years as those children grew up and public attitudes about racial minorities had become more tolerant. Most recently, the program was providing educational and occupational support for those children who were now entering university and the workforce. Several other programs that had been heavily invested in service provision to the elderly in the 1990s had changed their focus to single mothers after Moscow authorities increased pensions for its residents to a level that elevated most retirees out of abject poverty.[11] And finally, faith-based organizations some-times enjoy a degree of privilege and leeway for their presumed moral and institutional superiority in terms of addressing need.

When asked, recipients in faith-based assistance programs repeatedly assured me that they believed there was something special about the fact that religious groups were providing services. One man commented, "It's important because I think only the Christian church has the strength and power for doing this work," while another man told me, "Yes, [it] is very important because whatsoever come[s] from God can never be move[d] by any man on earth." Another simply stated, "A church is a charity organi-zation, and [I] think helping people should be their ultimate goal." Pastor Ivan, a Russian minister whose Protestant congregation was known for its work with Russian orphans and prisoners, summed up these reasons when he explained that no matter what an individual person's religious conviction might be, it was a human universal to want to share and help others. Pastor Ivan reflected that as a society, "we (i.e., Russians) do not provide organized opportunities," but churches do, and they make it pos-sible for people who want to help to give money and their hearts and to share with others.

Although each of these reasons is part of the puzzle, I think there is something else at play that is less about *what* work faith-based organiza-tions do and more about *how* they do it. Specifically, it is the emphasis on faith that animates the ideals and practices of these organizations and the many different people who come together through their activities. As will become clear in the cases that follow, this is not faith in the sense of a belief in a particular doctrine or deity, a conviction in a particular truth, or even as a claim to a moral framework. Rather, as seen through the activi-ties of Moscow's faith-based communities, faith is a commitment to believing and trusting that goodness will prevail (see also Jeavons 1994: 50–51).[12]

For the many individuals who had struggled through the 1990s and 2000s to move social welfare and justice concerns to the forefront of Russian policy and individual practice, they have sustained their deep convictions that the work did matter and would have significant, profound consequences into the future. Specifically, what has kept Moscow's faith-based assistance providers going is faith as an optimistic belief that there is a bigger purpose in life and that things will get better. This is akin to what Cheryl Mattingly terms "hope" in her ethnography of communities of care among poor American families with chronically ill children. For these families, hope is a fight against despair in an effort to imagine and create possibilities (Mattingly 2010). Similarly, in her ethnography of post–Hurricane Katrina recovery in Louisiana, Vincanne Adams (2013) has described faith as what reassured and propelled aid seekers and aid providers forward into imagining, and in some cases realizing, improvement. Yet as both Mattingly and Adams have noted, hope and faith are predicated on doubts, anxieties, and uncertainty: faith and hope are practices of optimism and possibility but do not guarantee absolute or predictable outcomes. As Mattingly (2010: 15) asserts, "Hope lives in an uncertain place. . . . It points us toward a future we can only imagine" (cf. Elisha 2011; Rudnyckyj 2010).

As one physician who volunteers with several faith-based charities told me:

> Every day our faith is tested. It is harder to believe than not. When you are actually looking at a world falling apart, it is hard to believe in an all-powerful, all-just God. Yeah, that's hard. You could do the easy thing and wall yourself off from religious stuff or from problems. If you believe in truth as all relative, then you will never expect anything and are not disappointed. But I have to believe in the Truth. I cannot explain everything that I see or be satisfied, but I keep going and I keep loving. Faith is a challenge every day. But I would rather keep fighting that fight than give up that truth or ignore the obvious.

The Nigerian ambassador, a devout Christian who supported several of Moscow's churches and their charities both personally and in his professional capacity, explained the nature of faith through similar references to futility and struggle.

> If Jesus came to such a country [i.e., Russia], what will his first question be to us as Christians? . . . We as Christians wait for problems to grow, like that big tree. Then we try to move the tree. . . . [But] as Christians and believers we will keep on addressing problems. But too often we fold our hands and close our eyes and lips. So the big question is, when does a Christian's social responsibility come in? The church must always keep on kicking and never give up.

For individuals like these deeply devout men, faith is a forward-looking optimism, a clinging to goals that they would likely never themselves witness being reached, as has been the case with some of my informants, who have died over the past twenty years or moved away from Moscow, never seeing for themselves the outcome of their work. Yet it is precisely this uncertainty that is important for professions and practices of faith among Moscow's aid providers. As another minister told me when I asked him about the uncertainty of faith, he described it as a profoundly beautiful experience of witnessing the unfolding of a future over which one does not have ultimate control.

Such perspectives do not mean that individuals involved in aid work are abdicating control or responsibility over their actions or the outcomes of their actions. Rather, these individuals do not identify practices of faith and care as conditions for producing particular results. Unlike the conservative American Christian evangelicals described by Omri Elisha (2011), whose interest in putting their faith into practical action, most notably social services, was geared at helping their recipients adopt new behaviors and beliefs (both material and moral), the individuals who participated in these Moscow assistance communities separated what they could reasonably achieve (i.e., provide care) from any personal assurances of the greater consequences of those actions.

For participants within these Moscow faith-based social services programs, faith that is put into practice becomes a future-oriented, dynamic, generative quality that mobilizes action and produces results. Faith circulates through an affective economy of kindness, compassion, and love. As such, it is external to any one individual but becomes a form of capital that can expand, grow, and produce results (Adams 2013; Ahmed 2004; Miyazaki 2003; Muehlebach 2012). Faith produces results, whether actual ones in the here and now or merely hoped-for results in a not-yet-realized future, much like the forms of hope that guided Miyazaki's Japanese arbitrage workers (2003, 2006) or the millennial capitalists described by Jean and John Comaroff (2000). When it is a divinely inspired Invisible Hand at work, faith is an optimistic, generative force that produces and shapes an entire political economy grounded in ideals of kindness, compassion, and justice (see also Muehlebach 2012: 26).[13] Faith does not simply imply potentiality and promise, but it is an energy that produces real, tangible results in this-worldly struggles against injustice.

This point came through clearly in my interview with Father Thomas, a Catholic priest, when he reflected on the nature of charity and care.

> Do we engage people in difficulties? Yes. Do we look out for them? [Yes.] Do we try to draw them in like flies to honey? No. Do we help them? Yes. We do things because they seem to be the right things at the right time. Were those things planned? No. Things happen; they seem to be part of events. Is that altruism? I don't know. These were just the things that happened. You just take these things as they go along.

Ultimately, as the examples described in this book show, faith represents people's commitment to trying to find and enact goodness and decency in daily life, even when the realization of those efforts seems doubtful. While personal convictions may be bolstered by religious practices that allow individuals to appeal to higher powers or to draw evidence of goodness from Biblical teachings, people's daily actions are embedded more explicitly in ideals and discourses of social justice and human rights. Ultimately, the people who comprise this community share a belief in the inherent goodness of people and the necessity of rightness as an ethical responsibility to make sure that all creatures—human and nonhuman alike—can flourish. Thus it is faith that sustains them and their work and enables future possibilities and opportunities.

This is a provocative and perhaps counterintuitive way to think about faith as a principled stance and technique of transforming optimism into reality, especially in a context such as Russia, where scholars, religious leaders, and politicians alike have tended to render faith as a distinctively religious or spiritual practice, albeit for different purposes (Hann and Goltz 2010; Metropolitan Hilarion 2013; Wanner and Steinberg 2008; cf. Berger 2013). Yet it is precisely this optimism and belief in a future goodness that illuminates the ways in which faith is more than belief but a practical activity with profound and tangible effects (Adams 2013; Mattingly 2010). At the same time, it is not simply a utopian dream but a practice that people enact and experience in very tangible ways.

In the discussion that follows, I treat faith as a form of practice that community members talk about, strive to enact, and then credit for the changes they witness. By focusing on faith as a distinctive feature of religiously affiliated compassion projects, I trace the contributions that this community has made to Russian civic life. Both in terms of political and economic activities, I examine how and why faith has played such a significant and consequential role. My discussion is organized around various permutations of the practice of faith as a mode of civic engagement, the forms of civil society and civic person these modes take, and the uncertainties and precarities that are revealed by the practical actions of faith.

I begin by considering how the secular humanist and public service orientations of faith-based assistance groups and their members have produced both a philosophy of social justice and a strategy of cooperation that I am calling ecumenism. This ecumenism rests on interfaith partnerships and has transformed the nature of religious life in Russia today. I then turn to an examination of the place of faith-based groups within Russian practices of public service and civic engagement, with particular attention to the ways in which compassion is a practical experience of shared intimacy, a perspective that informs how participants conceive of both justice and spirituality. The discussion then situates faith-based organizations and the values of compassion and kindness on which they draw within the larger context of Russian development projects. A key aspect is the contributions of faith-based organizations to civil society initiatives, most notably through their emphasis on civility and humaneness as something greater than humanitarianism or human rights. As civil society actors, members of Moscow's faith-based assistance communities promote principled practices of service that belong to a longer history of the ways in which faith-based organizations have worked in partnership with the state. As such they are engaged in practices of "ethical citizenship" that promote care for others, not just as an essential quality of human decency but as a critical right and responsibility of being a citizen of the nation-state, what Muehlebach (2012: 11) has described as "citizenship to be lived with the heart" (see also Malkki 2015).[14] I then turn to the consequences of this focus on service with regard to Russia's political economy, with particular attention to the ways in which kindness, goodness, and compassion more generally have generated a robust compassion economy that is both productive and problematic. Finally, I turn to the precarity of faith and how as faith-based proponents increasingly take on explicitly human rights work, they must navigate a delicate balancing act between preserving humaneness while safeguarding rights that calls into question their personal beliefs about both social justice and religion.

MOSCOW'S FAITH-BASED CHARITABLE ASSISTANCE WORLD

The questions and issues that animate this book have emerged out of my ongoing research in Russia. During that research I have been captivated by how and why ordinary people expend time, energy, and resources to help the people around them in an effort to make the immediate world around them a little better for all who live in it. In the mid-1990s, I began conducting fieldwork among several church-based social services charities in Moscow. That research was unplanned but fortuitous, as my initial research project in the early 1990s was meant to examine Russia's emergent consumer society by focusing on how Muscovites were experiencing the country's transition to a post-Soviet, neoliberal capitalist economy.[15] Just as I entered the field, the Russian economy suffered a setback, which prompted several years of economic stagnation and widespread shortages of money and consumer goods. In response, charities and other social services programs expanded their reach, and in so doing found themselves inheriting the role of social welfare providers that had formerly been the domain of the state. As a result, rather than focusing on consumer growth, I found it more interesting and timely to look at how post-Soviet consumers dealt with scarcity and their relationships with these new social welfare providers. This led me to a community of Christian congregations that were among the most active in Moscow's social welfare sphere (Caldwell 2004).

Over the past twenty years, even as I have engaged in other research projects in Russia, I have continued to follow members of this community as they have modified and expanded their services, navigated Russia's changing political and cultural currents, and more generally established themselves as reliable actors in Moscow civic initiatives. By the mid-2000s, the growing politicization of Russia's religious landscape was marked by what appeared to be growing closeness between the Russian

Orthodox Church and the Russian state and the concomitant marginalization, even ostracism, of non-Orthodox religions, especially other Christian communities. The passage of new laws and regulations defining which religions were "traditional," and thus "legal," marked most non-Orthodox groups as not legally recognized and therefore in constant danger of being closed or, in the case of groups with foreign members (which included several of the churches I had been following), having their members deported.

Within this context, the network of religiously affiliated social services providers that I had been following not only expanded their programs but gained legal recognition, which in turn endowed them with certain protections by city and state authorities. Most intriguingly, at a time when the leadership of the Russian Orthodox Church, often in coordination with conservative political parties, was publicly promoting religious and cultural isolationism, these social services programs and the non-Orthodox churches that sponsored them had established formal, albeit often very quiet, working relations with their Orthodox counterparts, including in the offices of the patriarchate. I became deeply curious as to why these religious communities and their social services programs were able to weather these events and even thrive in some cases, and my curiosity repeatedly brought me back to these communities, following them as they changed over time.

Thus, the research on which this book is based began in the mid-1990s, although the majority of events and issues described here came from fieldwork conducted between 2005 and 2010, with follow-up visits in 2011, 2014, and 2015. Having the vantage point of twenty years of ongoing field research has been both advantageous and challenging. As I have described elsewhere (Caldwell 2005), in a setting like Moscow that is characterized by people in transit and organizations in flux, I have been one of the most regular and constant features of this community. I have watched as clergy, parishioners, and staff of churches and social services programs have cycled through (one church community that I have followed has rotated among at least six clergy over the past twenty years, while others have had the same clergyperson for the entire duration of my research). In other cases for charities that I have been tracking, I have watched competing dynamics as, on the one hand, volunteers have moved up through the ranks to paid staff over the course of one or two decades, while other volunteers have come and gone. As a result of this length of time, I have been fortunate to be able to recognize patterns at different scales, both short-term and long-term. I have also been fortunate to develop deep and abiding friendships and collegial relationships, and I have had a front-row seat to important life cycles of children growing up, parents aging, romantic partnerships forming and dissolving, and friends dying. In many ways, despite working in a city of more than fifteen million people, I have been able to enjoy some semblance of the classic, albeit mythical, village anthropology.

At the same time, this long-term research within these communities has necessarily kept me involved in their affairs rather than venturing further afield to other topics or other regions of Russia. While this may indeed be a shortcoming, the fact is that these communities have changed dramatically in many different ways, and they are not the same communities that they were twenty years ago. They have expanded, moved in new directions, and created new networks and identities. Virtually all of the social services programs that I have been following over the years have thoroughly reinvented themselves, as has more than one of the churches described here. It would be a grave anthropological misstep to presume that these communities remained static over time. Perhaps most notably, in the case of programs that started in the late 1980s and early 1990s with the help of "foreigners," they have firmly established themselves within Moscow as local communities, including with legal registration identifying them as "Russian" entities. As a result, my deep temporal investment in this world offered contacts and insights that would not be possible in a new community after only a year or two.

At the heart of these communities is a network of assistance programs that includes the church that was part of my original research in the 1990s: the Christian Church of Moscow (CCM). In the 1990s, the CCM like many of its counterparts, including other groups described in this book, tended to operate more or less alongside but separately from other organizations. Since then, as the faith-based charitable sector has expanded, both religious and nonreligious organizations have increasingly forged religious and assistance partnerships, thereby facilitating a vibrantly multicultural and eclectic community that traverses religious, secular, and governmental lines. As a result, the CCM has become one node within a much larger network of partners, affiliates, and supporters that extend across Moscow and beyond.

Other nodes in this larger faith-based assistance network represent a diverse set of Christian and non-Christian communities: Orthodox, Catholic, Anglican, Lutheran, Presbyterian, Methodist, Baptist, Quaker, the Salvation Army, Jewish, Muslim, and Hare Krishna, to name just a few among a large community. In some cases, individual congregations sponsor social services as part of their outreach programming, while in other cases formal aid projects have been formed and administered through partnerships among multiple congregations. In still other instances, groups of volunteers from a variety of religious backgrounds come together formally and informally under ecumenical, even secular understandings of social action. One of the most active and visible of these ecumenical groups is the local chapter of Sant'Egidio, a street ministry started in Rome by a Catholic priest that attracts socially progressive, young adult Russians from a range of religious backgrounds, including atheists. Additionally, formal and informal partnerships bring together individual congregations and transnational denominational development agencies such as the Catholic agency Caritas, Lutheran World Relief, World Vision, and the Jewish Joint Distribution Council.

These communities rarely work in isolation from one another. The multifaceted work that religious and social services organizations pursue brings them into relationships with diverse partners across the religious/nonreligious spectrum. In some cases, partnerships reflect logical synergies between closely related religious denominations. Within Moscow's Protestant community, Lutheran, Presbyterian, Methodist, and Baptist communities have long worked together, finding common ground in spite of historical divisions, such as those between Russia's indigenous German and Ingrian Lutheran communities or between liberal and evangelical and even Pentecostal congregations. In other cases, partnerships span more sharply defined and publicly visible ruptures, such as those forged by Russian Orthodox and Russian Catholic communities, or between Christian, Jewish, and Muslim groups. One of the curious details that emerged during this research was the extent to which ministerial work was a profession and not exclusively a denominational affiliation, as clergy from different denominations often knew one another professionally and personally from having studied together at prominent ecumenical seminaries in the United States or Western Europe.[16] For these individuals, bringing their congregations together for shared projects was a natural extension of their own preexisting friendships and partnerships, which they saw as being based on shared experiences, not necessarily identical values and perspectives.

In fact, it was not uncommon for clergy ordained in one denomination to be employed in a service position in another denomination, as the ongoing interfaith dialogues and working partnerships forged by different religious communities illuminated the extent to which denominational traditions and theological differences were less significant than expressing compatible viewpoints on the types of services to provide and the system for administering those programs. Despite the Russian Orthodox Church's official rhetoric of exclusivity and its often public face of hostility to other religious traditions viewed as "competitors" (e.g., Knox 2008), the patriarchate's service programs employed staff who had been ordained in other faiths.

Collaborative relationships with other religious communities were supplemented by partnerships with nonreligious organizations, including governmental agencies and international humanitarian and development organizations that have shared interests. For instance, the Russian Red Cross, the United Nations High Commissioner for Refugees, and regional and provincial-level welfare offices have supported poverty relief programs sponsored by church groups in Russia, while staff from USAID and the American, British, Irish, and Nigerian embassies, among others, have worked closely with religious communities that offer health care services to low-income and homeless Russians.

I would note that one formally organized community largely absent from the network I have been following is that of Muslim groups. Although I have attempted to document the role of Muslim groups in social services over the past decade, this has been a surprisingly difficult task. Development and assistance providers in Moscow whom I approached for help in making contact with Muslim service providers repeatedly told me that they did not know of any such providers working in this area. Most intriguing was that several development/assistance programs I approached had significant Muslim communities among their recipients—all of whom received services from Christian communities. The imam of one of Moscow's mosques was in fact a registered aid recipient with one of the Protestant churches described here. The arrival of the Aga Khan Foundation in Moscow in 2009 was an exciting development precisely because aid providers saw it as the first instance of Muslim assistance in Moscow. In fact, this was how the director of the Aga Khan Foundation announced their presence—as their first venture in Russia proper. In 2014, a colleague related that the Gülen movement was just starting to become active in Moscow.[17] Nevertheless, as I discuss later in this book, whether or not Muslim groups were active in Moscow social services work is not critical as a detail in and of itself, since one of the fascinating developments from faith-based welfare has been the creation of interfaith, secular theologies of compassion and social action.

The individuals whom I have interviewed and shadowed come from across the assistance spectrum: recipients and their family members, volunteers, staff, clergy, congregants, donors, attorneys, social workers, Russian government officials, foreign diplomatic staff, and random strangers, among many others who inhabit Moscow's assistance world. Collectively they represent an equally diverse set of legal, economic, ethnic, racial, and national backgrounds: Russian and foreign; religious, atheist, and avowedly secular; university students, pensioners, undocumented economic migrants, professionals, and the homeless, among many, many others. With them I have attended church services, church council meetings, and church fellowship activities; volunteered in and visited a broad array of social welfare programs, funding agencies, international aid and development organizations, and governmental offices and programs; attended meetings at attorney's offices, with real estate agents, business managers, and corporate executives; and participated in seminars, workshops, and roundtables sponsored by federal and international organizations. To accommodate the fluid nature of this research, I have had to conduct interviews in Russian, English, German, and French, at times tracking the shifting linguistic registers of conversations between individuals from different backgrounds as they talked with one another through multiple languages. In some cases I became the translator for people who were talking with one another; at other times I accompanied staff and volunteers who did not speak the same language and then observed as they carried on conversations through another multilingual staff member who served as a translator.

Working with these individuals and groups has taken me into some unexpected places far beyond people's homes and workplaces: press conferences at the ITAR-TASS news agency; meetings at the offices of the International Red Cross, International Organization for Migration, and the Aga Khan Foundation, some of which were attended by high-ranking Russian officials; interviews and events at foreign embassies, including the offices and personal residences of ambassadors; a reception hosted by the US ambassador for the American Secretary of State; black-tie gala events; supermarket aisles and managers' offices; public parks; and the patriarchate of the Russian Orthodox Church.

TROUBLING CONVENTIONS

One of the threads of this book examines how the work of Moscow's faith-based assistance programs and their members proceeds precisely because they exist and operate in a civic zone of compassion and assistance that straddles multiple registers of public and private, governmental and non-governmental, commercial and nonprofit, religious and secular. In this respect, to practice forms of social action faithfully is to inhabit spaces of uncertainty and confusion and to find opportunities and potentialities within those "borderlands" (Mattingly 2010). As a result, as a mode of foreshadowing some of the uncertainties and messiness that follow, I would like to offer a few preliminary notes about some of the words, phrases, and concepts that will appear in the discussions to come.

The first instance of categorical messiness is that of trying to parse out what constitutes "religious" and "secular" or "not religious" among the individuals and programs detailed here. In terms of their focus on "religious" concerns such as belief, theology, practice, and identity, religiously affiliated assistance organizations cover a broad spectrum. At one end are organizations with explicitly religious origins and affiliations (for example, congregational social ministries or the development department of the Russian Orthodox Church) and at the other are groups that are adamantly secular (for example, Habitat for Humanity and Oxfam). Faith communities can also differ significantly in regard to whether they explicitly couple assistance with the performance of religious obligation, whether on the part of service providers or recipients. Orthodox and Jewish programs in Moscow are among those that require recipients to declare their religious affiliation and

perhaps even to attend services (see also Tocheva 2011). While these conditions are acceptable to some Russians, including persons who might strategically claim religious affiliation (or more than one) without committing
completely to any one congregation, others find them too limiting (see
Caldwell 2010). Russian Orthodox churches have come under particular
scrutiny for restricting services to enrolled members rather than to all
Russians. Staff with the development office at the patriarchate confided that
while these regulations were necessary for practical reasons, they were
undesirable in terms of providing assistance to those individuals who were
truly in need, regardless of their religious backgrounds. These requirements
for religiosity are in sharp contrast with communities such as Oxfam and
Habitat for Humanity whose religious origins have been largely forgotten
and who do not demand religious affiliation or activity from either supporters or recipients.[18]

More common, however, are groups that do not disguise their religious
origins or institutional affiliations but implement their social services programs as secular programs. The Christian Church of Moscow is like many
congregations that have created explicitly secular assistance organizations
for ideological reasons, namely that it is an ethical responsibility to help
anyone in need and to attract volunteers regardless of their personal religious backgrounds. Similarly, although the employees in the Moscow office
of Caritas were practicing Catholics, including several priests, their work
was explicitly nonreligious. They worked independently of any of the
Catholic churches in Moscow and provided their services through spaces
rented or borrowed from local government agencies. Recipients were largely
unaware of the program's connections to the Catholic Church, a detail that
Caritas's staff were keen to maintain given anti-Catholic sentiments in
Russia. Staff and volunteers with nonprofit programs administered by other
religious congregations have even reported that their recipients were completely unaware that they were being helped by a church, thinking instead
that the program was operated by the regional government.

The term "secular" poses similar problems. As I will discuss later, there
are no easy distinctions between "religious" and "secular" in Russian terminology or practice. Although the word *svetskie* is the word most commonly used to mean "nonreligious," in practice Russian organizations
and laws have created a complex and shifting terminological system to

designate nonreligious organizations as nonprofit (*nekommercheskie*, noncommercial) or nongovernmental (*nepravitel'stvennie*, nongovernmental, or *obshchestvennie*, social / community, among other renderings) entities. As Sonja Luerhmann (2011) has documented, "secularism" has a very particular political and historical context in Russia. Most notably, the Soviet project of secularization prioritized a human-centric approach by removing nonhuman (including mystical) agents from daily life and recalibrating people's affective frames of reference for moral, cultural, and social relations. Thus, while Soviet-style "secularism" shares some similarities with movements described by Talal Asad (2003) and Charles Taylor (2007), it also derived from a very different set of political and philosophical contexts. Therefore, I use this term carefully, either to reflect its use by my informants or to capture what seems to be the most important features of a particular organization at a given time, rather than to make a clear statement about whether a group or action is definitively aligned with a religious or nonreligious sphere or approach.

It is worth noting that although most of the religiously affiliated charities that operated as secular entities described here did so for ideological reasons, this had pragmatic ramifications because it satisfied Russian laws governing the interaction of "foreign"—that is, non-Orthodox Christian— religious communities with Russian citizens. Moreover, because of their secular nature, these types of faith organizations also tended to work closely with other national and international assistance and development organizations, both religious and nonreligious, as well as with Russian and foreign governmental agencies. As such, they enjoyed both a greater degree of security and a more diverse set of partners than either their explicitly religious counterparts or international development agencies.

Distinctions between "foreign" and "domestic" or "Russian" constitute the second layer of categorical messiness. One interesting feature of Moscow's faith communities is that many have occupied dual roles as both beneficiary and donor, as over the past twenty years they have simultaneously relied on assistance to support their own programming as religious communities and on funding for their public service activities. As I heard from numerous clergy whom I interviewed about their congregations' charitable activities, some of their own congregations were the recipients of international and domestic humanitarian aid during the initial period of the post-Soviet transition when foreign congregations sent considerable sums of money, material resources, and personnel to Russia in order to create or rehabilitate religious communities. Although American ministers and churches that sent aid and missionaries to Russia for evangelism and church-building activities, such as Billy Graham and his ministry, have been the most publicly visible and recognizable, denominational bodies and individual congregations from Western Europe (Germany, Finland, and the United Kingdom, in particular), Asia (especially Korea and Japan), and Australia have also been active in these areas (see Caldwell 2015).

At the same time, faith communities have also received support from Russian sources, including governmental bodies, primarily in the form of the return of real estate and other property that had been seized from religious communities by the state during the Soviet period. In some instances, post-Soviet Russian authorities have returned church buildings, synagogues, mosques, seminaries, monasteries, and other religious property to their former owners, or the successors to these religious communities, although by no means has this been a comprehensive policy. The Russian Orthodox Church has perhaps been the most visible recipient of these returns, but Russia's other faith communities—Baptists, Lutherans, Anglicans, Catholics, Methodists, and Jews, to name just a few—have also had property returned to them. Faith communities have also benefited from grant funding and other forms of financial support from nonreligious development programs and private donors geared at restoring religious heritage and values.[19]

Perhaps more significantly, despite persistent presumptions by both Russians and outsiders (including skeptical anthropologists) that non-Orthodox Christian churches are "foreign" congregations in the sense that they are denominations that were not indigenous to Russia but were introduced from abroad, largely as part of the massive proselytization efforts of the 1990s, this is not necessarily true, especially for the communities described here. Lutheran, Baptist, Methodist, Anglican, and Catholic denominations, among many other Christian faiths, existed in Russia for several centuries before the Bolshevik Revolution and are now reclaiming and rebuilding their historical legacies, even as they are creating ties with their denominational counterparts abroad. These liberal, progressive denominations are among the most active congregations described here. Consequently, it would be inaccurate to presume that these congregations are not Russian. Pastor Ivan related that one of his greatest frustrations was convincing Russians that his Korean-Russian congregation was in fact "Russian" and not "foreign."

Third, if congregations were constantly confusing categories of Russian and not-Russian, so, too, were the individuals who moved through these congregations and the larger social services networks. Although during the earliest phases of this research in the 1990s, the congregations and charities I followed typically had more foreigners than Russians, this has changed over the years. Some congregations are balanced between foreigners and Russians, while others are primarily or exclusively Russian. Most have experienced fluctuations in their congregations and programs over the years, reflecting larger demographic and migration trends within and beyond Russia as foreign expatriates, students, and asylum seekers have entered and left Russia, and as Russian citizens have emigrated abroad or found other interests to occupy their time.

As for non-Russians involved in this work, there are several general patterns. Most were resident in Russia for long periods—some for four or five years at a time, but many for ten to twenty years or longer. These longer periods of residence were most common among the African students and asylum seekers who had come to Russia in the late 1980s and then created lives for themselves, including marrying Russian citizens and having children who were Russian citizens. Other long-term foreign residents were businesspeople who had come to Russia during the same time period and remained for family and other personal reasons. On the other end of the spectrum were Russian citizens who had left during the periods of openness in the late 1980s and early 1990s to study and work in Europe, North America, and Asia, and then returned after many years of living abroad. In some cases, these returnee Russians had less cultural and linguistic capital than their foreign-born counterparts. Within this shifting identity terrain, I have used names that are in keeping with a person's background—for instance, an English name or a Russian name. Yet even these conventions are at times ambiguous, such as with Korean-Russians who have Anglicized their names, German-Russians who have Germanic names, Africans who have adopted Russian names after marriage to Russian citizens, and Catholic priests who have adopted saints' names after ordination.

As a result, because even the category of "Russianness" cannot be taken for granted, the question of who is authentically Russian is perhaps not as important as the issue of how the beliefs and actions of individuals involved in these communities are contributing to a particularly Russian civic sphere.

Fourth, referring to and describing any particular individual's legal status in Russia is tricky, especially as Russian laws have different policies governing the rights and responsibilities of citizens and noncitizens. One important detail is that citizens are required to be legally registered to a place of residence as their official address. Through this address, citizens are registered to a particular district, where they are entitled to receive public services such as access to schools, medical care, and other welfare services. As a result, to lack a legally registered address is to exist outside of legal structures.

In American activist discourse and scholarly and media writings, the term "illegal immigrant" has largely been replaced by "undocumented migrant" (or even "undocumented person"), reflecting the moral idea within US immigration debates that people cannot be illegal but they can be undocumented (e.g., Dumon 1983). Yet the phrase "undocumented migrant" does not easily capture the everyday reality for many persons living in Russia today. For the case of economic and political migrants, who come both from other republics in the former Soviet Union and from foreign countries, most notably sub-Saharan African countries, China, Vietnam, the Philippines, Bangladesh, Iran, Iraq, Syria, and other Middle Eastern countries, the problem is not that they are undocumented. Rather, the problem is that their documents are not legal. Russia's foreign borders are very rigid, and the majority of foreign visitors are required to get a visa for entry. Yet it can be relatively easy to purchase an entry visa for Russia, especially education visas given that some university faculty disgruntled by their paltry salaries have supplemented their incomes by "selling" student sponsorships to would-be economic migrants. Other brokers sell business visa invitations to would-be migrants with the promise of a job in construction, transportation, the market, or other sectors, even though most of these jobs never materialize. Thus most individuals enter with legal documents and as legally recognized visitors.

Once foreigners arrive in Russia, they must register their documents at an official place of residence or work. Few economic or political migrants have an official place of residence, however, and few landlords are willing to "write in" migrants to their apartments, because of the danger that persons who are "registered" to a residence could eventually claim possession. (And often landlords are reluctant to do this even for visitors with fully legal documents, such as a fieldworking anthropologist.) Thus, it is very common for economic and political migrants to become "illegal" quickly; while their documents are legal, they themselves are not registered and so have become illegal. The final step on the path to "illegality" in Russia is that foreigners cannot leave the country without an official exit visa, which requires proof of continuous legal residency registration. Foreigners who have failed to register their residence or who never received an entry/exit visa in the first place do not have legal rights to leave the country.

Qualities such as "illegal" versus "undocumented" become further muddled because of the common practice of sharing documents among economic and political migrants, especially in the African migrant community I worked with most extensively. People who possessed fully legal documents shared them with relatives and friends who were searching for work, needed medical care, or needed to travel either within Russia or abroad. During the summer, it was very common in the African community with which I worked for legally documented individuals who had secure housing and employment in Moscow to lend their documents to other persons who then used them to work in the summer resorts along the Black Sea. In a claim that I heard from numerous Africans, they believed that Russian officials were so racist that all black faces looked alike.

By contrast, Russian citizens could be undocumented, which was especially true for the homeless population, as well as prisoners and former prisoners, children living in orphanages, former orphans, and even persons who had been hospitalized. Poor record-keeping and lack of secure storage are rife across institutions, which has meant that many people have had their documents lost or stolen while they have been institutionalized. Upon release, a lack of documents prevents Russians from accessing housing—or even reclaiming their own legally registered property—and other resources. This forces many people into homelessness until they can accumulate the funds to begin the lengthy process of regaining their documents. Being undocumented can also affect citizens who have had more mundane experiences, such as squabbles with roommates in a shared flat that result in them being forcibly evicted without their documents, being robbed, or even getting divorced and being forced to move out and unregister from the residence they formerly shared with their spouse. In the latter instance, while a divorced person might have a legal passport, he or she might lack the official registration stamp, which makes him or her illegal.

Consequently, possessing legal documents, possessing legal registration, and being "legal" are not coterminous states. It was far more common for foreigners to possess truthful documents, even if only at certain moments, than it was for Russia's homeless, orphan, addict, and prison communities to do so. As a result, foreigners could be documented but not legal, while Russians could be both undocumented and in tenuous and shifting states of legal existence. In most cases, Russians were "legal" but could not prove their status until they were able to produce the necessary documents.

In this book, I try to avoid using terms such as "undocumented" or "illegal," but when I do, it is for very specific reasons relating to the distinctions explained above. It is not my intention to be drawn into debates about American immigration policies, both because those circumstances are vastly different from instances that I describe here, and because the morally laden terminology used in American immigration debates and discussions simply does not work for the Russian case.

More generally, as will become clear in the following chapters, trying to classify and describe fully the activities, philosophies, and approaches undertaken in these communities is complicated, not just because there is such a diversity of groups and projects, but also because there is no neat terminology with which to describe and categorize these communities, their projects, and their legal status and classification. Scholarly traditions, including but not exclusively anthropology, have typically distinguished among social welfare, charity, philanthropy, development, humanitarianism, human rights, and social justice as distinct sets of practices with their own philosophies about interactions between aid givers and aid recipients, the types of assistance that flow between partners, the organizational structures, funding sources, and even temporal modes (see, for instance, Bornstein 2012: 12; Fisher 1997; Redfield and Bornstein 2010).

As for Russian programs described here, faith-based organizations and their affiliates have at different moments described themselves or have been officially classified as charities, nongovernmental organizations (NGOs), nonprofits, noncommercial enterprises, development organizations, social services agencies, social welfare programs, social justice groups, human rights organizations, or even humanitarian groups, among many other terms. Moreover, these organizations often pursue many different things simultaneously, sometimes in separate realms. Consequently, they cover a broad spectrum of the types of activities, philosophies, and approaches.

For instance, while Pastor Ivan described his congregation's activities in terms of both spiritual ministry and humanitarianism, his colleague Pastor Mark from another congregation described his congregation's activities in terms of social justice and human rights, acknowledging that these terms reflected the theological perspective of his denomination. A conversation with a woman who created her own food relief program that was subsequently administered by a church reflected this shifting terrain in her response to my question about whether there was necessarily something special about religious organizations doing charitable work. She commented that while some organizations do good things, there is often a *noblesse oblige* connotation with charity, whereas social justice evokes a different sensibility. In her view, for the people doing this work there was a significant difference: "[For] a lot of religious people [who are] true, devout believers, people do charitable work, social justice work, [they] do it because they believe it is God's work." She went on to note that these are more than just "earthly" activities, but are perceived as divinely inspired.

Perhaps the best evidence of the ambiguous nature of Moscow's faith-based groups is their role as connectors between programs, oftentimes to fill gaps created between other projects. Even though Moscow's religious communities are becoming increasingly structured and even bureaucratized in terms of how they administer their programs, most retain an inherent flexibility that allows them to take advantage of unique circumstances and even to access communities that secular NGOs and governmental agencies miss. Above all, religious communities can connect at a more intimate level—specifically, with individual people and the minutiae of their daily lives. As noted by Eloise, a British national who served as a development director for the charitable projects of one Moscow-based church, the legal aid groups that served the same set of clients served by her church tended to focus on court-level activities, such as changing laws and filing class-action lawsuits, whereas her organization responded to individual cases that were often too messy and ambiguous for class-action work. Unlike larger legal aid groups, her organization could use personal connections to find an attorney, who could often be persuaded to work pro bono, to take on a case involving a single individual.

One such organization was Humanity (*Chelovechnost'*), a secular NGO that focuses on human rights issues in Russia. Alla Mikhailovna was one of the most senior attorneys and had worked with Humanity for almost a decade. Over that time, her organization has partnered with many other groups in Russia and abroad to document human rights violations, especially those against religious, ethnic, racial and other minorities. One of their most active and important set of partners has been an interfaith consortium of churches and faith-based organizations that support racial minorities, including both minorities who are native-born Russian citizens and nonwhite migrants from other parts of the former Soviet Union and from outside Russia.

Given the perilous nature of human rights advocacy and documentation, Alla Mikhailovna and her colleagues rarely met in person and worked from their homes. Alla Mikhailovna was the most public face of the organization and periodically emerged from the privacy and security of her home to make public statements or appear at public events. As a result, she frequently received death threats and confided to me at a workshop on tolerance hosted by an international NGO that she fully expected to be killed for her work. Given these constraints and real fears, Alla Mikhailovna's organization, despite their many accomplishments and the tremendous acclaim they enjoyed, was limited in their ability to pursue all the work they wanted to do. Yet their interfaith partners offered possibilities for working around these constraints, a feature that Alla Mikhailovna identified as one of the most compelling and productive strengths of faith-based work and advocacy in Russian civic life. This is the topic to which I turn in the next chapter.

2 Faith in a Secular Humanism

In 2013 I attended a workshop in Vienna focusing on interfaith dialogue and action between Russian Orthodox and non-Orthodox Christian communities both in Russia and abroad. In his keynote address, the sociologist of religion Peter Berger argued that one of the most important challenges of the modern period has not been secularization but pluralism. With the diversification of religion in the contemporary period, "every religious tradition loses the quality of taken-for-granted plausibility," forcing "individuals [to] make choices between [the] different religious possibilities available" to them. As Berger explained, this diversification and choice effectively turned religious institutions into voluntary associations to which individuals elected to turn their attentions (Berger 2013; see also Berger, Davie, and Fokas 2008).

Berger's provocations were noteworthy for several reasons. First, by casting religious institutions as voluntary associations, he provided a way to separate the "religious" from the "secular," and by so doing to recognize that people not only can shift between religious and secular registers but can keep those two positions separate. Citing the example of a colleague who is an Orthodox Jew and a surgeon but not necessarily both at the same time, Berger noted that "most religious people . . . switch back and forth between the secular discourse and their various religious relevancies." Second, by foregrounding pluralism, Berger opened up possibilities for rethinking presumed relationalities between religious and secular registers as neither fully absolutist nor fully overlapping. Third, and perhaps most importantly, Berger made these arguments to an audience of clergy, including the Metropolitan Hilarion of Volokolamsk, the highest-ranking representative of the patriarchate of the Russian Orthodox Church in attendance, and other officials from the patriarchate in Russia, as well as high-ranking officials from several of Europe's largest Catholic dioceses and Protestant denominations.

As a participant in the workshop, I found the exchanges among other participants fascinating, especially as they responded to the provocations raised by Berger and other religious leaders and scholars. Above all, the two-day workshop was infused with a sense of mutuality and shared perspective and experience, even as participants debated doctrinal, historical, and political differences. While I heard privately uttered grumbling from a few participants who either wanted more attention paid to doctrinal differences or were skeptical that a true interfaith effort could be realized, the general consensus at the end was that the event was successful in finding points of convergence within such a diverse field.

I find these efforts to discover moments of shared concern useful for illuminating some of the complexities of the phenomena that I have observed among Moscow's faith-based assistance providers. As has been evident in the efforts of members of these groups to work together and find common ground, there are few absolutes, and most people and programs operate in spaces of messy in-betweenness where they try to reconcile, but not eliminate, differences. In fact, it is this in-betweenness that is prioritized in many ways and is what enables much of this work to occur.

One of the most striking developments within Moscow's faith-based assistance world is that assistance workers have managed to create a robust social justice sphere that appears, from the outside at least, to be a relatively cohesive, or at a minimum a cooperative, community with shared visions and goals where clergy, staff, volunteers, and supporters circulate among projects and groups. By moving beyond theological and historical differences in the pursuit of a shared commitment to social action, these groups have produced an interfaith or transfaith approach to social justice that attracts staff, volunteers, political advocates, and even congregants.

Yet the journey to this shared commitment has not been easy and is very much a work in progress, as Moscow's religious institutions and religiously affiliated organizations have at different moments struggled to define themselves and their relationships with one another. In many ways, staff and clergy have confessed that relationships with nonreligious organizations have been much easier to create and maintain than relationships with other religious organizations. Over and over, clergy and staff members with faith-based organizations and religious institutions described their struggles when trying to work with their counterparts in other religious institutions. Curiously, as my respondents told me, it was not so much a sense of competing over "souls" or jockeying for position within Moscow's political or social circles that was the problem, as it was the difficulty of trying to achieve consensus about appropriate forms of service and ethics of social justice across denominational and philosophical differences. As one minister put it, one of the biggest challenges facing Moscow's Christian community, which included Orthodox churches, was "how to develop a community."

The question of what constitutes a "community" in the context of interfaith collaboration illuminates a somewhat unfamiliar perspective on the nature of religious life in Russia today. Since the late 1980s, the field of religion in Russia has been transformed both by the expansion of Christianity and by the shifting relationships of cooperation and competition that have emerged among Christian denominations. Studies of postsocialist religious life have typically been framed around individual religious traditions, an analytical tendency that highlights and reinforces the idea that religious traditions are set apart by unique beliefs, rituals, and denominational histories and that theological or doctrinal features are the most significant elements of ritual life (e.g., Hann and Goltz, eds. 2010; Steinberg and Wanner, eds. 2008; cf. Caldwell 2005). Most notable in accounts of these changes are the doctrinal and political issues that have at different moments simultaneously divided and united Christian communities, particularly the complicated relationships of sympathy and hostility, cooperation and competition, that reportedly exist between the Russian Orthodox Church and non-Orthodox Christian denominations (Knox 2005, 2008; Wanner and Steinberg 2008: 13–17).

An alternative strand in accounts of Christian communities in Russia rests on a largely unproblematized dichotomy between Orthodox and non-Orthodox denominations, a move that homogenizes an incredibly diverse set of Christian traditions into a generic category often presented as "foreign," which in turn is a gloss for "evangelical," "fundamentalist," and other explicitly proselytizing movements. Although Russia has indeed witnessed growth among evangelical and fundamentalist Christian movements, both homegrown and foreign, this gloss misrepresents a much broader religious spectrum that includes very liberal, progressive denominations—including the majority of congregations and programs that comprised the faith-based assistance world described here. These misrepresentations produce a further misunderstanding of religious pluralism by presenting it either in terms of doctrinal or theological distinction and separateness or in terms of religious homogeneity, rather than through accounts that acknowledge religious syncretism, overlap, or, even more intriguing, mutual misrecognition or even outright elision, such as when different Russian Orthodox churches refuse to recognize each other as legitimately Russian or Orthodox.

Consequently, because scholarly and popular accounts of the complicated relations among Christian communities have primarily highlighted antagonistic relations between Orthodox and non-Orthodox communities on the one hand, and among non-Orthodox Christian denominations on the other, little attention has been given to the dynamics by which Russia's religious communities, Orthodox and non-Orthodox alike, have engaged one another in dialogue and action around a common set of interests beyond those of theology and ritual. This siloing of Russia's religious communities was, in fact, one of the factors motivating the "Interfaith Dialogue" workshop attended by Berger, Metropolitan Hilarion, and other religious leaders.

Within the larger, diverse faith-based community described here there has been a shared commitment to overcome, or at least work around, differences in order to promote social justice causes that are not necessarily tied to any one particular religious orientation. In many respects, the religious component has become a relatively minor feature within the activities of the religious organizations that do assistance work, if it exists at all. As a result, a somewhat different version of Christian religious life has emerged and flourishes in the spaces of intersection and negotiation among diverse religious traditions as the members of these communities forge a broader and more flexible notion of Christian practice through their collaboration on social justice projects, a phenomenon observed by anthropologists working among faith-based communities elsewhere in the world (e.g., Adams 2013; Muehlebach 2012). As will become apparent, what has emerged through these interfaith collaborations is a project of universalist humanism (cf. Muehlebach 2012: 46), what I am calling a secular theology of compassion. This is a practical form of ecumenism that focuses on assistance and justice rather than on doctrine, belief, or religious identity, and illuminates Berger's argument that in a pluralist society, religious institutions are transformed into voluntary associations that provide different opportunities for individuals to pursue their interests (Berger 2013; see also Putnam 2001).

SINGULAR HUMANISM

In fall 2008, during my first official meeting with Nina, the director of the development division within the patriarchate of the Russian Orthodox Church, she presented me with a video about the church's social services projects before describing the challenges that the church has faced in reviving its historic focus on *Diakonie,* or social work. Commenting that even though social ministry has always preceded the church (i.e., historically the church as an institution has focused first on addressing social issues and second on spiritual issues), Nina said that it has been difficult for the post-Soviet church to reinvigorate this tradition of helping. As Nina put it, initially in the post-Soviet period, there was "a kind of boom" in religious life, as Russians were keenly interested in the church and wanted to find someone who had all the answers to their questions. The church suddenly found itself the object of people who wanted answers and of newly formed congregations that demanded help. When people came to the church, she said, they brought with them their own backgrounds, most notably an atheist perspective. As a result, people had "different anticipations and expectations" about religion and the church. These developments put the church under significant stress because it did not have the infrastructure to meet the demand, and there was internal fracturing within the church. According to her account, this was a period of great instability and difficult rebuilding as the church struggled to reinvent itself and reclaim its role as Russia's central spiritual and cultural institution.

Yet Nina also acknowledged that within this period of confessional turmoil, there were some bright spots, including a 1992 roundtable that brought together different groups from within Russia's religious faith communities with the explicit aim of getting them to work together. This was part of a larger project of a simultaneous "social revival" and "social work revival," she said, as the church worked to encourage a diaconal initiative that helped Russians channel their individualized efforts to perform assistance and humanitarian work into more organized and long-term sustaining projects. In describing these efforts, Nina stated, "Humanism is one [i.e., a single] confession."

Although Nina framed her account of the ROC's experiences primarily through the Orthodox perspective of Russia's religious revival in the 1990s, when there was a widespread perception that "foreign" religious movements were threatening Orthodoxy's position as Russia's dominant religious tradition, she was also invoking an idea of a more general Christian orientation that superseded denominational or theological distinctions. As she continued with her account, she referenced other non-Orthodox Christian programs that were active in Moscow, as well as the close working relationships, both formal and informal, that she enjoyed with representatives from other denominations. In fact, long before we met in person, we had heard of one another via several clergy and parishioners from other congregations, as well as through assistance workers with other faith-based programs, none of whom were from the same denominational background as each other or the ROC. (Nina and I met again in 2013 at the "Interfaith Dialogue" workshop in Vienna, where she was part of the official delegation from the patriarchate.)

Nina's invocation of humanism as a single confession was echoed by others from very different perspectives. A devout Christian physician with a faith-based medical clinic stated that he chose to work with other Christians because he believed they all started from the same worldview and assumptions about how to help other people. He commented that when he talked with others who were involved in faith-based assistance, even from different denominational backgrounds, they frequently found common ground talking about how to "model the fruit of the Holy Spirit personally." In another case, one of the staff members for the Christian Church of Moscow's programs for African migrants commented that very few of their recipients and regular volunteers belonged to the CCM. Instead, about half belonged to one of several Pentecostal congregations, while the remainder were Muslim. In fact, during my interviews and surveys with the CCM's African and Middle Eastern recipients, most did not identify themselves as being of the same denomination as the CCM or even Christian but yet noted that helping other people was simply a natural role for all religious organizations.

The timing of my first meeting with Nina was fortuitous as scarcely a few months later, on December 5, 2008, when I was back in Moscow for a short visit, Aleksei II, patriarch of Moscow and All Russia, passed away at his residence outside Moscow. The news quickly spread via telephone, text message, the Internet, and e-mail, and I was soon caught up in discussions with friends and colleagues. Within hours, several Russian television stations were broadcasting commentaries and retrospectives of Patriarch Aleksei's life and career. In both public and private conversations with my friends and colleagues, succession seemed to be an issue of paramount importance and rampant speculation, as observers debated who would assume the role of patriarch and in what direction the new leader would take the church.

The issue of succession especially concerned Russia's non-Orthodox Christian community, as clergy and parishioners alike wondered about the impact of this transition not only on the status of their own congregations and religious practices, but also on the interfaith partnerships they had forged with one another. Within Moscow's non-Orthodox Christian faith-based community, clergy, church staff, and parishioners alike seemed certain that the next patriarch would be either of two men who were highly placed clerics and patriarchate insiders. Although my acquaintances regarded both men as effective and charismatic leaders, they were more concerned with the clerics' personalities and perspectives on Orthodox theology and tradition, including the church's role as a national institution. As became clear during conversations and correspondence, while my acquaintances viewed one man as progressive, amiable, and supportive of a broader ecumenism in Russia, they viewed the other as somewhat mercurial and aligned with a more conservative, traditionalist vision of Orthodoxy and religious exclusivity.

In January 2009 Metropolitan Kirill of Smolensk and Kaliningrad was chosen as the next patriarch. Accounts of Metropolitan Kirill's selection furthered the uncertainty over the future of the Orthodox Church's attitudes and policies toward non-Orthodox Christian religions. While Metropolitan Kirill was described as a supporter of religious tolerance, he was also lauded for his dedication to promoting Orthodox tradition and heritage in Russia. Religious communities both within Russia and abroad pondered whether these two orientations could work productively together to foster simultaneously the continued revival of the Orthodox Church and a greater ecumenism within Russia, or whether this "tolerance" would be reserved for Orthodoxy within Russia and ecumenism would be promoted only with denominations outside Russia.

Perhaps most important of all was the concern among Moscow's faith-based organizations, both Orthodox and non-Orthodox, that the election of this particular man as the new patriarch might lead to a more politically aggressive church that would not only hinder their ability to engage in social work, but also transform their work, against their will, into an explicitly religious project. Acquaintances expressed concern that the otherwise nonreligious civic work they performed might be transformed into a politically salient symbol for perceived religious intrusion. In other words, what they feared most was that their faith-based programs would be drawn into religious battles.

These concerns were not unfounded, and clergy from several denominations related accounts of social and political hostility that they claimed had been initiated by the ROC. Most accounts focused on the personal actions of individual priests from parishes located in neighborhoods where these non-Orthodox churches provide social services. The most commonly told stories focused on priests who either chided parishioners or would-be parishioners about participating in non-Orthodox programs. Although these stories strongly resembled "urban legends," in a few cases interlocutors corroborated these accounts, including one close friend who described having recurring disagreements with the local Orthodox priest about her decision to be an advocate for a Protestant charity. Probably much to the priest's dismay, my elderly friend—a woman who had spent most of her life advocating for the elderly and disabled and standing up to authority (including her KGB ex-husband)—apparently informed the priest that she found that Protestants did a better job of caring for people than the Orthodox did.

More generally, however, non-Orthodox clergy usually invoked the experiences of the Salvation Army as evidence of the problems caused by the ROC. During my earlier research in Russia in the 1990s and early 2000s, the Salvation Army, along with the Hare Krishnas, had been branded as hostile and foreign entities and effectively forced out of Russia. I was thus not surprised to hear clergy reference these two groups when providing the "quintessential" example of confessional infighting within Russia. By the time of this research in the late 2000s, however, the Salvation Army had returned and even enjoyed their own building where they offered extensive social services. The pastoral staff were especially welcoming and modestly proud of their accomplishments, even as they acknowledged that it had been an arduous journey to reestablish themselves in Russia. As one of the senior officers told me, "Our relationship with the Russian Orthodox Church is probably our biggest weakness." She went on to describe how the Salvation Army was denied legal registration in 2002, and then appealed the decision: "We were the first to take an appeal all the way to the European Court of Appeals and win, but it took three years to actualize." She explained that there was "a legend" that a Russian priest told a territorial leader that "the Russian souls are ours [i.e., Orthodox] and we have paid for them with our blood." The officer continued by commenting that she understood their concerns and the history of martyrs in the Orthodox Church. But even though they had shared interests in terms of the social problems they wanted to solve, because the ROC was not friendly to the Salvation Army, it was difficult to make connections with them. She finished by commenting that other clergy in Moscow had been helpful in making introductions and advocating for them, but that as a church, they still lacked a formal strategy for working with the ROC.

Despite the fact that the Salvation Army and the ROC were still struggling to find common ground and ways to interact productively with one another, they belonged to the larger community constituted of other con-gregations and individuals who acted as liaisons and nodes within that larger network. One of the strengths of this larger, flexible network was that it could accommodate multiple perspectives and practices without reducing them to either a singular Christianity or a singular approach to social work. Even when individual congregations or clergy were not engaging one another directly, or were directly hostile to or dismissive of one another, they were still invested in a larger project of forging a singu-lar humanism, as Nina described. Much like Simmel (1903) has described about conflict or Myerhoff (1978) has described in her classic ethnography about elderly Jews who argue and squabble with one another at a com-munity center, conflict is itself a form of social interaction and solidarity in which the negotiation over differences can create a broader form of social interaction and cohesion. As for Moscow's religious communities, it was their struggles alongside and with one another to reconcile their dif-ferences in ways that did not eliminate them or create a generic Christianity that have cultivated a new form of religiously inspired social justice.

FORGING INTERFAITH TIES AND COMMON RIGHTNESS

Over the past ten years, the quiet efforts by Russia's religious communities to forge an explicitly collaborationist approach to charity and social advo-cacy have generated productive, albeit sometimes surprising, partnerships across denominational differences. In some cases, congregations from one denomination support the charitable projects of a congregation repre-senting another denomination by providing money, material goods, and volunteers. In other cases, several congregations have joined forces to operate welfare programs together. Clergy, church staff, and laypeople meet regularly to share ideas and strategies and to help one another on projects. Local interfaith initiatives are supported at the international level by international and transnational ecumenical institutions and fund-ing organizations. The denominational affiliations and histories of these local initiatives are not always matched by the denominational diversity of the ecumenical organizations, as when the Presbyterian Church supports the Baptist Church with funds and staff expertise and when support from

Lutheran World Relief finds its way to individual Catholic congregations. In still other cases, these cooperative ventures are manifest in face-to-face encounters, as clergy, staff, congregants, and other volunteers gather for meetings and work activities, as well as in virtual encounters, with people meeting and communicating through social media.

Despite the Russian Orthodox Church's official stance of theological separatism from other Christian denominations, some individual Orthodox congregations are very much part of these new interdenominational collaborations. One of the more progressive Orthodox churches in downtown Moscow has long enjoyed close relations with its Protestant counterparts. For many years this Orthodox church sponsored a feeding program that operated in the same space and at the same time as a feeding program sponsored by the Christian Church of Moscow. The two churches ordered the same meals for their clients, and their clients were drawn from the same demographic of elderly and disabled pensioners living in the same neighborhood. The only visible sign that there were two separate programs operating simultaneously in the same place was that staff from the two programs were seated at separate tables. The registration cards that clients from the two programs presented to receive their meals were so similar in shape and style that at first glance it was difficult to notice the difference.

Moreover, Moscow's Christian clergy and congregants have actively pursued opportunities to bridge denominational differences in order to create and present a more unified and cohesive sphere of interfaith social action. In spring 2007, the newly arrived minister at the Christian Church of Moscow set up a series of appointments to meet his counterparts at several other of the city's Christian congregations. Several factors motivated the minister's networking. First, as an American, he had only recently arrived in Moscow and was interested in understanding the larger religious landscape. Second, he had quickly discovered that Moscow lacked the tight community of religious professionals he had enjoyed in his previous posting, and he was particularly interested in establishing closer ties with fellow clergy in hopes of initiating pulpit exchanges and joint fellowship events with other congregations. A third factor was that the minister's congregation was in the planning stages for a new program. Members of the congregation felt strongly that their newest project should be a more ecumenically collaborative venture. At the congregation's urging, the minister wanted to meet with clergy in other congregations in order to gauge whether they would be interested in joining with his church in charitable programs.

By midsummer the minister had met with many of his counterparts throughout Moscow, not just with clergy serving congregations with large non-Russian populations, but also Russian clergy serving Russian congregations, notably the Baptist Federation, the Russian Lutheran Church, the Russian Catholic diocese, Korean-Russian Methodists, Korean-Russian Presbyterians, and Russian Orthodox clergy. He and his colleagues had also already begun visiting one another's church services in pulpit exchanges, and congregation members were visiting with one another through shared fellowship activities, including joint excursions to local monasteries and other tourist sites.[1]

At the same time, the congregations had also begun working closely with one another on charitable projects. In one case, a Protestant church and several Russian Orthodox parishes had joined forces to expand their homeless outreach programs. Members of the Protestant congregation had previously donated time, services, and money to assist programs sponsored by several Orthodox churches. One reason for these forms of assistance was that the Protestant church was not able to provide the same services in its own church building because of legal restrictions. Now, however, church members were interested in pursuing the possibility of setting up programs for shelter and medical assistance in their own building. Clergy and members of the Orthodox churches began contributing their own expertise and resources to reciprocate and help the Protestant congregation pursue these objectives. In other cases, youth groups from several congregations served as volunteer support staff in summer camps for underprivileged families operated by yet another religious community.

Collaborative ventures of these kinds require congregations and religious institutions representing different theological perspectives to find common ground in how they structure their programs, determine eligibility for recipients, provide services, formulate their expectations of volunteers, and even in how they present service programs to the public. When clergy, staff, and volunteers from different congregations meet to discuss joint activities, conversations typically revolve around how to reconcile their denominational and theological differences in pursuit of a common goal. Much like at the Interfaith Dialogue, I have been privy to privately uttered complaints from participants in these efforts, as they voiced disagreement or exasperation with the views of their counterparts. Yet the affective dimensions of these frustrations typically remained "offstage" such as in personal chats on the metro after meetings or quickly suppressed eye rolling or sighing. Public encounters were generally collegial, with participants politely questioning one another or ignoring potentially divisive comments. Noticeable exceptions occurred during a series of roundtables sponsored by international development organizations that I attended in 2009 and that I address more fully in chapter 4.

One of the charitable initiatives launched by the CCM, the Russian Lutheran Church, the Russian Baptist Church, and the Russian Catholic community is an excellent example of these efforts to reconcile differences in pursuit of a common good. In summer 2007, representatives from these communities held a series of meetings to explore opening a joint feeding program to serve single mothers with large families. This was a completely new program for each of the three communities, because until that time the CCM had specialized in working with the elderly, the Catholic community provided support primarily to low-income families and refugees, and the Lutheran Church was most proficient in small-scale parish outreach programs such as working with the homeless and offering educational support. Together the three communities hoped to mobilize their respective contacts among Moscow's social workers and welfare officials, local businesspeople, and their volunteer and donor pools.

Over the course of several planning meetings, clergy, staff, and volunteers worked together to blend their communities' respective strengths. Talking with one another through translators (Russian, German, and English were the three languages at play), the participants discussed how their respective religious communities approached, both theologically and practically, issues ranging from defining need, the appropriateness of assistance, and the ethics of personal responsibility to the logistics of launching a new program and securing commitments of assistance. During the planning stages, participants agreed that they shared similar, if not identical, views on the need to help the less fortunate. From their shared perspective, assistance was understood to be an essential part of the spiritual journeys of their respective congregations, even as they admitted that their own denominations had different degrees of experience with the practical implementation of such projects. For instance, the Christian Church of Moscow was the most experienced congregation in terms of knowing how to procure funding and volunteers for welfare projects, attract and motivate volunteers, and ensure the long-term oversight and maintenance of active welfare programs. Although the staff of Caritas had far less experience starting and managing formal welfare programs, including administration and staffing issues, they had established strong working relationships with social workers and other administrators in the city administration, connections that the Christian Church of Moscow lacked. Staff from the Lutheran Church, meanwhile, had little experience operating welfare programs or working with local administrators, but they did have connections with state-level public officials and politicians and with officials of international religious bodies (one of the ministers in President Putin's Cabinet was an active member of the congregation). Although the Baptist Federation had been invited to participate, it did not play an active role in establishing the project. Senior pastors and the outreach director of the Baptist Federation admitted that their community was not yet experienced in social welfare work, and so they could not take a leadership role in the initiative, yet they reassured their colleagues that they and their members were committed to the idea of the program and pledged to help in any way they could.

It was when representatives from the various constituencies discussed the "religious" aspects of the social work that the truly complicated work of forging commonality emerged. In this particular case, there were three different moments in which the participating clergy, staff, and volunteers had to negotiate their religious differences in order to find common ground and move forward with their joint project.

The first moment came during a discussion of the degree to which the social services project should be "religious" in terms of its message and activities. While this was partially a discussion of whether the partners would reveal any religious dimensions to recipients, the greater concern was about how to pitch the project to potential donors and volunteers. One serious issue pertained to whether the social work programs should include any kind of religious activity for recipients. Pastor Gustav, the

Lutheran minister who also served as assistant to the Bishop of the Russian Lutheran Synod, favored including an explicitly mission-oriented approach in the programs, and he argued strongly for publicly promoting the idea that the program would focus on transforming people materially and spiritually. His views were not shared by his colleagues, who politely acknowledged the idea but then moved quickly on to other details.

More problematic for the ministers was the discussion over the precise language to be used in the announcement of the joint project. Pastor Mark from the CCM had written the announcement in such a way as to emphasize the practical nature of the project: the types of services that would be provided, the number of clients served, and the expenses. Pastor Gustav took issue with this approach and described it as too workmanlike. He said that the document was "too serious" and did not focus enough on the spiritual and moral aspects of the project. Instead, he wanted to create a message that was spiritual in order to reach and appeal to persons who might at one time have had a religious orientation or training but were not necessarily religious at this point in their lives. Specifically, Pastor Gustav said that he wanted a message that would appeal to people's deeper feelings and inclinations without being overtly religious. During this discussion, Pastor Andrei, the other Lutheran minister present, answered a telephone call from Father Vasilii, a Russian Catholic priest, and reported to him the nature of the conversation. After Pastor Andrei hung up, he reported back to Pastor Gustav and Pastor Mark that Father Vasilii felt strongly that they needed to bring the regional welfare office into the discussion about the materials, a move that would necessitate the further scrubbing of religiously oriented language and references from the documents.

The second moment of negotiating occurred several weeks later at another organizing meeting. During this encounter, Pastors Gustav, Mark, and Andrei engaged in a protracted debate about whether to include prayers and other explicitly religious references in the ceremonies to mark the opening of the project. The three disagreed with one another about whether it was necessary or even advisable to incorporate explicit displays of religiosity in an otherwise secular event that would include governmental officials. Ultimately, a compromise was reached to limit the expressions of religiosity at the events but to ensure that the clergy themselves engaged in spiritual activities behind the scenes, such as sharing prayers together. Yet even as the three ministers reached a consensus to use the Lord's Prayer, which was common across the Christian denominations represented, it quickly became apparent that there were numerous variations on the phrasing, depending on the specific congregation or theological tradition. They eventually agreed to a plan in which participants would recite the Lord's Prayer together but using the phrasing that represented their own respective theological traditions.

It is important to note that while religiosity was a critical point of debate and disagreement, in general doctrinal differences rarely emerged during the course of planning meetings, and typically only as interesting scholarly points of comparison among clergy who came from different denominations. When such conversations occurred, they most frequently entailed comparative parsing out of minute differences in the meanings of words or practices in their respective liturgies and prayers. Throughout the meetings, participants repeatedly reassured one another that these theological differences were so minor as to be inconsequential and thus not an impediment in the larger task of collaboration. For instance, although every planning meeting began and ended with a prayer led by one of the clergy members, with each participant following the prayer in his or her own way—such as making the sign of the cross, invoking Jesus or the Holy Trinity, or using gender-inclusive or gender-exclusive language—these performances of denominational difference seemed to be relatively inconsequential to the participants. Recitations of the Lord's Prayer were conducted in multiple languages and cadences, as they were in virtually all of the church services that I have attended in Russia.[2] The prayers became a means for participants to affirm their common practical objectives while recognizing their different religious traditions. Thus, for the most part, the planning meetings for the clergy and their volunteers focused almost exclusively on the concrete issues at hand: for instance, locating a cafeteria to provide food services, compiling a list of eligible recipients, training volunteers, and ensuring sufficient funding. In this respect, the clergy and their volunteers shifted modes from being spiritual advisors to their professional roles as specialists in assistance activities (Berger 2013; Malkki 2015).

The third moment that highlighted how consensus and collaboration required delicate maneuvering around differences came with the program's opening festivities several months later. The opening festivities for the new feeding program were planned to be an overtly ecumenical affair. Clergy and congregants from the Christian Church of Moscow, the Lutheran Church, the Catholic Church, the Anglican Church, and the Baptist Federation, among many others, were invited to attend and participate in the opening celebration, with clergy from different congregations and denominations taking turns leading different parts of the worship service. The event was also attended by officials from local government agencies, representatives from supportive nonreligious, nongovernmental organizations, and diplomatic staff from embassies that worked closely with some of the congregations.

The most notable absence was that of the Russian Orthodox Church. Although officials from the patriarchate had been invited, they had declined. Yet while their absence could, at first glance, be interpreted as a sign of the ROC's continuing distancing from, and even hostility toward, Moscow's non-Orthodox Christian congregations, the reason had less to do with theological differences with non-Orthodox Christianity than it had to do with political problems within the Russian Orthodox community. Even as the patriarch's office officially declined the invitation, the patriarch's staff unofficially sent a message to their counterparts at the Lutheran Church that the patriarch supported the venture but regrettably could not send anyone to attend the festivities publicly because of ongoing political problems with the Russian Orthodox Church Abroad, which is based in the United States and comprised primarily of diaspora Russians. The ROC and the ROCA have long been engaged in a protracted battle over which church is the legitimate spiritual and political home for Russia's Orthodox believers. As such, the patriarch of the ROC could not risk being seen—or having one of his representatives seen—in public with a representative from the ROCA, even if they both supported the same goals. While the patriarchate's position on social justice activity aligned with that of these congregations, and even of the ROCA, the larger political issues that emerged from internal theological differences prevented the Russian Orthodox Church from demonstrating its support publicly.

The ecumenical diversity and interfaith collaboration displayed in the events leading up to the creation of this social services program are not unique but play out in many other activities across Moscow as individuals from different religious backgrounds find ways to work together on faith-related matters. Catholic-inspired social programs such as the Sant'Egidio street ministry and Sisters of Mercy similarly attract a theologically diverse set of volunteers who either set aside doctrinal differences or find ways to reconcile them as they work side by side. In the case of Sant'Egidio, after volunteers deliver meals and chat with recipients, they gather together for a shared meal and worship service. The worship service reflects the diversity of participants: Catholic hymns sung by participants who bring with them their own liturgical traditions—Catholic, Anglican, and Orthodox during the service I attended—and prayers that incorporate multiple liturgical and national languages. Although ushers handed out hymnals and songbooks, worshippers consulted them merely for suggestions on wording, not for tunes or for a singular form of prayer. Through singing together, worshippers found and engaged each other sonically, creating their own harmonies and counter-harmonies that in turn produced a shared experience forged from difference, a phenomenon similar to the practices of Dutch Syriac Orthodox Christian choir members described by Sarah Bakker Kellogg (2015) and among Orthodox Christians at the Estonian-Russian border described by Jeffers Engelhardt (2010).

RECONCILING DIFFERENCE IN CHRISTIAN JUSTICE WORK

Beyond creating opportunities for interfaith cooperation, Moscow's faith-based groups are also cultivating more ecumenical forms of religious life, within both individual congregations and social services programs. One of the most intriguing features common to the social justice–oriented faith communities described in this book is that individual congregations have each attracted staff, volunteers, donors, and other supporters from outside their denominations, including Jews, Muslims, Hindus, atheists, and non-practicing individuals. Few of the CCM's most dedicated volunteers belong to the CCM's congregation, but instead come from many other religious backgrounds and congregations, including non-Christian ones.

In each of the programs that I have followed, clergy, staff, volunteers, and recipients alike described both their activities and their desire to work with particular programs in terms of aligning their personal beliefs and practices of social action into a set of tenets based on a common understanding of social justice. Although some informants did explain their views in terms of religious motivations or theological requirements, most consistently framed their perspectives in the languages of socially correct action: "human rights," "humanitarianism," "social justice," "love," "friendship," and more simply "the right thing to do." This significance of common rightness is illuminated in informants' responses to questions about why they directed their time, labor, and other resources to a specific program. Although factors such as social networks, time constraints, and distance were important considerations in how clergy, staff, and volunteers made decisions about which projects to support and in what ways, these issues seemed in many ways to be secondary to another factor: the perceived "rightness" of a particular social program. Ultimately, the ability and willingness of faith communities and their participants to conform to norms of social action and social justice becomes in some ways more important than theological orientation in how faith communities are evaluated in terms of their value and contributions to Russian society.

Clergy, staff, and volunteers revealed that they evaluated not only whether the interests, goals, and methods of social programs appealed to their personal sense of appropriate social work, but also whether these programs were consistent in how they pursued their objectives. For example, one of the qualities of the CCM's food sharing programs that most appealed to volunteers was that the community consistently and reliably met its goals. As volunteers and donors have told me, this consistency has given CCM's programs an appearance of stability that many volunteers, donors, recipients, and other supporters found reassuring. In turn, that stability informed the CCM's reputation as a successful and compelling leader in the field of Russian social justice work.

Attributes of consistency and reliability also informed the social value of other successful interfaith programs. Most notable are the activities of a progressive Orthodox church that sponsors numerous social programs, often in partnership with non-Orthodox Christian congregations, including some of the ones described here. Although it was rumored that the congregation had at times been under pressure from the patriarchate for not adhering to church policy regarding theological interpretation and relationships with non-Orthodox congregations, the church continued its social work in partnership with a broader ecumenical community. The church's commitment to adhering to its own principles of social action appealed to observers who saw this consistency as evidence of the church's moral authority. More recently, rumors that this congregation had run afoul of the increasingly conservative stance of the patriarchate merely signaled to supporters that this church remains true to its principles and practices.

In summer 2015, when I returned to Moscow, acquaintances told me that the church had closed one of its programs for the elderly, allegedly because the church's liberal politics had angered the patriarchate. While it was public knowledge that the program had closed, I was unable to verify the rumors about the reasons for its closing. One day, just a few blocks away from this church, I walked past another Orthodox church that was sponsoring pro-Palestine political groups, including non-Orthodox Christian groups, in an organized community outreach demonstration. Tables with political materials were nestled among booths selling Palestine-made artisanal food and crafts projects. As I was only in Moscow for two weeks, I was unable to find out how long the demonstration continued or learn whether it might have generated any responses from the larger Orthodox community.

While ideals and practices of conformity may be more familiar coming from materialist-oriented accountability regimes, especially those that are prevalent in highly bureaucratized systems like development programs and neoliberal systems, they are part of the moral systems that are embedded within Russian religious life (Garrard and Garrard 2008; Steinberg and Wanner, eds. 2008). Although religious institutions have never been the sole sources of morality in Russia, especially during the Soviet period when the state promoted its own vision of a secular morality, in the post-Soviet period morality has emerged as an important venue through which religious traditions and religious practitioners can articulate their roles in this new society and attract followers (e.g., Rogers 2008; Zigon 2008). As religious institutions and traditions assume status as the repositories and conduits of moral sensibilities, practices of theological distinction are being reframed as practices of moral distinction. In other words, individual religious communities are distinguished from one another not simply through their respective beliefs or doctrinal practices, but through the particular moral systems with which each is associated (Caldwell 2008; Hann and Goltz, eds. 2010; Mitrokhin 2004; Rogers 2008; Zigon 2008).

Ultimately, what is at stake is the extent to which any particular religious institution or tradition can lay exclusive claim to a specific moral system. More important than the efforts of religious communities to stake out their claims within a field of moral systems, however, are their efforts to stake a political claim as the most legitimate, perhaps even sole, authority on morality in today's Russia. The Russian Orthodox Church has been particularly active in asserting its moral authority through extensive morality campaigns covering such diverse issues as sexuality, abortion and reproductive politics, family relations, drug and alcohol use, gambling, immigration reform, and national security, among many others. Debates over moral authority also shape efforts by such institutions as the Russian Orthodox Church and the Russian state to determine legally and socially the status of the many different religious traditions that exist in the country.

Within the Christian realm alone, Russian Orthodox, Anglican, Lutheran, Methodist, Baptist, and many other congregations and clergy have engaged in extensive public relations outreach efforts to introduce their specific visions of the moral and good life to potential followers. These efforts to promote religious movements are reflected not just in the increase in the number of churches and church services, but also in the religious publication of Bibles, prayer books, meditation guides, spiritual self-help manuals, and other guides for denominationally or spiritually specific moral living, television and radio programs devoted to instructional conversations about religion, and more informal person-to-person outreach. Such guides are meant not simply to introduce potential followers to a particular religious tradition, but to provide them with a coherent framework for orienting their beliefs and practices to that religious tradition. Muscovite acquaintances who purchased religious tracts, "how-to" books and videos, and other such items told me that they found them useful guides for knowing how to act and what to believe in particular denominational settings.

Contestations over defining and legitimating particular combinations of religious and moral sensibility, coupled with the attendant issues of how individuals align their personal beliefs and actions "correctly" in accordance with theological policy and practice, comprise a "politics of right-ness." Practitioners are concerned not simply with fulfilling the conditions of their respective religious traditions, but with fulfilling them properly, according to the rules of how that fulfillment should occur.

This notion of rightness redirects the analysis of the values informing social action beyond a dichotomy between doxa (beliefs) and praxis (practices), and between the ethical and the moral, to focus instead on the normative systems of both doxa and praxis. Jarrett Zigon (2007) has argued that the difference between the moral and the ethical is a distinction between doxa and praxis. That is, the moral refers to repertoires of knowledge that shape actors' beliefs and perspectives. These repertoires are deeply embedded systems of knowledge, whether subconscious or unconscious, and thus not immediately knowable or accessible to actors even as they shape their beliefs and actions. The ethical, by contrast, pertains to the moments and processes of awareness and reflection in the repertoires of knowledge and the circumstances in which they are evoked and engaged. In contrast to what Zigon has suggested, however, for the case of the faith-based organizations discussed here, doxa and praxis are both entangled in the politics of rightness, with neither one separated out as moral or ethical. They are both parts of the same whole, an orientation encapsulated in the perspective of faith-based social justice activists that their work is faith in action.

In distinguishing between orthodoxy as a system of "correct belief" and orthopraxy as a system of "correct practice," James L. Watson (1998) calls attention to the fact that there are coherent, delineated forms and procedures inherent in both belief and ritual systems. For religious rituals or beliefs to have meaning and efficacy, followers must adhere to the proper or correct enactment of these forms and procedures. In the context of Moscow's faith communities, participants are concerned with how the proper enactment of belief and practice reflects the moral order of Christian social justice work, so that social activists are careful to create a common framework of rightness underlying their activities and the values they attach to those activities. Thus in the logic of orthodoxy and ortho-praxy proposed by Watson, these faith communities become meaningful and productive in Russian religious life because they are properly adhering to the rules of doxa and praxis for social action. By extension, it is this conformity to the norms of social action—rightness, in other words—that enables these communities to stake out claims in the field of morality.

The issue of efficacy raised by Watson (1988), and similarly by other theorists of ritual (e.g., Turner 1969), is critical to understanding not just how Christian social justice activities work, but also whom they serve and benefit. Anthropological studies of religion emphasize the ways in which belief and performance are directed at the self, at a deity, or at both simultaneously. Fenella Cannell (2006: 20) argues that "personal interiority" is a recurring theme in understandings of Christianity, and more particularly Protestantism, so that the motivation for Christians is a process of self-making as an expression of efforts to imitate God, to become Godly (see also Miller and Yamamori 2007: 2). Redemption, salvation, and transcendence are all states oriented to particular relational configurations between the self and a deity.

Curiously, anthropologists and other scholars of religion have not fully considered how orthopraxy and orthodoxy might be directed toward others beyond the self or a deity—most notably toward other members of society and toward society itself. This orientation to society, especially a civil society, confuses conventional distinctions between this-worldly and other-worldly religions (e.g., Weber 1946). Although such practices as tithing, alms-giving, and charity may be framed as a means to articulate and attain a presumed relationship between the giver, in this case a religious practitioner, and the deity, the same activities are also directed, whether explicitly or implicitly, to a this-worldly social community of real individuals who in turn comprise a this-worldly political economy (Caldwell 2008; Coleman 2006; Parry 1986). Social action, by contrast, presents a possibility for a simultaneous orientation to both an other-world and a this-world larger than the Self.[3] The efforts of Moscow's religious communities and their supporters to help other people thus present a different way of understanding conventional categorical distinctions between worlds and participants, as well as the very nature of "religion" itself as a distinct category and phenomenon (Adams 2013; Bakker Kellogg 2015; Berger 2013).[4]

Framed within these perspectives, rightness can be understood as proper adherence to a set of practices and beliefs about social action in order to bring about benefits simultaneously to oneself, to others, and to a higher being. These interpretations of rightness are crucial for constructing the pathways that allow religious communities to forge a shared set of social justice orthodoxies and orthopraxies, even from diverse and conflicting theological perspectives. The importance of rightness for constructions of morality emerges perhaps most strikingly in the views on social and moral decay that have appeared regularly in both public discourse and private conversations in Moscow (see also Zigon 2008). Beneath complaints about decay and moral decline are fears about the disarray and disintegration of the very structures and codes of norms that comprise Russian social order. In other words, concerns about moral decay are, at heart, concerns about order and rightness, as Russians debate the extent to which individuals and institutions conform to or deviate from social norms of appropriate behavior.[5]

As for the specific case of social assistance and social action, Muscovites' concerns about immorality arise when they criticize those who are believed to be withholding assistance from family and neighbors. Immoral individuals are those who violate social norms of mutual assistance and reciprocity by keeping money and other resources for their own purposes rather than sharing with people presumed to be in their social networks (Caldwell 2004: 86–99). In other words, selfishness is immoral because it fails to conform to cultural norms of mutual support. This understanding of immorality as a lack of conformity to norms is similarly evident in public attitudes, mostly negative, about New Russians, *biznesmen*, and other political elites who are suspected (or known) to have violated the standards of social and economic propriety. Intriguingly, Russia's mafia is often valorized because, unlike the state, it is believed to provide social order and stability (Ries 2002).

Moralizing discourses were evident in the frustrations of Muscovites who criticized state agencies and state workers for being apathetic or even hostile to the needs of the less fortunate, thereby deviating from expectations about compassion and care. Even aid programs risk criticism for not meeting public expectations about assistance. When I first began working with the feeding programs of the Christian Church of Moscow in the late 1990s, donors frequently gave the community small food and personal hygiene items (e.g., candy bars, instant soup packets, soap, toothbrushes) to distribute to recipients. On some occasions, there were enough donated items for every client to receive more than one; on other occasions, items were limited to one per person. Clients became accustomed to receiving these free items, and on days when supplies were limited or, even worse, were depleted early in the morning, it was not unusual for them to become angry and berate staff and volunteers for treating them improperly and unfairly. Clients who manipulated the system to receive more than their fair share were similarly accused of impropriety by other clients. Russian Orthodox churches in particular have been sharply criticized as immoral and, more precisely, corrupt because of their social action policies that are often seen as violating a sacred trust with the nation (Caldwell 2010). By allegedly failing to uphold proper norms of social action—that is to help others—the church had failed to conform to standards of rightness.

Hence it is the ability of institutions and individuals to conform to orthopraxies and orthodoxies of social action that determines whether they are perceived as moral or immoral, and by extension, successful. Interfaith projects seem particularly well positioned to demonstrate their moral authority, because all of their efforts to create truly collaborative partnerships are ultimately oriented to minimize individual differences in the mission of achieving conformity with a shared set of values and practices about social action. Through careful negotiation of theological and political differences, churches forge a new common ground that, in turn, sets standards to which they can adhere and demonstrate their moral authority. As a result of these projects of alignment, social justice activities have become the arena where Russians look to a set of cultural guidelines and social norms regarding proper actions and beliefs. This attention to qualities of correctness, appropriateness, and rightness is important for understanding the complicated nexus of morality, religion, and spirituality not just in Russia, but also in studies of Christianity and other religious movements more generally. Ultimately, it is the ability of religious groups to deliver social justice work that provides a vantage point for evaluating the place of religion and its moral authority in Russian life today.

RECONSIDERING CHRISTIAN MORAL EXCEPTIONALISM

With regard to religious life in Russia, interfaith social justice projects challenge and complicate more familiar accounts of religious institutions as moral authorities by revealing how the qualities of morality come into being and how authority is achieved. Interfaith communities directly challenge perceptions of Christian moral exceptionalism in which some denominations or congregations are accorded special legitimacy as sources and arbiters of moral authority, a tendency that is particularly relevant for popular and scholarly attitudes toward Russian Orthodoxy.

Attention to interfaith social action projects also reveals that Christian communities are not necessarily moral in and of themselves. That is, it is not their status as religious institutions that endows them with the status of moral authority. The enactment of particular norms through the realm of religious activity may give them greater cultural valence, but their value is not derived specifically or exclusively from religion. Rather, morality is a state that must be achieved through a process of conformity. When seen from this perspective, morality is disarticulated from religion. The movement of morality outside the exclusive domain of theology and doctrine thus facilitates ecumenism across religious boundaries in pursuit of a shared theology of compassion and social action. As for Russian Orthodoxy, the disentangling of theology and morality enables Orthodox churches to resolve the conundrum of Christian exceptionalism. Individual churches from diverse denominations can work together on a common project of moral action separate from the issues of faith, belief, ritual, and identity that would otherwise divide them. This working together across differences is what allows them to pursue and achieve what ROC's development director Nina called a "singular humanism." It is also what allows faith-based organizations to become "secular" institutions, both legally and practically, a detail that becomes more apparent in their interactions with government agencies and international development organizations.

The bigger question that emerges is whether this is a religious humanism, an interreligious or interfaith humanism, or perhaps even a secular humanism? Benjamin, the British director of Oxfam's Russia division, noted the tension between religious life and social justice when he commented: "Social development is supposed to be secular." Although he was not advocating that religious organizations should not be involved in social justice projects, he succinctly stated the crux of the matter: despite the utopian visions promoted by social development and social justice ideologies that promote the creation of another, better world that is distinct from the miseries of the here and now, these activities are always deeply grounded in this-world realities. This is the tension that Moscow's faith-based organizations navigate in their efforts to work together to care for their fellow humans. By paying attention to the rules and norms of belief and behavior for social justice we see a different dimension of religious life that encompasses both practical, this-worldly interests and spiritual, other-worldly interests.

Consideration of the nontheological aspects of religious social action opens new interstices and spaces for considering how and where both common Christianities and common moralities might take shape. Interfaith social justice activities remind us that multiple orthodoxies and orthopraxies pertaining to different registers of religious life are always at work. Just as rituals do not have meaning and transformative power in and of themselves but only through their proper enactment (Turner 1969), morality acquires power and significance only through its proper enactment. For Moscow's faith-based assistance providers it is this claim on propriety that motivates and sustains their faith that they are doing "the right thing," even when they cannot see the results of that work immediately or concretely. The nature of this "right thing," as it is rendered as an object and mode of care, and how Moscow's faith-based assistance providers struggle to articulate it and realize it, is the subject of the next chapter.

3 Practical Love

[To work] with love . . . is a good thing.

—Natalya, director of a Russian human rights NGO,
  Red Cross–UNHCR Roundtable, 2009

The efforts of Russian religious communities to engage ever more intensively and publicly with matters of "care" over the past twenty years have coincided with a turn among anthropologists to focus on human suffering and responses to this suffering. Ethnographic accounts of crisis, poverty, inequality, welfare, development, humanitarianism, and human rights have all emerged as materially and ethically urgent ethnographic topics that have, in turn, contributed to an ever-expanding field of theoretical and applied work.

In this era marked by concerns with inequality, vulnerability, and victimhood (Farmer 2003; Fassin and Rechtman 2009; Kleinman 1997; Malkki 2015), the terrain of daily life has changed dramatically, as has the fundamental nature of the person. After urban anthropology in the 1990s enlarged the scale and geographic scope of the "village" that was so fundamental to ethnographic inquiry, the anthropology of inequality and suffering has similarly generated new settings and landscapes. Simultaneously emplaced and displaced, fleeting and enduring, sites such as refugee camps, homeless shelters and encampments, and aid distribution centers have become long-term and even quasi-permanent structures around which regular communities and cultural worlds have formed (e.g., Cabot 2014; Desjarlais 1997; Malkki 1995; Smart 2001; Song 2006).

The movement of the most invisible and vulnerable segments of society—those who are poor, homeless, disabled, addicted, or undocumented—from the margins of their respective societies to center stage in ethnographic accounts has profoundly reshaped the ethnographic features that define societies around the world and how we view them (see especially Bourgois and Schonberg 2009). In other words, what we know about different societies changes dramatically when the vantage point shifts from the mainstream and the comfortable to the margins and the vulnerable, and when the point of view is not one of pity or contempt but of empathy and even outrage on their behalf (e.g., Farmer 2003).

These shifts have also changed the nature of the ethnographic subject, now that social actors are no longer divided into those with power and those without, but into those who do and those who have been done upon (Caton 2006; Robbins 2013: 448). Didier Fassin and Richard Rechtman's (2009: 140) observation that trauma came to be constituted as a category of experience and quality of personhood—"trauma had become an essential human value, a mark of the humanity of those who suffered it and those who cared for them"—is equally applicable to experiences such as inequality and vulnerability. In response, this repositioning of suffering, crisis, and trauma as defining features of humanness has inspired new modes of analysis and impulses for action (e.g., Bornstein 2012; Redfield 2013: 28n26; Fassin and Rechtman 2009: 153).

Above all, this focus on suffering and assistance has raised questions about particular types of subjects and the theoretical and methodological means to identify, reach, and understand those subjects. Perhaps the most immediately recognizable subject is the figure of the marginalized, disenfranchised, disempowered person, most visible in their status as victim, refugee, the invisible, and the anti-citizen. Key to understanding and rescuing this figure, both as practical and ethical projects, have been theories about oppressive structures and the ways they separate and distance persons from themselves, their fellow humans, and their fundamental nature and rights (e.g., Agamben 1998; Farmer 2003).[1] Yet even as this figure of the stripped-down, bare life individual that features so prominently in recent accounts of suffering reveals particular logics about today's world, most notably in terms of how resources and power flow partially and unevenly, it is still only a partial glimpse into this world and the possibilities for new modes of analysis and activism.

The vulnerable, suffering subject has been accompanied by the new figure of the person who provides aid and care. Represented in various guises—social worker, health care provider, professional aid worker, and volunteer—this caretaker is what Liisa Malkki (2015: 2) has described as the "humanitarian subject [who is] characterized by a desire to help" (see also Bornstein 2012) and Andrea Muehlebach (2012) has termed the "moral neoliberal." In a global neoliberal order where care has been privatized and outsourced from states to individuals—this "humanitarianization of the public sphere" (Muehlebach 2012: 46)—the motivation to care is presumed to exist as an intrinsic part of the good citizen.[2] As virtues such as compassion become resources that support state needs and goals, the responsibility to care about and for others thus becomes a technique of governance, and self-governance more precisely (Muehlebach 2012; Rudnyckyj 2010). Yet as Malkki (2015: 164) has pointed out, it is never clear if the compulsion to care comes from a position of power or a position of vulnerability or need, thereby further complicating any clear understanding of the relationships that might hold between those who provide aid and those who receive it.

This humanitarian turn in anthropology has prompted some scholars to question whether attention to suffering, marginalization, and disempowerment has come at both a practical and intellectual cost. In his rejoinder to what he sees as anthropology's privileging of "suffering" as a human problem and ethnographic topic over the past two decades, Joel Robbins (2013: 448) has called for an "anthropology of the good." For Robbins, anthropologists' ethnographic and theoretical preoccupation with social problems, political disenfranchisement, physical dislocation, and misery and despair may have obviated our ability to engage in critical engagement with these issues. Robbins's concern is not with the value of these topics, but rather with the possibility that anthropologists might lose their critical, objective distance and detachment from the people they study. For Robbins (2013), within this anthropological vision of suffering as a human universal lurks the potential for anthropologists to imagine a shared experience, even a sameness, with their ethnographic subjects.

Certainly within anthropology, efforts to imagine and create connections with ethnographic subjects have been essential to the fieldwork experience, whether as a methodological technique or as a reality for researchers who can claim a position of insiderness to the communities they are studying. Yet among some scholars working on suffering-related topics, there has been an explicit push to "go native" in an effort to document and understand better the experiences of subjects. As Seth Holmes has explained for his research among Mexican migrant farmworkers, this was partly a methodological decision to understand firsthand the lived realities of the danger and suffering experienced by his subjects, and partly an ethical necessity, as he could not in good faith do his research from the comfort of his privileged position (Holmes 2013: 8–10; cf. De León 2015). This is a stance that seemingly resonates with Michael Jackson's (2012: 5) caution about the limits of conventional anthropological training, in which merely reading about theories and methods "will not help you reach an understanding of others unless you share in their lives as a fellow human being, with tact and sensitivity, care and concern."

Robbins does not discount the power of empathy as a critical lens, either methodologically or conceptually, but he suggests that imagining sameness might lead not only to the loss of a distinct Other, and therefore ethnographic confusions where the anthropologist's position and experiences trump those of their true subjects, but also to a pessimistically inclined anthropology where the only possible cultural realities to be revealed and examined are misery. Instead, Robbins (2013: 457) challenges anthropologists to retain a sense of optimism—to suspend our critical cynicisms about a world in decline and despair—and instead to "focus on the good." By critically questioning the work done by the "suffering subject," Robbins reminds us of the productive potential of objectively practiced empathy and compassion to illuminate other people's lives.

What Robbins is calling for is a critical empathy and compassion that retains both intimacy and distance simultaneously between the anthropologist as self and the subject as Other. This is the stance illuminated by Michael Jackson (2012: 2) in his inquiry into humanness as being caught up in the "interplay between being a part of and apart from the world," what he calls the state of being "between one and one another." Grounding his perspective in the idea that humans are fundamentally social creatures who are constantly interacting with other people, Jackson (2012: 3) observes that "neither complete detachment nor complete engagement is a real ontological possibility . . . . Rather, these contrasted terms suggest that while human existence is profoundly social . . . it always entails a sense of our own singularity and aloneness." Relationships, then, are always dialogical oscillations between registers and perspectives.

Finding the space in-between, what Mattingly (2010) has called "border zones," is what becomes productive, not only for anthropologists but also for assistance providers such as the individuals described in this book. Members of Moscow's faith-based assistance world used numerous terms to describe the nature of their interactions with the people they tried to help. Some of these were more practical terms that defined forms of assistance: support (*podderzhka*), defense (*zashchita*), and help (*pomoshch'*). More frequently, however, were terms that evoked affective relationships of intimacy and familiarity: friendship (*druzhba*), love (*liubov'*), and compassion, empathy, and sympathy.[3] As for compassion, empathy, and sympathy, the terms are especially revealing, because they deliberately invoked qualities of shared experience: *sochuvstvie* (to feel something with another), *sostradanie* (to suffer something with another), and *soperezhivanie* (to endure something with another). Rarely did I hear distancing terms such as pity (*pozhalet'*, to have pity on) or blame (*vina*, or *vinovatyi*, to be guilty). Above all, the diverse terms that were routinely used by assistance workers and recipients alike all invoked the idea that care work was very much something which conveyed simultaneously affective and practical qualities of an experience and relationship that was shared while maintaining distinctions between individuals. These were practical modes of accompaniment and of co-presence as much as, or even more than, they were modes of co-feeling (Kundera 1984).

From this vantage point, care, whether rendered as empathy, compassion, love, social justice, or human rights, was understood to be intrinsically connected to a quality of humanness, and most specifically to a form of intersubjective sociality, a perspective echoed by other scholars who have explored empathy and compassion. Echoing Shott's (1979) notion of sympathy as a "social emotion," Catherine Lutz (1988) has argued that emotions are simultaneously subjective and intersubjective because they bring individuals into dyadic relationships. In his work on spiritual economies in Indonesia, Daromir Rudnyckyj (2010: 161) has observed that affect has a "transitive quality" when it produces "relations practiced between individuals," while Omri Elisha (2011: 157) has described the compassion work of Tennessee evangelicals as aimed at "a desire to collapse or transcend the boundaries of human intersubjectivity."

Reminiscent of Adam Smith's concept of "fellow-feeling," these affective relationships are formed through an active "taking [on] the role of the other" (Clark 1997: 27). These acts of "taking on" might be ideational or physical, or both. Douglas Hollan and Jason Throop (2008: 393) have described the intersubjective dimensions of empathy as "a type of metacommunication among people." More specifically, in his work on Yap experiences of suffering and compassion, Throop (2008) has elaborated on how it is physical experiences that link individuals, both those who experience the pain and those who sympathize by re-experiencing that pain through their own perspectives. Drawing on philosophical inquiries into the nature of empathy as a form of transference and access between individuals—the one who has the initial experience and the one who seeks to understand it—Throop (2010) argues that compassion is a moral act of trying to know and make sense of another's experiences. Hollan (2008: 484) adds that the value of knowing one another is the recognition that it brings: "empathy unfolds in the transitional space between those who seek to understand and those who can still imagine being understood." When individuals take on the experiences of another as their own, intimacy becomes an intersubjective merging of difference.

If acts of compassion are truly social acts, however, they require social systems in which to be enacted, a detail that raises intriguing questions about the nature of these social interactions as well as the types of social and cultural institutions that make empathy, compassion, and charity possible. For Hollan and Throop, among others, these are social institutions of communication, and empathy or compassion are ultimately projects of knowledge and imagination that seek to bridge difference. Yet bridging difference is not precisely what either Jackson or Robbins is promoting. Rather, both of them are seeking to preserve those moments in which difference and distance are made and made meaningful, because it is acts of doing that define both the anthropological project and the nature of humanness itself.

At the same time, Moscow's faith-based assistance providers would argue that simply knowing another's experience is not enough. For them, simply knowing another's circumstances and imagining how another must feel will not bring about change in the world. Nor will distinguishing between those who act upon others and those who are acted upon. Rather, as Moscow's faith-based assistance providers would argue, these spaces and moments of in-betweenness are full of potential that may or may not be realized (see Mattingly 2010). As such, because aid work is always partial and fraught with doubts, anxieties, and missed connections, both accidental and deliberate (Bornstein 2012; Cabot 2014; Mattingly 2010), compassionate relationships always require a delicate balancing between intimacy and distancing (Malkki 2015). Consequently, because good is never guaranteed, it is more important to consider instead how ordinary people act with one another to bring good into the world, why they do so, and how they explain those efforts in ways that deliberately invoke the simultaneously intimate and distant dynamics of being "between one and one another." Members of Moscow's faith-based assistance community struggle every day to put co-fellowness and co-presence into practice in ways that not only celebrate the dialogical relationship that inheres in every social relationship but also contribute to something with forward momentum that is both deeper and bigger than any one person.

BEING WITH ONE ANOTHER

Standing and walking have been intrinsic to the experiences of the people I have followed, and to the fieldwork encounter itself, as I have followed people through the many spaces and relationships of their daily lives. For Muscovites of all backgrounds, movement through and out of city spaces has long been a deeply social, even political experience that is far more than a form of conveyance from one place to another. Strolling along city streets or through forested parks offers a sense of intimacy and relaxation for friends, while standing in lines cultivates a shared experience of communalism (whether desired or not). Despite the frequency of subway trains and other forms of public transit, the sheer number of people riding together ensures that most passengers do much of their traveling—and other personal activities such as reading, talking on their phones, or even sleeping—throughout the city while standing up. Until the relatively recent introduction of a system whereby passengers pay before entering a mass transit vehicle, standing-room-only buses and trams encouraged a spirit of trust and responsibility as riders passed money and tickets, from one hand to another, between fellow passengers to the driver and then back again.[4]

For Moscow's most vulnerable residents who lack adequate resources for the necessities of daily life (eating, sleeping, bathing), movement and standing still, often as states of being in constant interplay, have acquired additional significance as defining features of their everyday lives. Aid seekers and recipients find themselves forced to move about constantly in an effort to cobble together assistance from various programs and to generate income from odd jobs, begging, or even scavenging for recyclables that they can resell. As city authorities clamped down on fare-evaders on public transit, it became increasingly difficult for the poor and the dishonest alike to "ride like a hare" and catch a free trip on the bus or trolley. As a result, despite age, disabilities, or other hindrances, it was not uncommon for the aid seekers with whom I came into contact to be in a seemingly perpetual state of walking as they navigated the city. One elderly woman I knew was rarely home because she was always walking around Moscow in order to frequent the various organizations that were dispensing free meals and clothing. For those who were homeless or forced to share inexpensive quarters with many other poor people, walking around the city afforded a sense of privacy and security that they lacked elsewhere. Not surprisingly, shoes and socks were highly desired objects, and one's personal housing or financial status was often evident in the state of one's footwear.

For aid workers, this perpetual motion was problematic, both because of presumed fears about the toll of constant movement on the physical health and safety of already vulnerable persons and because it meant that recipients did not always reliably turn up for those appointments for which they had to travel far. For organizations that served homeless populations, staff were never entirely sure where to find their recipients on any given night and sometimes had to add extra time to their schedules to drive or walk around until they found them. When staff from several religious groups that worked with African migrants recognized that their drop-in programs were often the only time that recipients might have stopped moving in several days, they added chairs and couches to give weary recipients a chance to take a nap or put down a heavy bag.

At the same time, the protocols of assistance programs often require recipients to wait, most typically by standing in line, first to show the identification cards that entitle them to services and second to receive the actual services. While aid providers do their best to reduce the amount of time that recipients spend standing and waiting and to provide a few chairs for the most needy, standing is an unavoidable reality as the number of recipients often exceeds the number of staff and volunteers or the seats available. In the late 1990s, when the Christian Church of Moscow opened a new soup kitchen in central Moscow, a long line of both enrolled and would-be recipients formed several hours before the program opened, filling the dining room and overflowing into the cramped vestibule and on to the sidewalk outside. After the program's staff started the registration process, the scene was crowded and chaotic as staff from the CCM and local welfare office attempted to confirm those individuals who were actually enrolled and write down the names of individuals who wanted to be enrolled if spaces later became available. In an era before regular computer use in Russian social welfare offices, the lists had been handwritten the night before by staff in the municipal welfare office. With names largely illegible and not in alphabetical order, the process was time-consuming and forced hundreds of elderly and disabled Muscovites to stand in line for hours. Individuals who were turned away had no choice but to walk across the district to the welfare offices where they could appeal their case. The same scene played out every day for the next week, until the rosters were finalized and organized. Recipients at other programs encountered similar standing routines. In fact, it was often easy to identify program distribution points not by marked signs but by the clusters of people standing and waiting for services.

Walking, standing, and waiting were not activities exclusive to aid recipients but also structured the daily routines of aid workers. Many programs depended on staff and volunteers who spent hours standing while sorting boxes of donations, handing out clothes, or serving food to recipients. The centerpiece of several faith-based programs was their street ministries. Several nights a week, volunteers walked Moscow's streets, delivering meals to homeless people and engaging in casual, friendly conversation with them, sometimes for an hour or so at a time. When I accompanied Salvation Army volunteers on their nightly rounds, we first spent almost an hour driving around a remote Moscow neighborhood, searching for signs of the people who formed their primary recipient community before finding about forty individuals waiting in a small neighborhood park, some by themselves and others in clusters of three or four people. After serving the recipients, we loaded up the van and set off again in search of the next group. In her description of the nature of the Salvation Army's approach to social work, Captain Alexandra explicitly referenced movement to connect their on-the-ground activities with the expectations placed on professional Salvation Army social ministry staff: "We are used to being able to be transient. The attitude of the Salvation Army is 'I'll go where the Army needs me.'" She noted that for some new Salvation Army members this was a difficult philosophy to put into practice, especially for native Muscovites whose families had always lived in the city and no one had ever moved away.

The Christian Church of Moscow's long-running program to pack biweekly food bags for refugees was another project that depended on the willingness of volunteers to devote considerable time and energy to walking to buy and collect groceries and other items to be included in the bags. For many years, one group of dedicated volunteers and staff made a weekly trek to several city markets located in different regions of Moscow. In order to stretch the program's budget as far as possible, the volunteers bought staple items at the markets where they were cheapest—frozen chickens in one market, rice and oil in another, and soup packets in yet another. Traversing the city by food and public transit and toting the increasingly heavier bags required a full day of physical stamina. More recently, a warehouse supermarket chain offered to provide the supplies, some at a discount and others as a donation. Although this provided a one-stop-shopping solution, it still required volunteers to spend several hours driving in heavy Moscow traffic and then an hour or more walking around a large warehouse to load their carts with the necessary items, before returning to the CCM's distribution center where another set of volunteers stood to unload the vans and then sort and package the food items.

Even as standing and walking were physical expressions of the everyday reality of inequality and its responses, they were far more than this. Rather, for participants within Moscow's faith-based assistance world, they were also modes of being that were simultaneously professional, ethical, affective, and even spiritual. During conversations with aid workers, the frequency with which themes of standing and walking emerged as ways of explaining their philosophies and practices of compassion and social action was striking. Repeatedly, staff and volunteers explained that they saw their role as being to "stand with," "walk with," or more generally to accompany others on their journey—whether it was a journey through poverty and suffering, a spiritual journey, or a professional journey with other religiously inspired aid workers who were developing their own programs and techniques for assistance.

Susanna, an American and ordained Methodist minister who worked for and with the Russian Orthodox Church as an official liaison between it and other Russian religious communities, summed up this perspective best when describing her responsibilities: "We do not solve [their] problems. [Instead] we stand beside them. We help them so that they [become] strong so that they can help those who are weak. . . . [It is] not our job to save the drowning ones. . . . We don't have the language [i.e., cultural communication skills] [to do that work], so we help those who do."

The language of accompaniment is common in Christian social ministry philosophies, both as an ethical stance of solidarity and as a practical means to provide support and safety (e.g., Gubi 2015). Above all, it is an explicit invocation of a social relationship predicated on shared humanity and humaneness. For aid workers like Susanna, accompaniment is the most ethical and logical way to work together: "It is a ministry of presence more than a ministry of doing," she added. Yet even though Susanna's de-emphasis on action was not shared by her colleagues in Moscow's other religious communities, and certainly not borne out by the very real, tangible results of her work with social justice communities in Russia, what Susanna was emphasizing was the idea that members of this community—those who provide assistance and those who receive it—are brought together by a shared experience of sociality, and specifically the shared social experience of being human. As such, the accompaniment model as it was presented by members of this community is not just a model of cooperation and mutual support, but a form of co-presence, affirmation, and even practical empathy that resonates with the approaches promoted by social justice activists in other contexts around the world.

This accompaniment is not limitless, however, but restrained by recognition of the dangers of losing objectivity. In a conversation about accompaniment with Pastor Charles and his wife, Claudia, a retired medical professional, they both started laughing. Pastor Charles then turned to me and explained that within church circles there is an inside joke that while it is necessary to walk with people, one should never walk off the cliff with that person. Thus while assistance is critical and necessary, it should never be done blindly and at risk of danger—whether physical, emotional, or spiritual—to oneself or to one's values.

Embedded within accompaniment models and rhetoric are intriguing and important questions about the nature of the relationships that exist between individuals and communities who come into contact with one another through acts and ideologies of care. These are of crucial importance for aid workers and their beneficiaries, because the terms of their engagement with one another inform not only how they work together—cooperatively or antagonistically, in a manner that is egalitarian or hierarchical—but also the results of that work. Although anthropologists and other observers have critically questioned the ways in which aid projects are grounded in hierarchical power dynamics where funders and aid workers determine the directionality and outcomes of their interactions (Escobar 1995; James 2010), aid workers themselves, and even their beneficiaries, might have a different perspective on their relationship and whether the different positions of various actors affect the practical and ethical dimensions of their interactions. Certainly within the religiously inspired assistance communities that I have been following in Russia, I have regularly encountered the perspectives of accompaniment, mutuality, commonality, and partnership shared by various participants.

A more profound, philosophical question that is raised by the accompaniment model has to do with the possibilities and limits of a shared experience. In other contexts, Susanna and her colleagues raised questions about the possibility of achieving a sense of shared humanity with other people—the people with whom they worked professionally and the people to whom they provided assistance—and whether a sense of shared humanity was beneficial. Most commonly, the conversations focused on how striving toward a shared humanity was part of treating others humanely and with dignity. These conversations were also suggestive that they were all a part of something bigger than themselves, whether that was rendered as "all God's children," or as a belief in a universal humanism.

FRIENDSHIP AND LOVE

Forging a sense of shared humanity was critical to how Moscow's faith-based assistance providers perceived their activities and their responsibilities to their recipients and to themselves. The human rights director from one of Moscow's most prominent religious NGOs attributed her organization's success in attracting donations, volunteers, and respect from other organizations and city authorities precisely to supporters' inclinations to "do good." As she explained, "the religious aspect is important, but it's more the voluntary nature of the people who get involved. They are dedicated and passionate about social justice, human rights, and providing for the needy. It is the energy of the people." Interjecting, her colleague put it more simply in terms of a basic human connection: "I always like working with people. [I like] putting smiles on their faces."

This sense of making a difference by engaging people is not simply about minimizing difference and distance as a practical or ethical matter, so much as it is an experiential reality of accompaniment. To accompany others on a shared experience, even if from different positions, is something that moves beyond simply providing aid and gets to an understanding of what it means to be a person embedded within social relationships.

In some cases, these social relationships are ones grounded in shared experiences, as was common in organizations in which former or current recipients took on roles of helping other recipients and used their personal experiences as forms of expertise in providing guidance or a sense of "having been there." After arriving in Moscow in the early 1990s from a refugee camp in Ghana, Joseph became an active member of the CCM's congregation, singing in the church choir, serving as music director, and sharing his boundless enthusiasm and many talents with the church and his fellow

congregants. Despite coming from a refugee camp, Joseph was more privileged than many of the CCM's African members because he had won a
scholarship to a Moscow university, where he completed undergraduate
and graduate degrees, including a PhD. He first started working with the
CCM's assistance programs as a volunteer, occasionally receiving supplementary food assistance that augmented his meager student financial aid
stipend, and then was offered a more formal, paid position as a director of
one of the church's soup kitchens. Eventually, after many years of dedicated service, he was appointed director of the social services outreach
center.

Joseph was known for being fair in how he interacted with recipients at
the soup kitchens and the outreach center, even as he often had to make
difficult decisions to curtail or deny services for individuals. Moreover,
Joseph was very aware of the difficulties inherent in different positions
within the assistance relationship, as he himself had shifted from someone who received assistance to someone who provided assistance. For
Joseph, this shifting positionality was important for his ability to do his
work. He reflected that if one wanted to help and to be able to understand
other people, it was necessary to try to put oneself in the position of living
among other people for a period of time in order to understand what they
were going through, what they felt, and what they thought. As he told me,
"I know when people are in need; I know what it is. . . . To work with people who have gone through what you yourself have gone through, it's a
blessing, a blessing."

Repeatedly, themes of blessings, friendship, and love emerged from
assistance workers' descriptions of acts of compassion and doing good for,
to, and with others. In some cases, this was about building a community
or family of assistance providers with shared beliefs in the relationship
between faith and social action and then projecting a model of that faith-
inspired social action outward. Pastor Mark invoked this idea when he
told me, "What the Church needs is a body of believers who are able to
come together as a family. We see each other as closely knit together
because of a shared relationship with Jesus Christ." This idea was even
more explicit in the comments of Dr. Valerii, a physician who divided his
time and skills between two different faith-based medical programs. Dr.
Valerii was steadfast in his belief that faith and care are not separate

things. By way of explanation, he invoked the first question from the Westminster Catechism from the Presbyterians, which asks, "What is the chief end of man?" He then told me the answer: "To glorify God and enjoy Him forever." By way of further expansion, he explained that this goal of glorifying God looks like enjoying Him: "By doing things close to God's heart, so that we're satisfied and content." He finished his thoughts by saying, "When I'm with the other people I work with we frequently talk about model[ing] the fruit of the Holy Spirit personally—that is, love."

This idea of a faith-driven compassion is also about building a community of intimacy and sentiment between assistance providers and their recipients. Even as Moscow's faith-based assistance providers acknowledged how important it was for them to find like-minded people with whom to pursue projects together, perhaps more important was the commitment to finding ways to connect with the people to whom they were providing assistance that went beyond the more practical, structural dimensions of exchanging aid. Being a friend, a loving family member, and a good neighbor with and alongside those who required assistance were also deeply personal and meaningful matters of faith, and most notably the tangible manifestations of putting a faith-driven social justice into action. Father Alexei put it directly when he told me, "What we do is we respond."

Building on this theme of responding, Pastor Mark described the imperative to reach out to others: "Social ministries are an important part of what God wants from us. I am never just a pastor. There is more to it than that. It is important to be involved in the social reality that surrounds us. As a pastor, it is about reaching out for those around you, reaching out for your neighbor, as Scripture would say." Making explicit this idea of being a good neighbor as essential to being a person of faith, Pastor Mark went on to relate that in the Presbyterian Church before ordination,

It is necessary to answer a question about whether you love the Lord your God or do you love your neighbor. But it's not possible to separate the two; you cannot do one without the other. You can't just love God without loving your neighbor. I have always felt this so strongly and seen it in so many contexts. It is intimately linked together, where if you are a follower of Jesus Christ . . . and there is recognition of what God has done for you, you have to respond. One way to respond is to reach out to your neighbor.

A more explicit take on the notion of friendship and love came from volunteers with Sant'Egidio, the Catholic street ministry that provides meals to homeless people. With its explicitly stated focus "Friendship with the poor," Sant'Egidio promotes "solidarity with the poor" as an expression of a Christian ecumenism that recognizes what Pope John XXIII described as "the Church for all and particularly the poor."[5] Paulina, a non-Catholic but longtime and regular Sant'Egidio volunteer whom I met through Susanna and several other assistance workers and parishioners affiliated with various Protestant groups, exemplified these ideals in her actions and reflections. In her mid-twenties, Paulina had spent several years studying English in Europe and had returned home to Moscow, where she was earning her master's degree while working full-time as a human resources manager in a mid-sized international company. Although Sant'Egidio was her primary volunteer activity, she was active in her own church's community and supported their social ministry projects.

I first accompanied Paulina and her friend Margarita one night as they made their rounds to meet regular recipients and look for newcomers who might need assistance. We met at the group's headquarters, a large multi-room apartment that was buzzing with action. In the small kitchen, several volunteers were busily making sandwiches and wrapping them in plastic bags, while others were ladling hot soup from an industrial kitchen-sized soup pot into large thermoses. Still others were packaging bread and pouring hot tea into smaller thermoses. In the outer room, volunteers greeted arrivals and sorted food into carrying bags.

After Paulina, Margarita, and I had gathered our bags, we left the apartment and went down to the busy street. We first walked over to the underground pedestrian crossing that led to the nearby metro station. Paulina and Margarita saw a man standing inside the dark, dirty hallway and whose clothing and bags suggested that he was homeless. After a quick look between themselves, they approached him and asked him if he would like something to eat. The man assented. Although they tried to engage him in small talk, the man was not responsive. After a few words of goodbye, we walked off in a different direction.

As we walked, Paulina and Margarita explained to me the group's philosophy by way of describing their relationships with one another and the people they helped. They did not simply provide meals to people in need.

Rather, they wanted to provide friendship and love with others. In order to support their perspective, they described several occasions in which Sant'Egidio volunteers and recipients had gathered together to share special occasions, such as major national holidays like Easter and International Women's Day.

Most notable was the recent wedding of one of Sant'Egidio's volunteers. Over many years of volunteering, the young woman had developed close relationships with her fellow volunteers and many recipients. Because it was imperative for her to have her closest friends and family with her, she hired a bus to transport a group of volunteers and recipients to the wedding and reception. At the reception, the Sant'Egidio guests had a place of honor at the head table with the bride and groom, whereas other family members and friends were displaced to tables elsewhere in the room. Paulina and Margarita described how some of the elderly women who were Sant'Egidio recipients tried to assert their moral authority as community elders—*babushki*—by rearranging the table decorations, directing the dances, and enforcing the behavior of other guests. The two women laughed as they remembered how disconcerting this was to some of the non-Sant'Egidio guests but endearing to the bride and groom and their Sant'Egidio family.

This emphasis on building a family that shared intimate moments was supported when we met some of the recipients with whom Paulina and Margarita visited most frequently. The first was an elderly woman whom we met on the street outside Sant'Egidio's apartment. I had first passed the woman in the passageway leading from the metro, where she had been begging. Now she approached Paulina and Margarita, and the three greeted each other familiarly with hugs and kisses. After they introduced me to her, the three of them quickly began catching up on news. The older woman asked them about the volunteer who had recently gotten married, and they shared other personal news before taking leave of one another.

A few minutes later, we passed two people huddled within makeshift cardboard shelters. I had passed these same figures over the past several days as I walked through the neighborhood and had never noticed any movement. Paulina and Margarita paused near the figures and exchanged a few words with one another: they thought they recognized the figures; should they try to initiate a conversation with them? Paulina and Margarita first decided not to stop and walked past, but then after brief consultation they reconsidered and went back. Paulina gingerly approached one of the figures and tapped her on the shoulder. The figure did not move. But after several moments of gentle tapping and back rubbing, accompanied by soft murmurs of reassuring words from Paulina, the figure slowly unrolled from the tightly held position. Once the figure had stretched out, her face was visible, and she peered at Paulina, recognizing her with a big smile. The two women greeted one another fondly, and the other woman told her companion, a younger woman who was her daughter, that it was safe to reveal herself. As Paulina and Margarita told me later, the two women were migrants from Central Asia who had been living in Moscow for a long time in an effort to find work. Although they found occasional work, they did not have a regular place to stay, and so their usual "home" was along that stretch of sidewalk.

The four women then engaged in a long conversation. The older woman had deep black-and-purple bruising on her face, and Paulina and Margarita questioned her, asking her what had happened and whether she needed assistance. The woman related a story of being beaten while living on the street. Paulina and Margarita repeatedly asked if they could provide assistance for her injuries, but she declined. The conversation then shifted to a more general chat about each other's lives. The older woman asked about Paulina's and Margarita's summers and whether they had had their holidays, as well as about the recent graduation festivities for another volunteer. In turn, Paulina and Margarita told the two women about the recent wedding, which prompted the two women to express their joy and request to pass on their best wishes to the newly married couple. Eventually, after twenty to thirty minutes of conversation, Paulina and Margarita offered the two women some food and drink, which they accepted. After making our goodbyes, we continued walking along the sidewalk.

The care and affection with which the four women interacted with one another was evident and deeply moving. They did not shy away from personal topics of discussion or physical contact. In fact, they each seemed to relish the physical contact of touches and embraces. While we continued our rounds, Paulina and Margarita continued to discuss the circumstances of the mother and daughter, trying to figure out if there was anything

Figure 3. The value of friendship as an essential component of social service is evident in this billboard promoting volunteer opportunities working with disabled persons through the "Best Buddies" organization. Potential volunteers are encouraged with statements such as "Come be friends with us!" and "We are best friends!" Copyright Melissa L. Caldwell.

more they could do, or whether their interactions were enough, for the moment. In the end, they seemed to agree that even though they wanted to do more to help the women materially, the ability to engage one another in friendship was just as valuable and meaningful a goal.

Several nights later, over dinner, Paulina and I discussed her work with Sant'Egidio more fully. Because of Sant'Egidio's strong emphasis on friendship, I asked Paulina to explain what this meant to her. She began by detailing her own personal journey as a person of faith to understand friendship. As she told me, there are different levels of friendship that entail different degrees of awareness and intimacy, but also recognition of what it means to be fully human. Echoing a perspective I had heard from several other volunteers the evening I spent in the Sant'Egidio apartment, Paulina explained that the commitment to intense personal relationships is difficult and dissuades many would-be volunteers. While the organization has a tightly knit community of dedicated volunteers, they struggle to attract new volunteers, especially foreigners with limited Russian language skills, who are not comfortable engaging homeless people in extended, personal conversations. Paulina confessed that when she first joined Sant'Egidio, she had to overcome her discomfort when talking with someone who lived on the streets. Once she made this initial move of becoming more comfortable with homeless people, she was excited and felt that she loved that other person. Other volunteers who were more experienced, however, advised her that she did not yet understand love and needed to continue her journey.

For Paulina, that journey was exemplified by two relationships that she had developed over the course of her volunteer work, first with Babushka Valya, with whom she now had a relationship of more than six years. For the first two years of their relationship, Babushka Valya always seemed to her like a small woman, always on the verge of tears. Paulina confessed that at that time, she did not know what to do to help Babushka Valya. Paulina helped her get into the hospital, but when the older woman was discharged, she still had problems. Paulina and others took her to Mother Teresa's Sisters for assistance, and then visited her there. After that, Sant'Egidio rented an apartment for her, where she now lives. Now, after all of this time, Paulina sees Babushka Valya differently: she sees Babushka Valya's strong character, her ability to fight, to scheme, her strong dislike of some people and her strong like of others. "It does not happen overnight, but if you are open to it, it can happen," Paulina said. Paulina then followed this example with a story about another woman who moved into the rented apartment. According to Paulina, this woman was "really homeless"—she smelled bad and she was uneducated. Paulina reflected that at first it was difficult to love her, but then it changed and she could see that the other woman was an open and kind lady who is thoughtful to others.

In her candid reflections, Paulina was not suggesting that the other women had changed but rather that she herself had changed in terms of how she saw them. Specifically, she had changed from focusing solely on their problems or seeing them as people she had to force herself to like. Instead, over time she realized that she was focusing on the whole person and getting to know these women as real people with both good points and flaws. In the process, Paulina learned more about herself and her own good and bad points. When she has moments of doubt, she reminds herself of the Christian emphasis on the need to cross boundaries. Working with the homeless was a boundary, she remembered, because it was dirty and scary for her.

For Paulina, being a true friend also meant recognizing other people's limitations and not trying to fix everything for them, a perspective echoed by Father Thomas, who said that what he has observed and perceived within his own parish is the coming together of people who would not normally come together. He has seen them grow in understanding, love, and affection, even as they had to work through normal human fallibilities such as quarreling with one another. Paulina commented that although she had developed a sense of responsibility for other people, she also had a sense that she could not do everything for them, that maybe there will never be a perfect solution that truly helps them and fixes all of their problems. In the meantime, she reflected, there is always human contact, spending time together doing small things like sharing laughs with one another. She found that her minister's mention of Christian hospitality helped her to remember that with Sant'Egidio she is part of a community, and that they are friends even outside of a religious context: "When it is my birthday, I spend it with friends [like those from Sant'Egidio]. It is a fun thing, it makes me happiest. . . . It makes me more human in some way, a little less self-centered."

Pastor Mark offered a similar perspective when he commented that Scripture shows that "God is present in a divine way in the poor and the powerless and the oppressed. We have a responsibility to be there for those people." Presbyterians call it a "mutual mission," he said. The idea is that you are not the missionary, but rather that "you are the one who is in mission with the person that you are ministering to." They fill your needs as you fill theirs: "You have to be invested in the person personally. There should never be a disconnect."

As Paulina explained, friendship and the compassionate interactions that it brings do not (and should not) entail a collapsing of difference into a sameness. Rather, it is about finding ways to bridge difference while still retaining a sense of distinction, respecting the unique circumstances and perspectives of one another's lives, and celebrating the fact that to be human is to be different and even flawed.[6] Through the simultaneous distancing and intimacy of compassion, when people are "between one and one another," relationships of care are transformed into affective relations of friendship and love.

Father Thomas, a Catholic priest whose apartment in Moscow has over several decades turned into a quasi-transitional housing dormitory for young men in search of work, expanded on this notion of love when we discussed the nature of assistance and charity. He said that for him, it was important to think about Pope Benedict's statement "God is Love" because this goes back to the original Latin, "God is Charity." As Father Thomas explained, this idea of love is not just agape or eros, but *caritas,* which is practical love. Thinking of practical love, he continued, leads people to service, and specifically service in the sense of God's labor. He noted further that teachers in the church have emphasized this duality, such as equating service of one's neighbor and love of one's neighbor: the move from loving your neighbor as yourself and then on to feeding your neighbor. In a separate conversation, Pastor Mark added that it was important to think about the related concept of Emmanuel, "God with us." The key to understanding what occurred when a person was being helped or served was realizing that it was potentially God being served. As he explained, God was always present in acts of care.

Ultimately, for practitioners of faith-based assistance, the cumulative effects of compassion based on friendship and love are stronger and more

Figure 4. This banner hanging outside a Russian Orthodox church encourages people "To love your neighbor as yourself" as part of cultivating a "Holy Russia." Copyright Melissa L. Caldwell.

powerful than what is possible outside the world of faith. Pastor Mark noted this in his comment that "The social has to be driven by the spiritual. If it is not, it may do good, but it is empty from both sides." In other words, for Pastor Mark, the social and the spiritual can never be disentangled from one another. Pastor Fedor, a Baptist minister, put it in more personal, but equally powerful terms: "I left a [Russian] government job to come to the ministry because here it is possible to serve people. When I was alone [i.e., working in a government agency], I could not do anything. But when we have a group, we can do things together."

FAITH-FULL COMPASSION

For faith-based assistance providers, care as a form of practical love is clearly divinely inspired, even as individuals may disagree with one another about whether that practical love is part of their responsibility as people of faith, most notably Christians, or whether it is simply a part of being human that brings a deeper spiritual experience, either to them or to their beneficiaries. When I asked Doctor Dmitrii, a Salvation Army physician highly praised by his colleagues for his skills and his insight into patients, if he was satisfied (*dovol'nyi*) with his work, he immediately responded that it gave him great satisfaction to help people. As he put it, his ability "to work from the soul" as a doctor made helping others especially meaningful to him.

When Paulina reflected on what Christian beliefs brought to social action, she claimed that it was essential to compassion. She stated that God creates friends, although she qualified that this idea is hard to understand because it is an unequal relationship. The Christian part is not about doing miracles all the time, she continued, but rather about feeling compassion, which is more important than changing things. By way of elaboration, she noted that Easter was a very important holiday for Russians, and during Holy Week she and many other Russians take off Maundy Thursday and Good Friday as spiritual holidays. She explained that what is important about Easter is that it invites people to talk about what it means to stand at the Cross, because to be a friend means to learn not to turn away from others but to be there with them. Stating that the love for the poor started from real love, as in facing the Cross, she commented that Christians have their own way of doing things, and it is a Christian way, but it is a way that is important for them. She finished by saying that she cannot imagine any Christian group that would not help someone else, including if the other person was not Christian.

For faith-based assistance providers who found direct inspiration in Scripture, there were many examples of compassionate care, especially those of Jesus. Father Thomas noted this when he stated that the figure of Jesus was very powerful because he was a model of service, specifically a model of loving one's neighbor. Father Thomas found many parables in the New Testament about service and trying to gain an empathetic perspective. Referencing how the figure of Jesus was represented in the New Testament, Father Thomas explained that what Jesus talks about is a straightforward, interactive, immediate reaction. Pastor Fedor's Baptist colleague Pastor Vitalii made a similar point when he observed that it was important to ignore critics who thought that faith-based social action was merely religious "propaganda" and not divinely inspired and necessary social work. Punctuating his views on faith-based compassion and care work with frequent expressions of "*Slava Bogu*" ("Thank God" or "God Bless"), he stated, "The Bible is full of other passages where the disciples were doing other things [i.e., besides ministering or proselytizing]." To engage in social justice work was, in his words, "absolutely Christianity" (*eto deistvitel'no khristiantsvo*).

Perhaps the most revealing set of comments came from Father Thomas, who was frustrated by policy and scholarly attempts to reduce care and compassion to terms such as altruism. A widely read scholar of both theology and social theory, Father Thomas complained that the recent turn in postmodernism was replacing ethics with studies of power, so that helping others has become transformed into exercises of power. The reductive logic of these approaches based on power could not capture the realities and complexities of what happens in relationships of care. Where do these things spring from then? he asked. Answering his own question, he stated that the nature of God is always involved, as are the things that God has created. People are independent beings who have free will and are attracted to the company of others. We like the company of other human beings, he said, and love is a natural thing. More importantly, love is a creative activity of human life because we create the world around us. We have a profoundly creative element in everything that we do, he concluded.

For Father Thomas, even though people and their actions are decidedly products of free will, that free will is a gift from God, and thus ultimately acts of care are more than merely utilitarian, social interactions. "As a Christian, I say that it [i.e., service] is God-given. I cannot locate it in a biological need for satisfaction or survival. That is not enough, because it does not account for what engages me. . . . There is an awful lot of God-given action of the heart and soul. . . . I believe that if people treat others better, we live better, more humanely, more divinely. . . . [There is] no ungraced nature."

Within the logic of faith-based assistance this graced nature allows assistance providers to do what they, and their supporters, see is some-thing quite different from their non-faith-based counterparts. Despite invocations of spirituality and divinely inspired actions, theirs is very much a this-worldly approach that is recognized as more attuned to basic needs, whether those are material or existential, or even spiritual. More importantly and intriguingly, Moscow's faith-based assistance providers are focused on celebrating human diversity and flourishing by promoting a more holistic understanding of the person. This is not an idealized vision of the person but one that recognizes people—both assistance providers and recipients—as flawed individuals. Assistance providers admit to struggling with their own biases and assumptions about the people they help and about their fellow assistance providers. Nor is this a notion of an atomistic person; rather it is a person in community with, and responsible to, others, even when those individuals have profound differences among themselves. As Andrei, the Russian director of a secularly oriented reli-gious development organization put it, one of the key components of char-ity is to give people a sense of what is possible and the values behind these possibilities. The values may be various—"take your pick," he said—but they all go back to the true meaning of charity: freedom and happiness. And when faith-based assistance programs promote and foster practices and qualities of freedom and human flourishing, they intersect directly with Russia's public sphere, most notably its civil society.

4 Developing Faith in a More Civil Society

In summer 2009, members of Moscow's assistance community found themselves cycling through a seemingly never-ending circuit of meetings, roundtable discussions, and workshops. The US Embassy, USAID, the Office of the United Nations High Commissioner for Refugees (UNHCR), Caritas / Catholic Charities, and the Aga Khan Foundation were just a few of the organizations hosting these events, which drew representatives from the many domestic and foreign development agencies, funding organizations, nongovernmental organizations (NGOs), charities, and more informal social justice interest groups in Moscow.

The topics covered at these meetings were equally diverse: anti-racism / pro-tolerance initiatives, educational reform projects, health care for disenfranchised communities, strategic fund-raising and donor cultivation, and best practices for collaborating with city, federal, and international authorities to address social concerns such as elder care, maternal and child health and nutrition, and illegal migration, among many, many others. Participants included an eclectic mix of Russian and foreign political appointees, clergy, career development professionals, technology and media experts, and eager, untrained volunteers.

Despite fluctuations in attendance from meeting to meeting, there was still a sense of overlap and consistency, as participants frequently knew one another or one another's colleagues and partners, often from other such gatherings. The meetings followed similar agendas and were characterized by the same collection of stale packaged cookies, flimsy white plastic coffee cups, and easel-mounted paper flip charts, prompting participants at the roundtables that I attended to joke among themselves about having lost track of which theme they were supposed to discuss *this* time.

At each meeting, staff from the sponsoring organization first introduced the mission statement of the agency, identified and thanked the funders, described the institutional structure of the organization, and finally set concrete objectives for the meeting. After this introductory session, participants took turns briefly describing their respective organization's programs and what they hoped to achieve from the gathering. Once the participants were acquainted with one another's activities, the meeting's leaders attempted to moderate the discussion by aligning the groups' varied goals and strengths around a shared set of programming goals and opportunities for continued networking.

In each of the meetings I attended it was always at this last point in the proceedings that participants who were frustrated with the formulaic bureaucratic structures derailed the conversation to focus instead on the "real" problems that they were ostensibly there to resolve. Ignoring the organizers' flustered attempts to return to the set agenda and strict schedule, participants left the "script" and began commiserating with one another about their common problems and swapping news of other programs and colleagues not in attendance.[1]

What was particularly notable at these meetings was that when participants began talking in detail about the realities from their fields, they frequently singled out their colleagues from religiously affiliated programs for special attention. Over and over, participants claimed that their colleagues from religiously affiliated programs were more successful at doing the kind of work that mattered, not just in terms of the practicalities of fund-raising, service provision, and obtaining support from Russian authorities, but most importantly, in terms of providing client-centered services that were humane, compassionate, and emphasized the dignity of clients. Throughout the meetings that I attended, participants informed their hosts that rather than organizing yet another meeting, they should be paying more attention to the work of the religious organizations.

THE PROBLEM WITH FAITH-BASED ORGANIZATIONS

Despite the strong views held by a surprisingly vocal number of Moscow's development practitioners at the meetings that religiously affiliated organizations might be better suited and able to provide assistance services, the contributions of these communities have been largely disregarded and discredited by both scholars and Western development officials.[2] Outside observers have been quick to dismiss the extensive work done by religious organizations and faith communities across the former Soviet Union as "missionary activity," as I have heard in academic settings, or as "merely charity," in the words of one Washington, DC, development bureaucrat.[3]

For scholars working on religious assistance, the devaluing and elision of religion from discussions of development is curious, given the role that religious institutions and values have played in development practices around the world (Fountain, Bush, and Feener 2015; Salemink 2015; Tomalin 2015). As scholars working at the intersection of religion and development have noted, careful attention to these synergies would reveal not only new ways to rethink the politics of development, but also to rethink the politics of religion within development (Fountain, Bush, and Feener 2015: 21). Acknowledging the role and place of "religion" within "development" efforts and ideologies—at whatever scale and topic they are pitched—moves between simple dichotomies between church and state, religious and secular, and instead opens up possibilities for illuminating how different constituencies, institutions, and bureaucracies engage with one another and share (or not) responsibilities and practices of assistance (e.g., Adams 2013; Fountain, Bush, and Feener, eds. 2015; Muehlebach 2012; Rudnyckyj 2010).

The relative lack of attention given to Russia's religiously affiliated organizations is, in many respects, the product of a larger set of turf battles that have characterized Russian development projects in the post-Soviet period. Following the dissolution of the Soviet Union in the 1990s, Russia and other formerly Soviet countries became prime destinations for international aid workers and donors whose primary assistance objective was facilitating the transition from state socialism to a liberal, democratic, free-market economy. Representing a broad sweep of countries, organizations, and ideologies, international aid workers and donors created a field in which they were competing against one another to gain converts and bring their own particular vision of democratization and neoliberalization to life (Mandel 2012).

Within this politically charged field, where Russia's own history as a development agent was ignored and obscured, religiously affiliated organizations have proven problematic because they disrupt the dominant discourses of post-Soviet development. In many respects, religious organizations do not conform to the logic of Western development paradigms, especially those that came out of Washington, DC, in the early 1990s (e.g., Creed and Wedel 1997), a difference that makes them problematic and even dangerous because of their potential for calling into question the legitimacy and authority of Western development approaches.

First and foremost, rather than promoting the "democratizing" and "civil society" initiatives that were the hallmark of Western development projects in Russia during the 1990s (Urban 2010; Wedel 1998), religiously affiliated organizations have instead challenged the efficacy of these ideals and introduced competing philosophies for social order. By drawing on Christian development models of "civilized societies" and humanism that prioritize holistic and humanizing treatment of the individual (see also Cnaan 2002: 5), religiously affiliated organizations have largely turned their attentions away from large-scale projects such as overhauling Russia's judicial system or instituting new voting procedures.

Instead, religiously affiliated organizations have often prioritized smaller-scale, but equally pressing social problems such as poverty, homelessness, addiction treatment, medical care, and human rights (Caldwell 2004; Tocheva 2011; Wanner 2007; Zigon 2011). In the specific case of the Moscow-based faith organizations that I have been following, their staff and supporters have deliberately positioned themselves as presenting an alternative vision of intervention that is meant to protect Russian citizens from what they see as the destructive consequences of democratization and civil society initiatives.

Between 1997 and 2007, a theme that repeatedly emerged in my interviews with participants representing diverse faith organizations was the concern that ongoing economic decline was causing Russians to lose hope and optimism and prompting individuals to dull the pain of these losses through destructive behaviors such as alcoholism, drug use, and hyper-consumerism. In response to these perceived problems, faith organizations added programs for addiction treatment, financial counseling, marital counseling, parenting classes, and life skills seminars.[4]

Susanna, the Protestant minister employed by the ROC social services programs, commented that in her many years of working in Russia and with Russian colleagues, the new capitalist culture was at the root of many social problems. "Materialism is a huge problem, and people are over-working [themselves] to get a Western lifestyle. But this materialism is itself a social problem because it does not solve real problems, it does not heal the soul, and it does not bring happiness. In this new materialist moment, Russians care less and less about each other."

Aleksandra Petrovna, an elderly Russian who has volunteered for many years with several church-run charities that assist elderly and disabled persons, focused on the dangers of capitalism when she described signing up for an investment seminar run by a priest at the local Orthodox church. Given that she depends on a small monthly pension and had endured numerous bank collapses during her lifetime, she was keen to find a way to protect her money and perhaps even grow her investments a little. After signing up for the seminar, she was disappointed that the priest was demanding a fee for the seminar—an amount that, to her, represented a significant portion of her monthly pension. She complained that clearly the priest had learned the practices of capitalism too well if he was not compassionate enough to waive the fees for impoverished persons such as her, and instead praised the clergy and volunteers of the programs with whom she worked, most notably the CCM's programs, for always putting the person ahead of profit.

In very tangible ways, faith-based programs have publicly inverted the hierarchies of personal value and political efficacy articulated by secular development programs. Unlike development programs that have targeted a more socioeconomically elite population of Russians who are presumed to have sufficient financial means and acumen to be the bearers of the country's new political economy, perhaps most notably (and problemati-cally) the new business leaders described by Janine Wedel (1998), Russian faith-based programs have focused on those individuals who have been most excluded from the changes taking place around them. As a result, faith-based programs have typically served Russia's most economically and socially disenfranchised and have attempted to bring them into the new economy. As one assistance worker wryly commented, faith-based programs help the people that the development organizations do not even know exist. In so doing, faith-based programs emphasize that true development is fully democratic because it benefits all members of Russian society, regardless of class or position within the development relationship.

Moreover, the models of service promoted by faith-based programs take this inversion further by encouraging people of means to subordinate their needs and interests to those of the people they are helping. Vows of modesty and even poverty are not uncommon among those who work in the field of religious assistance in Moscow. Clergy like Father Thomas lived simply and spent their salaries on supporting, both formally and informally, social services programs and recipients. Father Thomas also shared his apartment with aid seekers, as did several of Sant'Egidio's volunteers. A frequent topic of conversation among social services staff and volunteers who had regular and generous incomes was whether it was unseemly to wear clothing or jewelry that might show how their material circumstances differed radically from the people they were helping. This was especially troubling for expatriates who enjoyed high salaries, private drivers, housing allowances, and other perks. Some foreign professionals I knew chose to live in working-class neighborhoods in Moscow, eschewing the modern conveniences of Western-standard renovated apartments in favor of apartments that more closely approximated those of their recipients. Other expatriates who were required to live in housing or neighborhoods catering to upper-class Russian and foreign elites, either because those homes were closer to their workplaces or to their children's schools or because they satisfied their employers' liability requirements, found ways to evade the trappings of their comfortable lives. One American man I knew was especially skilled at slipping away from his mandatory driver and hopping on public transportation so that he could reach his volunteer sites and ease into his work without attracting attention. Another tactic among expatriate volunteers was simply to delegate their drivers to take on tasks for the social services programs they supported: running errands, transporting recipients to doctor's appointments, transporting supplies.

The message that emerges—and one that was proposed by volunteers in several different faith-based programs—was that a progressive, financially secure middle-class lifestyle should not be maintained at the expense of the less fortunate, and that it was important to help the less fortunate achieve their own personal satisfactions. Given that the actual labor behind faith-based programs is performed primarily by volunteers and low-paid staff for whom the ethical mission is more important than financial compensation, faith-based programs have also not contributed to the creation of a professional class of development workers who are not suited for other employment and depend on development for their livelihoods and occupational progress (see Phillips 2008). This does not mean, however, that faith-based assistance providers, both paid and unpaid, did not approach their work as professionals. Much like the Red Cross aid workers described by Liisa Malkki (2015), faith-based assistance providers typically drew on their existing professional skills—writing reports, accounting, health care, legal advocacy, translation, and teaching, among others—to perform their assistance work. Unlike the development professionals produced in the early post-Soviet period, however, these individuals did not constitute a separate class of professionals who were only able to work as development staff.

At the same time, religiously affiliated organizations differed, at least initially, from their nonreligious counterparts in terms of their institutional structures and practices, especially the ways in which they approached issues such as impact, results, accountability, legal recognition, and networking. Departing from the more usual bureaucraft practices among nonreligious humanitarian and development programs that employed calculated diagnostic criteria and logics for determining assistance procedures and evaluating efficacy and compliance (see James 2010: 87–92), religiously affiliated organizations like the ones described here prioritized denominational ethics and institutional practices as well as the more general religious principles of seeing practical care as a spiritual matter (Bane and Mead 2003; Bosch 1991; Jeavons 1994). Knowing that one has made a good-faith effort to help others carries more value than balancing figures in a ledger book or checking off goals met on a planning document.

Another feature that distinguishes faith-based programs in the post-Soviet development field is the inherently transnational and even paranational features of faith-based programs. The prevailing Western development story is oriented around a West-to-East movement (Escobar 1995; Mosse 2004). Yet the development resources invested in Russia by faith-based programs reveal very different topographies and trajectories that in turn set up very different hierarchies of need and assistance. For instance, many Moscow Christian faith-based programs rely on African students and refugees to staff their programs as employees and volunteers (see Caldwell 2003, 2004), a reality that puts a twist on what Charles Quist-Adade (2005: 81) has described as the more usual picture presented by Soviet and Russian media of "blacks . . . [as] the objects of infinite white benevolence." This is not to say that there were more African than Russian or other nationalities represented among volunteers, but to note that African volunteers were noticeable within these communities.

Upon arriving in Moscow in the mid-1990s, I was surprised to discover a vibrant community of Africans who participated in the churches and social services programs I encountered. Roughly half of the CCM's 250-member congregation consisted of African students and refugees, and the church sponsored a biweekly aid program for African students and refugees that regularly attracted 200 people. From my observational data, Africans seemed to constitute a larger proportion of congregants in some other churches, especially Catholic churches and French-speaking Protestant congregations. African friends reported that there were several evangelical and Pentecostal churches that were almost exclusively African. Until the early 2000s, most Africans in Russia had arrived as part of the Soviet and post-Soviet state's efforts to build international socialism. During the Soviet era, the state sponsored many promising young scholars from its socialist allies in Africa, Latin America, and Asia with scholarships for educational and professional training. By the early 1990s, ongoing political troubles in Africa meant that many African students in Russia could not return home and became de facto refugees (many received official legal recognition as refugees). The expansion of Russia's for-profit educational sector meant that other African students came in as paying students. By the early 2000s, Russia had become a destination for economic and political migrants from many African countries. NGOs focused on race relations estimated that Moscow's African population was relatively small—several thousand at most—but many of these individuals had found their way to established communities of other Africans and then found their way to churches and faith-based social services programs as both recipients and assistance providers (sometimes occupying both roles simultaneously).

Africans who volunteered did so for several reasons: some who had received assistance expressed a desire to give back. For individuals who were churchgoing, participating in social services work was a logical extension of their church community and religious life. Still others saw the opportunity to engage in work, even if it was unremunerated, as a good opportunity to develop skills and contacts that they could potentially mobilize for paid work elsewhere. But perhaps the most common reason given by African volunteers was a social one: for people who were far from home and their families, the social services programs offered an opportunity to socialize with people who spoke the same language or shared similar histories.

The prominent role of Africans in the Russian development sector discomforts Russians who were accustomed to a moral hierarchy of aid in which Russia sent assistance to Africa but now find themselves on the receiving end of aid from Africans (Caldwell 2011). The presence of Africans as key staff and administrators in Russian assistance programs also challenges conventional occupational and knowledge structures in Western development models. African countries have often been classified as "hardship" posts that require development staff to undergo training but then reward them with extra compensation. Although the presence of African assistance workers could be interpreted as evidence of the "successes" of Western education and professionalization training in African countries, this has not necessarily been the case in meetings that I have attended, where Western staff assume that Africans are recipients and not providers.

Korean Christians have also long been a significant presence in Russian social services activities (Caldwell 2015), especially in terms of international partnerships between Korean-Russian and South Korean congregations, a detail that opens up a vantage point for recognizing other significant flows of development aid from East to West. For instance, by

2004, Japan had contributed 7.4 million euros to the European Bank for Reconstruction and Development (EBRD) for projects in Russia, Kazakhstan, and Uzbekistan (EBRD 2004); and by the end of 2005, Japan had contributed 134 million euros to the EBRD for the "Russia Small Business Fund" (EBRD 2007). In 2006, Taiwan sent 23 million dollars (US) in aid resources to Russia (Chang and Hsu 2006). By resituating the development story within the networks and flows in which faith-based programs are embedded, we see a more complicated set of relationships and directionalities as assistance moves West to East, East to West, North to South, and South to North simultaneously.[5]

FROM CONFORMITY TO RELIABILITY

The consequences of the alternative models presented by faith-based programs are profound, not just in terms of introducing new ethics and practices of assistance, but also in terms of changing the expectations about what assistance might look like and how it can be provided most effectively. Over the past twenty-five years, as development programs have come and gone in Russia, faith-based programs have weathered the storms and created reputations for credibility, legitimacy, and reliability. With these long-term successes, Russia's faith-based programs have revealed critical flaws in how "development," and assistance more generally, has been theorized and practiced in Russia.[6]

This has been especially true of how program priorities have been set and how funding decisions have been made. In Russian development projects, funding has followed ideological interests, often changing quickly and radically as international donors change their minds about the latest "need." In this "adhocracy" (Dunn 2012) environment, aid workers are always at the ready to improvise quickly to take advantage of ever-changing realities and pressures. Officials with Oxfam's Russia office identified this as a particular problem since funding objectives have forced them to shift away from traditional Oxfam concerns with poverty alleviation and food relief to programs geared at generating a new class of entrepreneurs and small business owners.

Even more problematic for aid workers in Russia has been what informants have described as the "short attention spans" of funders who redirect
their support frequently and in response to popular trends, thereby forcing aid workers to reinvent themselves repeatedly in order to compete for
funds within this shifting field (see also Hemment 2007). Staff at assistance programs complain that these constant changes present significant
obstacles to the implementation of long-term projects, a reality that
became apparent at the end of summer 2009 when a secular, Russian
NGO that was one of the largest and most comprehensive service providers to refugees and asylum seekers lost its funding, leaving staff, recipients, and partner organizations scrambling to secure alternate support.

In the case of this NGO, in the previous few years, although the NGO's
client list had swelled beyond existing capacity owing to ongoing violence
in the Middle East and Africa that was compelling families to flee to
Russia (among other destinations), staff had worked mightily to accommodate as many people as they could, often drawing on contacts and
resources from other secular and religious organizations. Despite this
growing need, the several foreign governments and international funding
agencies that supported the NGO decided that the program's existing
foci—supplemental food bags for refugee families, supplies of clothing,
diapers, and formula for infants and children of refugees, and a summer
camp for displaced children—were no longer pressing concerns. The NGO
was left with a small amount of funds to run a skeleton crew of staff who
handed out the dwindling supply of clothes and baby gear left in the
offices, while the directors attempted to create new programs that might
re-attract the notice and support of their funders.

During an interview that I held with two program managers, several
colleagues came through the offices to listen to the discussion and share
their views. What was most palpable was the sense of dismay that their
tremendous efforts had been discounted and that they were being forced
to reinvent themselves. One woman described all the now-locked rooms
that they had once used for children's services: speech therapy, physical
therapy, and parenting skills classes. Another woman pointed to the small
stack of baby supplies in the corner and said the need was unending. She
described how emotionally draining it was to tell new mothers that they

could take only one small pack of diapers. Yet another woman confessed that she was preparing to look for another job where she might have a better chance of being able to help people, rather than constantly writing grant applications.

Intriguingly, religiously affiliated programs have been far less susceptible to the fickle nature of funders, and many have transformed temporary charitable activities into permanent programs. For instance, after launching its programs in the 1990s by using rented cafeterias during off-peak hours, the CCM has since solidified and expanded its services and signed long-term leases for dedicated spaces that it has customized and used to anchor its programs permanently. The church has also begun investigating the possibility of purchasing real estate, a reality that came true for the Salvation Army when it was able to buy its own dedicated building after many years of moving between rented spaces and always on the verge of being evicted from Russia altogether. Two other religious communities were finally able to purchase apartments where they could provide both temporary and long-term housing for homeless clients. This is not unusual among the religiously affiliated programs I was tracking, as they were increasingly able to sustain their programs over decades.

More important, however, was the sense among Moscow's development practitioners and funders that religiously affiliated organizations were less doctrinal and more neutral, flexible, and even progressive than international development organizations in their approaches to identifying problems and devising solutions. During an interview with Alison, a US embassy official who brokers partnerships between American and other foreign funders and Moscow-based assistance programs, she reported that she preferred to work with faith-based organizations because they were not only the most reliable but also the least ideological in their motives. Alison commented that, in her experience, faith communities genuinely wanted to provide needed assistance, and not use assistance as an opportunity to promote a particular political agenda. She stated that although she had begun her appointment under US president George W. Bush, who had famously formalized a policy of "compassionate conservatism" that highlighted and even prioritized the work of American faith-based organizations, this did not affect her decisions about which programs to fund.[7] Rather, she had awarded grants to faith communities in Russia because they were doing, as she put it, "good work." The "faith-based" component of these particular organizations was, in her words, "tangential or irrelevant." Continuing, Alison commented that she suspected that the minister of St. James Protestant Church, one of her closest partners, was probably agnostic and that he was a minister only because it gave him the opportunity to do the social justice work he valued.

In a subsequent interview, St. James's minister did admit that his commitment to social justice ideals was a primary motivation for his professional career. A longtime Catholic priest in Moscow expressed similar sentiments during our conversations, which typically veered quickly from discussions of church matters and theological questions pertaining to service to more expansive discussions of political philosophies of social justice, which he found more helpful for understanding and explaining his own social action ideals and activities.

Interviews with staff and volunteers from St. James also revealed that many identified themselves as nonpracticing, and non-Christian in some cases, but participated in this church's activities because of the social justice orientation. One of the development directors for St. James's NGO Sosedi confided that although as a progressive Catholic she was not always comfortable with the theological views expressed by some parishioners at St. James during worship services, she connected closely with the liberal, progressive social values promoted by the congregation's NGO. I heard similar responses from staff and volunteers with many other faith organizations in Moscow: respondents claimed that they chose their assistance activities based on programs' respective social justice values, thereby easily distinguishing between beliefs that were personal religious beliefs (either their own or those of others) and those that belonged to a larger realm of ethical beliefs, a distinction that recalls Bellah's (1967) "personal religious belief" and "civil religion."

Such attitudes are far from universal within development circles, however; and assistance and development professionals acknowledge that faith communities fit uneasily within, and sometimes even disrupt, persistent stereotypes about faith-based organizations. Moscow-based program managers with development programs and funding agencies related numerous accounts of the challenges of reconciling assumptions about the motives of faith-based organizations that were common among

Russian government officials and foreign development officials with the actual approaches and impact of such groups. Michele, an American program manager for a Moscow-based, US government–sponsored funding agency that directed foreign grants and resources to Russian HIV/AIDS-prevention NGOs, reported that although faith-based programs were the most capable and reliable groups for administering health programs, it was virtually impossible to convince regional officials to work with these organizations. Michele complained that despite assurances by her staff that these faith-based organizations did not proselytize or promote religious agendas of any sort, regional officials preferred to forego the resources altogether, thereby sacrificing the well-being of their citizens.

I have encountered similar biases in presentations of my own research, as colleagues have been quick to presume sinister motives behind the activities of faith communities and faith-based programs and to assume that organizations such as Habitat for Humanity or Amnesty International represent "good" examples of nonreligious charity. (Both are, in fact, Christian in their origins.) Others have questioned whether people involved with these organizations are as nice as they are described (in most cases: yes). In one particularly memorable instance, a Washington, DC–based American development practitioner who attended a Kennan Institute workshop where I presented my research insisted that faith organizations did not belong within the same category as "true" development organizations like USAID, because, she argued, faith organizations were "merely charities" that enabled religious congregations to proselytize to vulnerable Russians.[8] Several months later, however, when I was in Moscow at a private brunch at Alison's home, I happened to meet a highly placed USAID professional who had worked in Russia for several years. When I asked the USAID official about her work and the role of faith communities in USAID's partnerships in Russia, she quickly responded that faith communities were extremely active partners and then effusively praised the faith-based organizations with which her office partnered for being nonideological and effective service providers.

Benjamin, the British director of Moscow's Oxfam office, described similar frustrations in working with Russian and foreign development workers who categorically refused to create partnerships with other faith-based organizations because they were convinced that these groups were interested only in converting Russians to their particular tradition of Christianity, even when that was not the case. Especially ironic for Benjamin was that these same development workers overlooked, or were completely unaware of, the fact that Oxfam was itself a faith-based organization.

As these experiences and reflections from within Moscow's assistance community reveal, faith-based organizations elude easy or definitive categorization. Neither wholly religious nor wholly secular, they must navigate a delicate balance between the perceptions of their supporters and those of their detractors. Both supporters and detractors further contribute to these categorical confusions either by attributing religious motives that may not exist or by overlooking the religious connections that do exist.

Collectively, these misrecognitions raise an important question about the extent to which these categorical confusions are unique to Moscow's faith communities or whether they are themselves part of a larger problem of confusion stemming from the overly bureaucratized nature of post-Soviet development and assistance more generally. At the same time, these categorical confusions are not necessarily unique to the post-Soviet world, a point made by Fountain, Bush, and Feener (2015: 21) in their call for "*seriously* taking religion seriously" in studies of development in Asia and elsewhere, in order to illuminate and understand how the categories of development are created, contested, and straddled (see also Salemink 2015).

Intriguingly, however, these confusions have not necessarily been constraining but have, instead, productively enabled Moscow's assistance communities to benefit from the ambiguities and ambivalences of existing betwixt and between and outside of expected categories. In their reflections on this bureaucratization, Moscow's development practitioners suggest that these misrecognitions actually create opportunities for action that faith-based organizations are better able to exploit than their nonreligious counterparts. Specifically, even as the institutional logics of conventional development paradigms have excluded, or at least misrecognized, the work of religiously affiliated organizations in Russia, they have, paradoxically, actually created opportunities for these same groups to carve out a productive niche for themselves. Staff and supporters of religiously affiliated organizations contend that their value and effectiveness derive precisely from their ability to address the gaps and problems within conventional development projects.

THE POLITICS OF CLASSIFYING ASSISTANCE IN RUSSIA

How, then, have Russia's faith communities been able to work with, against, and around both conventional development paradigms and popular stereotypes? Part of the answer lies in the "regimes of discourse and representation" (Escobar 1995) in which Russia's assistance world is embedded.[9] In particular, in order to identify and regulate organizations and people, Russian authorities have created a highly bureaucratized system of organizational management. A recurring theme in accounts of assistance organizations across the post-Soviet world is the "politics of differentiation" (Phillips 2008) that has classified and ranked issues, projects, types of institutions, and even clientele, effectively creating a competitive field for development organizations that must position and market themselves.[10]

Bureaucratic distinctions affect whether and how particular institutions and projects are recognized, both legally and culturally, at the same time that they demarcate fields of action and delegate authority for these activities to particular types of programs. Nevertheless, the effectiveness of classificatory systems is debatable, as distinctions can be arbitrary and create ambiguity rather than providing institutional clarity (Bowker and Star 1999). The experiences of Moscow's faith communities highlight well the ambiguities and productive possibilities of this institutional politics of classification.

Post-Soviet development and assistance activities have been marked by a dizzying proliferation of terminologies, each with its own lexicon, historical genealogy, and presumed philosophy and social value: development (*razvitie*), social welfare (*sotsial'naia zashchita*, literally "social defense"), social support (*sotsial'naia podderzhka*), charity (*blagotvoritel'nost', miloserdie* [referring to Russian Orthodox charity, mercy]), humanitarianism (*gumanitarnost'*), and voluntarism (*dobrovolets, volontery* [referring to the people who provide volunteer labor]), to name just a very few.[11] This diversity of terminology is exceeded only by the diversity of projects pursued by assistance organizations: artistic and cultural development; heritage preservation; Western-style civil society initiatives focused on capacity building, legal reforms, citizen empowerment, and voter education; economic reforms and incubator projects to stimulate new businesses; health care reforms; women's rights; educational reforms; cultural revival; and poverty alleviation, among many others.[12]

Which terms were invoked at which moment were revealing of deeper, more fundamental questions about the self-image that a particular organization wanted to project or about the networks in which it was operating. Even more challenging was that the terrain was fluid, and new terms were constantly being introduced to delineate new philosophies and approaches. From a methodological standpoint, it was tricky to ask questions in interviews because I was never fully sure which term was most appropriate for a particular organization or set of programs. Yet as I discovered, the flexibility of terminology and classifications actually benefited organizations by enabling them to take advantage of loopholes or to rebrand themselves quickly to apply for funding.

An illustrative case occurred during an interview at United Way Moscow in fall 2009. At the meeting, I asked Marina Andreevna, the Russian director, to comment on her agency's relationships with religious charities in Russia and to describe any differences she perceived between religious and secular aid programs. Given that my contact with United Way had come through a Moscow-based Protestant minister who worked closely with United Way and whose congregation was finalizing a proposal for a United Way grant to support several assistance programs, I was thus surprised at Marina Andreevna's emphatic reply that her agency does not work with or support religious organizations: "not any kind of religious organizations [*nikakie religioznie organizatsii*]," she stated.

Exchanging a meaningful look with her assistant, Marina Andreevna repeated the statement that United Way did not work with religious organizations, while simultaneously qualifying her statement with hand gestures and facial expressions to convey that her words were to be understood as an official "party line" statement, before going on to say that her agency worked very closely with "official nonprofit [that is, noncommercial] organizations [*ofitsial'no nekommercheskie organizatsii*]." She explained that federal regulations prohibited United Way from working with religious organizations because of the "religious propaganda [*religioznaia propaganda*]" allegedly promoted by religious groups, thereby limiting her agency's relationships to "secular organizations [*svetskie organizatsii*]."[13]

As if anticipating the apparent contradiction that I was about to note in my next question to her, Marina Andreevna then further qualified the category "nonprofit organization" by adding that this included the social ministries affiliated with the church whose minister had facilitated our meeting. Marina Andreevna praised the congregation for the scope and impact of its assistance programs, and then noted that this church and several other Moscow congregations each had a "charitable foundation [*blagotvoritel'nyi fond*]" that United Way supported. In her comments about the nonprofit status of religiously affiliated programs, Marina Andreevna used the names of the minister and his church and not the name of the officially registered secular, nonprofit NGO and charitable foundation through which they conducted their activities. Moreover, after having delineated the official semantic parameters of our interview, Marina Andreevna then went on to describe and praise in great detail the myriad assistance programs pursued by religious organizations in Russia, with special attention to projects affiliated with her agency.

Marina Andreevna's strategic move to delineate carefully the specific, official terminology by which our conversation could proceed was significant for what it revealed, both about the bureaucratic structures that produce, circumscribe, and manage the diverse field of assistance programs that currently operate in Russia, and about the ways in which officials and organizations within this field creatively navigate, and even transgress, these bureaucratic structures in order to pursue and support social services programs. When asked to explain why their organizations chose the terms and labels they did, staff and volunteers with both religious and nonreligious organizations typically grounded their responses in acknowledgment of the realities of funding and registration opportunities.

The decision-making process underlying St. James's process of registering its charitable projects with the Russian government in 2007 is illuminating. During the lengthy process of translating their activities into state-sanctioned bureaucratic language and structures, members of the church staff and church council found themselves debating the merits of different classificatory titles. They finally settled on the English term *nongovernmental organization* for their English-language materials directed to non-Russian audiences, including donors from abroad, and the Russian terms *nekommercheskaia organizatsiia* (noncommercial/nonprofit organization) and *blagotvoritel'naia organizatsiia* (charitable organization) for their application for official Russian registration and to appeal to donors within Russia. I never heard church staff use the word *miloserdie*, the word more commonly used for explicitly Russian Orthodox charity, either in conversation or written documents, although the term was used by their Orthodox partners. This distinction was evident in a conversation between St. James staff and their partners from the social development office at the patriarchate, as they moved fluidly back and forth between *blagotvoritel'nost'* to describe St. James's projects and *miloserdie* to describe Orthodox projects. Thus from the perspective of the Russian Federation and Russian funders, St. James's Protestant Church's NGO Sosedi was a completely secular, nonprofit development organization, and not a religious charity.

Although classificatory schema are meant to delimit the field of assistance into manageable units for greater effectiveness, including limiting and even excluding the participation by other, potentially competing groups, the reality is that institutions can creatively work around them. Faith communities are especially flexible, owing to the fact that their projects can take multiple institutional forms and draw on different institutional histories. It is worth noting that many of the non-Orthodox Christian communities at the center of the assistance network described here have struggled to gain legal recognition from the Russian government as official religious communities, even in the case of communities that satisfy requirements for historical authenticity.[14] Yet these same congregations report that they have found it far easier to register their assistance programs as official nonprofits and have received more welcoming overtures from Russian officials for their assistance projects, which has in turn facilitated greater official acceptance of their religious dimensions.

Ultimately, what the ambiguities of these classificatory schemas reveal are the tenuous and even contradictory parameters of Russian development and assistance trends, as well as the very ordinariness and even secularism of faith organizations within this field. In the terms they use, the expectations they hold, the partnerships they forge, and the recognitions afforded to both religious and nonreligious organizations, Moscow's actors in the assistance community consistently treat faith organizations and their nonreligious counterparts in ways that suggest commensurability.

This commensurability does not necessarily mean that distinctions between faith organizations and nonreligious organizations have completely dissolved. Rather, at the same time that Moscow's development practitioners include faith organizations as equivalent partners, they do so in ways that also recognize that faith organizations might have a unique role to play in the cultivation of a new Russian society. Most notably, proponents suggest that faith-based organizations promote an alternative vision of civil society that is more progressive and beneficial than the models that have typically been introduced by nonreligious programs.

THE PLACE OF CIVILITY IN CIVIL SOCIETY PROJECTS

One of the defining features of Western-inspired development models in the post-Soviet world has been the promotion of "civil society" as the means to address social problems and encourage the democratization of these countries (Aksartova 2009).[15] Although civil society is, as Chris Hann (1996: 11) points out, "closely linked to issues concerning the 'quality of life,'" civil society initiatives in Russia and other post-Soviet countries were oriented more to the structures of life through reforming the political and economic systems, notably by focusing on legal systems, market activities, civic education, the media, and, crucially, creating the mechanisms that facilitated the formation of NGOs (Sampson 1996; Urban 2010; Wedel 1998). By contrast, religiously affiliated organizations have typically come to development activities from different political philosophies about intervention and social stability. Members of Moscow's religiously affiliated organizations, for instance, have interpreted the idealized, Western-style civil society objectives as contributing to Russia's social, political, and economic problems, and hence as obstacles to improving "quality of life."

By invoking explicit critiques of the dangers of Western-style capitalism and democracy, religious communities have taken particular issue with the ways in which Western "civil society" models are predicated on a particular spatializing logic of a sphere that is separate from the state but yet operates as an intermediary between the state and its citizens (Ferguson and Gupta 2002).[16] Sometimes called the "Third Sector," this separate realm requires the creation of "mediating structures" to set it apart and energize it (Berger and Neuhaus 1977; Cnaan et al. 2002).[17] These "mediating structures" have typically been rendered as voluntary associations or, in the case of post-Soviet projects, nongovernmental organizations (Wedel 1998: 8). Through these spatializing logics, Western development models effected a distancing of the Russian state from its citizens, a move that was necessary for creating independent, autonomous, self-responsible citizens (Kornai 2001).

From the viewpoint of faith organizations, however, this type of move is a form of devolution in which the state withdraws from its citizenry and creates a gap (Cnaan, Wineburg, and Boddie 1999). In Russia, faith communities have interpreted this distancing of state from citizen through intermediaries not just as the abandonment of citizens by the state, but also as the violation of an implicit social compact between state and citizen. In sharp distinction from civil society models that credit the Third Sector with encouraging greater citizen activity through voluntary organizations, faith-based organizations see the creation of mediating structures as the deliberate exclusion of citizens from society and the fragmentation of an already existing community of service and care.[18] Consequently, the work of faith-based organizations is not so much geared at creating and strengthening a civil society sphere that exists between state and citizen as it is oriented to filling that space in order to protect citizens who are increasingly distanced from the state.

Describing their activities as antidotes to Russian citizens' perceived abandonment by the state and citizens' subsequent loss of personal connections with the state, clergy, staff, volunteers, and even recipients with Russia's faith-based organizations have prioritized the compassionate dimensions of assistance provision as the means to create a more holistic and humanizing construction of the relation between citizen and society (Cnaan et al. 2002; Elisha 2008). Ultimately, through this approach, religious communities seek to cultivate new forms of civility in Russian society.

As participants in religiously affiliated programs repeatedly explained, the vibrancy and vitality of Russia's new civic society depends on the cultivation, not of self-interested economic actors, which they perceive as the goal of Western civil society models, but rather of empathetic and compassionate citizens committed to the betterment of others as the way to better the self (cf. Muehlebach 2012). Consequently, by emphasizing a holistic treatment of individuals, religiously affiliated organizations seek to promote a more inclusive, egalitarian, and nonhierarchical vision of Russian society that they feel better represents the ideals of democracy.

Underscoring these concerns about abandonment and dehumanization, faith-based organizations have typically focused their attentions first on programs that address both material and social needs—most notably, poverty alleviation programs. Through these programs, faith-based organizations deliberately couple material assistance with social companionship. For instance, Caritas's support programs for single mothers and their children include not only food, financial support for expenses such as rent and medical care, and educational and technical retraining courses to help the mothers find better jobs, but also holiday parties and excursions to ensure that the children share normal childhood experiences. When Sant'Egidio's volunteers walk Moscow's streets to deliver sandwiches and beverages to the city's homeless residents, they make sure they spend time talking with the people they meet. Over time, volunteers have created close and mutually meaningful relationships with some of the people they have met, with volunteers and recipients celebrating birthdays, weddings, and other important occasions together.

Similarly, in 2007, volunteers with the soup kitchen program administered by Sosedi discovered that some elderly and disabled recipients were no longer able to attend the soup kitchen and that the regional welfare authorities no longer had the resources to provide in-home services for its shut-in citizens. In response to this perceived "abandonment" of citizens by the state, volunteers launched a "meals-on-wheels" program to provide food packages through weekly visits. As the volunteers described the program, however, it was clear that the food packages were secondary to the socializing component: volunteers were expected to make at least a one-hour weekly commitment to each recipient because the visits typically involved lengthy conversations over tea.

By responding to these perceived gaps and oversights in Russia's emerging civil society, Moscow's faith-based organizations propose modes of assistance that seek to restore and protect the humanity of citizen-subjects. These more deliberately humane approaches are acknowledged in the frequency with which the restoration of dignity and self-worth is invoked as an explicit aim by staff and volunteers with faith-based organizations (see also Höjdestrand 2009; Zigon 2010). By focusing on the potential for humaneness in assistance projects, faith communities create possibilities for thinking beyond simply a "civil" society to what several individuals suggested was a society with greater civility. It is precisely this approach that generated such excitement among participants at the roundtables described at the very beginning of this discussion and to which I turn in the following section.

INVITING FAITH-BASED ORGANIZATIONS TO THE DEVELOPMENT TABLE

In late summer 2009, the Aga Khan Development Network (AKDN) and the UNHCR sponsored two of the many roundtables that regularly brought together different actors from Russia's development field to discuss common interests and explore networking possibilities. I found myself at these two meetings at the invitation of staff members from Sosedi. As mentioned previously, like similar meetings described elsewhere, these roundtables were bureaucratically scripted and revealed familiar development concerns with legal reform, technology development, and networking.[19] Yet in both instances, participants challenged organizers to rethink their assumptions about the functioning of Moscow's development field, the feasibility of Western-influenced goals, and the significance of faith-based organizations.

The first roundtable was that sponsored by the newly opened Moscow office of the AKDN. Founded by His Highness the Aga Khan, Imam of the Shia Imami Ismaili Muslims, the AKDN is grounded in Islamic principles of social responsibility and compassion for the poor but is explicitly nondenominational and pursues projects that promote pluralism and draw together diverse groups of service providers.[20] This roundtable was an opportunity for AKDN staff to introduce themselves to Moscow's development community, especially those groups working in the area of medical and social services for migrants. Invitees included health care practitioners, social workers from state welfare agencies, professional staff and volunteers from nonprofit social services organizations, labor union leaders, and social sciences researchers from the Russian Academy of Sciences.

They were joined by consultants from a media technology firm and by program managers from both the local AKDN office and the organization's international headquarters. While the majority of participants were Russian citizens, several were foreigners, including the South Asian–American director of the Aga Khan's Moscow office and the American doctor and African staff person representing Sosedi.

In their opening remarks, Aga Khan's program managers described the purposes of the roundtable. With the recent opening of their Moscow office, the foundation's officials were interested in expanding their activities throughout Russia, beginning with the Moscow region. The two AKDN employees leading the meeting claimed that because their staff lacked the necessary experience and social connections to initiate programs in Russia beyond a small, preexisting program in Dagestan, they wanted to create a network of organizations and professionals who could help them and one another. In trying to determine how best to focus their initial efforts in Russia, AKDN staff had settled on medical and social assistance for migrants. They were particularly interested in assisting undocumented foreign labor migrants, primarily from Central Asian countries, who were at risk of exploitation and violence and unable to access material, legal, or medical aid. This was a timely issue, as in the preceding weeks Moscow authorities had engaged in raids of undocumented laborers in their workplaces and living quarters (Krainova 2009).

Each organization was allotted fifteen minutes for their representatives to describe their clientele, services, and goals for the meeting. In the first session, several scholars and labor union officials described Russia's immigration policies and general demographic trends among migrant populations. They focused almost exclusively on migrants from the former Soviet republics, which prompted agitated whispering among the Russian physicians next to me who insisted that this perspective excluded the even more marginalized and vulnerable populations they served: homeless Russians and Asian and African economic migrants. One physician commented that she found it difficult to take the presentations seriously when the data were so biased and incomplete. The second session featured several social workers and immigrant activists, who focused their attentions on the legal problems facing migrants and how their organizations helped clients deal with state policies governing visas, work permits, salaries, and mediation of labor disputes with employers. This was followed by a brief presentation from the media consultants, who reported on the online networking forums and online advertising projects that were their firm's specialty.

At this point in the roundtable, Inna Arkadievna, an AKDN program manager, commandeered the conversation and invited participants to brainstorm practical measures to provide and disseminate information about services, including how best to publicize the organizations that provided services and the funders that supported them. Several attendees commented that they were not familiar with most of the organizations listed in the sample brochure displayed. Other attendees questioned AKDN's proposal to reach potential recipients through the Internet. One of the social workers pointedly argued that while a listing of organizations and their funders was nice, migrant laborers would benefit more from accessible information about services, and not biographies about the funders.

This heated discussion about the shortcomings of conventional development priorities—such as networking and the ranking of information about services over the actual services themselves—allowed for a productive segue to the final session of the roundtable, which was devoted to three programs that provided medical services to migrants. As Inna Arkadievna explained, because AKDN was interested in opening or supporting a medical clinic, they had invited representatives from three groups with technical expertise in operating medical clinics for migrants. Not coincidentally, these three programs each had a connection to faith communities. The representative of one group was a physician who accompanies volunteers from the Russian religious charity Na Ulitse (On the Street, or Outside) on their "street mission" outreach with Moscow's homeless population in order to provide informal medical consultation services. Several other physicians represented the secular NGO Vrachi Druzhby (Doctors of Friendship), which provides low-income medical care in collaboration with physicians and staff from another, explicitly faith-based medical charity. The third group of participants were the physician and office manager from the medical consultation clinic operated by Sosedi.

Like other nongovernmental medical services programs in Moscow, particularly those affiliated with religious communities, these three programs attempt to keep their work quiet in order not to come into conflict with local authorities. Under Russian law, only licensed physicians are allowed to provide medical treatment in registered facilities to legal residents. Other activities can entail only "consultation," and physicians must refer patients to formal medical facilities for treatment. Despite recognition by local welfare officials that unregistered persons (both noncitizens and homeless Russians) desperately require medical services, and despite welfare officials' informal encouragement of NGOs and private physicians to provide this assistance, law-enforcement officials closely monitor these activities. Consequently, physicians who work in these more informal fields tread carefully in the types of services they provide, in how they represent their work, and in the extent of public visibility they are willing to permit.

Whereas the previous sessions had generated debate and, at times, irritation among the participants as they challenged one another to move past talking about problems to discussing how to solve them, this session elicited the most obvious and supportive excitement. More importantly, the discussions from this session provided strong examples of a very different model of the types of services that could be provided and how these services could be delivered to clients.

Svetlana Maksimovna, a physician from Vrachi Druzhby, went first. After identifying the populations her group served—illegal migrants and refugees, including many from Chechnya and Africa—she described the social assistance models that she and her colleagues followed. Beginning with the provocative statement "I do not practice medicine," she detailed a different set of technical procedures by which she and her colleagues first listened to their patients and then made referrals for emergency or other services if necessary. Her point was not that she and her colleagues denied necessary medical services to patients in need, but rather that they believed that treating their patients as humans who might wish to talk to a friendly and sympathetic listener took precedence over a more instrumental relationship of dispensing prescriptions. Continuing, Svetlana Maksimovna described a second, more interventionist model of assistance that also privileged a compassionate, humane treatment of the patient. These cases typically arose when they were approached by a person who was especially vulnerable, both socially and financially, such as a mother with a child or an invalid. In such cases, her organization had an agreement (*dogovor*) with a nearby polyclinic that provides tickets for specialists who volunteer their services. In response to a question about the precise, technical nature (including financial and legal) of the relationship between Vrachi Druzhby and the polyclinic, Svetlana Maksimovna responded that the relationship was solely one of goodwill (*dobrovol'nie*).

The next presenter was Anatolii Sergeevich, a physician who accompanies Na Ulitse volunteers on their visits to Moscow's homeless community. After describing how he meets patients, provides basic first aid, and then refers them to other services, he strongly criticized AKDN's plan for an online resource program by stating that it was impossible to expect homeless people to be able to use the Internet to access services. Instead, he argued, funding organizations needed to provide support for the actual needs of the people they were trying to help. In his comments, Anatolii Sergeevich insisted that homeless persons deserved to be treated in ways that recognized their unique needs and circumstances, not in ways that further marginalized them. The final presenter was Michael, the African office manager from Sosedi. After reminding participants that his organization was "a charitable and not a commercial organization [*blagotvoritel'naia i ne kommercheskaia organizatsiia*]," Michael noted that Sosedi helped patients without regard to their citizenship or legal status. He then introduced one of the program's doctors, who briefly described their services and Sosedi's partnerships with several other medical NGOs and private physicians. In illustrating how they worked with clients, Michael and his colleague referenced similar themes of treating the whole person rather than simply following a clinical diagnosis.

In the animated discussion that followed these three presentations, the other participants expressed enthusiasm for the range of services provided and the explicitly humanitarian ethos of these religiously affiliated organizations. Although participants posed numerous questions to these presenters about the difficulties they faced with legal regulations, funding, and outreach, their real attention seemed to be focused on the ways in which these physicians were able to integrate a human connection—a warm smile, a gentle touch, a listening ear—with the services they provided. Repeatedly, participants suggested that AKDN and other funders, other NGOs, and government agencies needed to learn from these groups the most effective and humane ways to provide development assistance to Russia's migrant populations.

Two weeks later, the Moscow branch of the UNHCR sponsored a round-table for organizations working with migrants in order to promote racial tolerance in Russia. Although Sosedi was the only one of the groups in attendance at the AKDN roundtable to be invited to this meeting, the UNHCR roundtable closely resembled the one organized by AKDN in terms of the types of organizations invited and the overall goals (especially advocacy and services for migrants, networking, and creation of an online database and advertising materials). The conversation at the UNHCR meeting was also marked by a sense of dismay among participants who lamented a lack of understanding by the large development organizations about the real issues facing potential recipients and the work that was already being done by local groups. Most significantly, echoing their colleagues from the AKDN roundtable, participants at the UNHCR meeting singled out Sosedi and the other religiously affiliated organizations for special commendation and invited their advice and collaboration. Repeating the views of several attendees, Alla Mikhailovna, an attorney and the director of one of Russia's most active human rights NGOs, as well as a frequent recipient of death threats from neo-nationalist groups, praised Sosedi's efforts to advocate for and assist Africans and other non-Russian migrants and commented, "They are able to do what we can only dream of doing."

Whether or not Alla Mikhailovna's statement was accurate—it was difficult, if not impossible, to ascertain whether the religiously affiliated organizations did in fact provide better, more extensive, or more effective services—her perception of this greater effectiveness was significant. Alla Mikhailovna was well known and highly respected throughout Russia's human rights networks, and she was frequently featured as an expert authority in national and international media reports about racial intolerance issues. Her opinion about the work of religiously affiliated organizations thus carried considerable weight in the court of public opinion.

Two themes that emerged from the AKDN and UNHCR roundtables were particularly noteworthy for illuminating the role of faith-based organizations in Russia's development sphere. The first was that precise boundaries between religious and secular do not necessarily exist—or even matter—to local practitioners, as participants described existing partnerships and expressed interest in pursuing more partnerships among religiously affiliated organizations and nonreligious organizations. In even more practical terms, distinctions between religious and secular were insignificant as participants at the AKDN roundtable described how physicians, volunteers, program staff, and hospital administrators moved between religious and nonreligious organizations in order to pursue a greater common good. The second common theme was that faith-based organizations were recognized for pursuing an alternative vision of social development. While representatives from the labor unions, media groups, and the other NGOs debated more familiar qualities of "civil society" pertaining to legal reforms, information and media networks, and the formation of citizen-focused social movements, what generated the most attention were the efforts of the religiously affiliated communities to encourage civility through holistic, humane assistance to the persons in their care. As the interactions at these two roundtables demonstrate, those individuals who are doing the actual work of providing assistance in Moscow perceive faith-based organizations as being able to do something very different, and more significant, than their secular counterparts.

RESTORING HUMANITY TO CIVIL SOCIETY

What, then, are the implications and consequences of claims by proponents such as those described in this chapter that faith-based organizations are not only legitimate actors in Russia's development sphere, but are also better positioned to work around conventional development paradigms in order to pursue a different set of goals? As faith communities intervene publicly and directly in the problems of everyday life in Russia, they complicate the more familiar conceptual civil society topography marked by state, market, and citizen. Rather than creating and colonizing the space between citizen and state in order to foster new types of civil activities and values, faith-based organizations seek to redress the problems they identify as caused by the Russian state's withdrawal from its citizens by bridging the social and material distancing that occurs with civil society initiatives.

What faith communities have done most effectively, according to the perspective of their supporters, is to protect and maintain the human connections through which civic life emerges and flourishes, especially during periods such as the current moment when many Russians—assistance providers, beneficiaries, and ordinary citizens alike—continue to voice concerns that neoliberal trends deemphasize these more subjective, "human" qualities in favor of impersonality and objectivity.

Reconsidering the place of religious communities as legitimate and protective civil society actors also provides insight into understanding why religious bodies—the Russian Orthodox Church, most notably—have historically played such a significant role in both ordinary Russian daily life and national political affairs beyond providing systems of morality and safeguarding cultural heritage (Hann and Goltz, eds. 2010; Mitrokhin 2004). By appropriating and reconstituting the civil sphere, faith-based organizations are actively transforming not just the relationship between religious and secular spheres, but also changing the tasks for which each sphere is responsible. Institutions and ideologies that may be more familiar to secular actors—state agencies, political parties, and businesses—are increasingly engaging in the work of policing tradition and morality, while institutions and ideologies more ordinarily associated with the religious sphere are increasingly engaging in the work of ensuring social stability. These reorientations of spheres conventionally delineated as "religious" and "secular" offer new lenses for considering the extent to which "religious" qualities such as faith and ideology can ever be completely absent from the work of secular development organizations, a point raised by observers of development elsewhere in the world (Comaroff and Comaroff 2001; Escobar 1995).

Moreover, the experiences of faith-based organizations provide insight into how domestic development is evolving in Russia. Despite the fact that aid from foreign governments and foreign institutions was most prominent during the 1990s and early 2000s in Russia, today domestic faith-based organizations are funding development projects both throughout Russia and abroad (Bernbaum 2006; Livshin 2006; Rakhuba 2006). The efforts of Russia's religious communities to cultivate ethics of tithing and donation among their congregants have inspired similar efforts among Russia's secular assistance and development organizations. In 2009,

Russia's newly created charity and development agency, the National Charitable Foundation of Russia (Natsional'nyi Blagotvoritel'nyi Fond Rossii), launched a broad citizen-focused fund-raising campaign and began issuing grants to domestic assistance groups, including faith-based organizations. After meeting with this agency's director during summer 2009, Sosedi's director of development reported not only the new agency's enthusiasm for Sosedi activities but also its strong encouragement for Sosedi to submit a funding proposal. The successes of faith-based organizations thus present striking alternatives for enlisting and sustaining grassroots support in ways that create permanent communities of caring.

Finally, the work of faith communities in Moscow invites questions about whether they are more effective than their secular counterparts. Issues of efficacy are impossible to measure objectively, however, as the diversity of assistance programs within Russia prevents precise comparison. More problematic is that even though both faith-based organizations and secular organizations must follow detailed accounting practices for the Russian government, their own organization's administrators, and their funders, Russia's long history of informal economic practices means that the accuracy of financial figures and personnel information is often questionable.

Nevertheless, one measure of efficacy may be that of official recognition from the Russian state. Over the past several years, the activities of NGOs operating in Russia have been curtailed, or even eliminated, through both official legislation and more informal means such as harassment, prompting high-profile development agencies such as the Ford Foundation and the Peace Corps (among others) to leave Russia. Curiously, during this same period, a growing group of faith communities, including St. James, have successfully navigated complicated federal requirements to register legally both their congregations and their nonprofit NGOs. While it is inappropriate to speculate on the decisions by Russian officials, these forms of official legal recognition raise intriguing questions about how the state might view—or misrecognize—the activities of these particular NGOs. In these cases, it appears that faith-based organizations have achieved some degree of success by capitalizing on the categorical confusions and misrecognitions that are endemic to development activities to gain formal recognition from, and a defined position within, the Russian state.

Whether this formal recognition is a benefit or a disadvantage remains to be seen, however. As faith-based organizations become more institutionalized and formalized, they may be vulnerable to the same problems affecting their secular counterparts. In the last several years, volunteers have become professionalized, resulting in their being promoted or poached to positions elsewhere, as has happened with development directors at several faith-based NGOs. In other cases, while faith-based NGOs have successfully competed for larger and larger grants from domestic and foreign funders, their internal contributions from congregational tithing have decreased sharply as parishioners believe that their support is no longer needed. In still other cases, the successes of these groups are attracting attention and requests for partnerships with other development programs, thereby prompting worries that faith communities are being stretched thin by trying to serve as many people and needs as possible.

Consequently, there are growing concerns among some clergy and staff at faith-based NGOs about the potential limits to their activities and whether they will lose the personal touch that they find so valuable. In the end, however, these new experiences facing Moscow's faith-based organizations only further illuminate the ambiguous and tenuous gray areas of institutionalized development and how that directly shapes whether vision and practice can actually align. In the next chapter, I take up the question of how Moscow's faith-based assistance providers and supporters are working to bring together vision and practice through a specific understanding of what faith-inspired public service could and should look like.

5 Living a Life of Service

"The more we serve, the greater we are." With these words, the lay minister in front of a large Christian congregation in Moscow began a sermon about the necessity of service as intrinsic to being Christian. Dressed casually in khaki pants and a polo shirt, the lay minister leaned into a lectern standing on a worn wooden stage under hot stage lights in the performance auditorium of Moscow's theater school. As he delivered his sermon, PowerPoint slides with selected Bible verses flashed by on the projection screens hanging on either side of the stage.

Distinguishing between "mature Christians" who engage in service and "immature Christians" who have a "serve-us" mentality, the lay minister argued that providing service to others is when people are happiest. "The Bible says that greatness and service go hand in hand. . . . A non-ministry Christian [is a contradiction]." He then outlined twelve principles for living a life of service, drawing on Biblical passages to support his thesis that service was a fundamental component of Christianity.

Coloring his sermon with statements such as "if we are called to salvation, [we are] called to Christianity, [and] then called to serve" and "It's not the duration [of service] that counts; it's the donation that counts," the lay minister repeatedly reminded congregants that the talents they had been given by God were not for their own benefits but to help others: "We are commanded to serve others." As he advised the congregation, "living a life of service" was what made possible a meaningful life both in this world and the next.

Well known in Moscow as one of the largest and most active Christian congregations, the New Life Christian Church was also one of the oldest in the sense that it was formed during the early transition period of the late 1980s and 1990s. The church's membership was diverse in terms of the national origins, ages, and denominational backgrounds of parishioners; and worship services were an eclectic mix of prayer, readings from the Bible, sermons, and contemporary Christian rock music. Although English was the primary language of worship services and Bible study groups, Russian was used almost as often in prayers and private conversations as the congregation was composed almost equally of Russians and foreigners. Although some foreigners were North Americans, Europeans, and Australians on short-term work assignments in Russia (2–5 years was a regular cycle), others were longtime residents of Russia (ten or more years) who had established businesses and created families, often by marrying Russian spouses.

Especially noteworthy was that many congregants were actively involved outside the church in Russian social welfare projects, either as paid staff or as volunteers. Female church members were especially well represented in two of Moscow's largest women's associations, which funneled considerable resources—financial, material, social, and political— into Moscow's charitable organizations. Congregants and visitors routinely used worship services and the fellowship hour that followed as opportunities for publicizing their social welfare projects and drumming up interest from potential donors and volunteers.

The deployment of public service as an intrinsic and necessary part of religious practice, and of Christian faith in particular, was one that was clearly visible in other congregations I visited across Moscow. Vestibules outside sanctuaries served as spaces where congregants and non-church-affiliated staff with nonprofit groups placed posters and other materials to advertise their programs, and the time devoted during worship services for announcements and "prayers of the people" became opportunities for ministers and parishioners both to commend the contributions of those who had served and to encourage others to get involved. A common church project during winter, especially the weeks of Advent leading up to Christmas, was to collect donations of bedding, blankets, coats, and non-perishable food supplies. In one congregation, the donations were placed neatly along the walls of the nave and the chancel in the sanctuary. Over just a few weeks, the donated items were so plentiful that they began obscuring the religious artwork hanging along the walls. In private, a minister affiliated with the church wryly, but affectionately, commented that the sanctuary looked more like a food pantry than a space of worship.

In describing the many different types of activities in which his church was involved and the transformation of his church, both physically and ideologically, into a setting for public service, Pastor Mark stated, "[You] can't separate what it means to be a worshipping community [from] a worshipping community in action." In a similar vein, Pastor Ivan asserted that it was crucial that faith communities do "social work or social ministry." He continued: "[it is] essential that faith [is] practiced in some real, helpful, visible way . . . [otherwise] we have no credibility without good work to accompany [us]." Carolyn from the Salvation Army put it just as directly when she told me that her church's first priority was spiritual: "We believe that God as Jesus Christ can make a difference in people's lives. Our social work comes out of that belief." Going on to clarify that it was a misunderstanding to interpret the work of the Salvation Army as evangelistic, she stated, "[We have a] belief in action. It's true. But we have a sense of purpose that we will change people's lives for the better."

This is the reality of religious practice in Moscow today, where public service is both the internal and external expression of a religious community, and where expressions of personal faith are manifest not in acts of penance or contrition but in publicly performed acts of social welfare. Figures such as Jesus, the Virgin Mary, and the saints are revered not simply for their spiritual qualities but for their dedication to helping the less fortunate. Ultimately, as many interlocutors described it, being a person of faith is about being an active, compassionate servant to the public good. Yet even as Christian figures, traditions, and philosophies were frequently referenced, the individuals involved in these service activities were almost unanimous in their assertions that Christianity was not necessarily intrinsic to social work. As Carolyn put it, the imperative to serve and help others could come from anywhere—Islam, Buddhism, or nonreligious traditions. In fact, my regular conversations with several Christian clergy often focused more on the work of political theorists and philosophers such as Habermas and Hume who espoused ethics of service than on theological precepts.

Above all, today's religiously affiliated assistance groups are focused on redressing inequalities, whether those are social, cultural, economic, or political. Working both in cooperation with official projects and governmental bodies and in opposition to regional and federal policies, religious communities are addressing issues and operating in arenas that have in turn complicated and expanded what counts as worship, service, action, and even the intended beneficiaries of their work. Summing up a perspective that emerged frequently in the comments of his fellow clergy across Moscow's Christian community, and that echoed Berger's (2013) notion of religions as voluntary associations, one minister stated the question of whether congregations should be churches or social programs was misleading because it suggested these as mutually exclusive orientations. Rather, he said, it should be taken for granted that religious communities were social programs, and thus the better and more important question was how could religious communities best serve and help their communities. In so doing, these organizations are positioning themselves not merely as "religious," "charitable," or "benevolence" groups but as forms of civic religion that are critical players in Russian national politics and international human rights matters.[1]

WHICH MASTER? CHURCHES IN THE SERVICE OF THE STATE

In many ways, contemporary religious communities in Russia are simply continuing the work of their predecessors by focusing not just on the personal lives of individual recipients but also on larger civic concerns. The religious imperative to serve in order to support the needs of Russian society extends back more than five hundred years, when religion was an indispensable component of the imperial government's efforts to create a unified, modern, and civilized society. As Russia's history shows, religion has long been privileged and used precisely for its ability to serve not spiritual needs, but civic needs.

Already by the sixteenth century, long before concepts such as poverty and destitution were "discovered" as social problems in Russia, religious persons and institutions were enlisted to promote state interests, primarily to help the state manage and regulate its empire and subjects. As historian Michael Khodarkovsky (1996, 1999) has documented for Russia's early modern period, Orthodox missionary efforts were crucial tools for the government's political and economic policies and procedures. With the expansion of the Russian empire between the sixteenth and eighteenth centuries, the country's territories grew to encompass a diverse population of subjects, most notably non-Russian pagans and Muslims.[2] From the point of view of the imperial government, conversion to Christianity represented an opportunity to incorporate Russia's newly claimed territories and peoples "into a single political and religious identity under one tsar and one God" (Khodarkovsky 1996: 269).

Although conversion was not necessarily voluntary, nor did it necessarily entail spiritual transformation (Khodarkovsky 1996: 268–69), it did mean a change in identity and status, which in turn was envisioned as a means of creating Russian subjects who would be loyal to the tsar. This was particularly significant during Russia's territorial struggles with the Ottoman Empire and the need to reorient the cultural and political fidelity of newly conquered peoples to their new Russian rulers. At different moments, missionaries promoted conversions through incentives (provision of clothing, education, money, land, rank and status, and release from taxation and military conscription) and disincentives (penalties for failure to convert included taxation or the closure of mosques, among others) (Khodarkovsky 1996).

At the same time that religious conversion was a means for the state to incorporate and assimilate diverse populations into a single nation, it was also a conduit for foreign policy: notably, the geopolitical boundaries of the Russian Empire could be shown through the official reach of Christianity as marked by the conversion of local communities and the creation of space designated as Christian and, hence, Russian (Khodarkovsky 1999). These acts of boundary making were more than symbolic, however, as Russian Orthodox missionaries, clergy, and followers also participated in early cartographic practices. Mapmakers who incorporated Orthodox imagery into maps invested those spaces with spiritual qualities and sensibilities, thus creating a uniquely social and spiritual world to be inhabited by particular subjects. In other cases, Orthodox missionaries and clergy played a central role in the physical expansion of the Russian territory by traveling and documenting the empire's resources and subjects (Kivelson 1999, 2006).

Beyond contributing to the government's geopolitical affairs, religion was simultaneously deeply enmeshed in domestic matters that contributed to state-building concerns, particularly supporting social institutions that in turn fostered skills and sensibilities that would equip the state with a stable, enlightened, and civilized society. At times, Orthodox conversion efforts were accompanied not just by distributions of material goods but also by educational and literacy programs (Khodarkovsky 1996). During this same period, other Christian denominations also performed duties in service of the state (Coleman 2005), including efforts by the Lutheran Church to promote coeducational opportunities, voting, and military service, as documented in the Lutheran Church in Russia's Statement of Faith.

Through its religious policies, the Russian Orthodox Church played a key role in regulating and managing important societal concerns such as household management, financial security, and legitimization of children.[3] Religious precepts established parameters for taxation, property ownership, and employment, while Christian courts investigated, adjudicated, and administered property disputes and marital relations, political fidelity, and even legal determinations of personhood (Kaiser 1998, 2003). In the case of marriage, which was recognized by Orthodox officials as both a spiritual and social institution, religious clerics and courts dealt with such issues as bigamy, underage marriages, and abandonment. Although the ROC's privileging of first marriages meant that church officials tried to prevent remarriage and forcibly return runaway spouses to their marital partners and homes, persons who had been abandoned could also petition the church for exceptions that would allow marital dissolution or to have runaway spouses declared legally dead (Kaiser 2003).

Religious institutions thus offered imperial leaders a productive channel for creating and implementing an ideal society composed of exemplary and loyal subjects. As the interests of state and church aligned, their shared emphasis on moral qualities such as personal responsibility and deservingness in turn shaped the nature of charity in Russia.

Beginning around the sixteenth and seventeenth centuries, charitable giving coevolved with churches' civic role. The growth of testamentary giving—that is, donations specified in wills—formalized an existing tradition of almsgiving that was practiced in Russian Orthodoxy (Kaiser 2004). Although there is insufficient evidence to determine whether giving of any sort was directly related to religious or spiritual influences, religious rituals inspired giving and religious institutions became recipients of such donations (Kaiser 2004; Lindenmeyr 1990). At the same time, the imperial government increasingly leaned on churches to monitor the allocation of assistance through organized means, such as formal assistance programs.

These two facets can be seen as the transition of charity from a personal, spontaneous act to an activity facilitated by institutional means. Not coincidentally, this was also the period in which "poverty" came into existence as a social phenomenon. Echoing Peter Brown's (2005) assertion that "the poor" do not exist until they become a politically salient category, Daniel Kaiser (1998: 125) has argued that "the poor" were made visible in Russia when charity became bureaucratized with the formal recordkeeping of gifts.

In the late seventeenth century "poverty" became not just visible, but more importantly transformed into a social problem requiring solutions. Although poor households were noted in sixteenth-century tax registers, they were not a formal identity category until the reign of Peter I (1689–1725). Peter I was particularly troubled by the poor, whom he saw as a blight on society and whom he believed were individuals, primarily able-bodied men, who were deliberately not contributing to the state's needs (Kaiser 1998: 127–29). In an effort to distinguish between degrees of deservingness, early seventeenth-century laws criminalized both begging and private almsgiving. Historically, Orthodox monasteries and convents had provided shelter and food to destitute persons in exchange for work (Mitrokhin 2004), but now churches were pulled into a more interventionist and punitive role for the state, as Peter's government required church bodies to pay attention to where beggars congregated so that they could be arrested (Kaiser 1998: 129–30).[4]

In the early eighteenth century these practices of assisting the poor and homeless were formalized when, during the 1720s, Peter introduced laws that required monasteries to create poorhouses and to provide shelter and care for disabled soldiers who could no longer work (Kaiser 1998: 131–37). By the end of the eighteenth century, poorhouses and their use to compel work from seemingly able-bodied persons were institutionalized and common. Within charitable institutions, work was emphasized as a solution not just to unemployment, but also to teach personal skills and cultivate personal habits that would make people self-sufficient (Lindenmeyr 1986). By the end of the nineteenth century, this push to make work socially and morally productive and necessary crystallized in the work relief movement, with proponents advocating that social reform could happen through social action (Lindenmeyr 1986: 2).

Two of the founders of the work relief movement were Christian figures: an Orthodox minister, Father Ioann, who had worked to replace almsgiving with organized charity and founded the first Industrial Home in 1882, and Lutheran Baron Buksgevden, whose personal aversion to begging and almsgiving inspired him to found an Evangelical Home through the Lutheran Church. Although the two differed in their attitudes—Buksgevden favored a more punitive approach, while Father Ioann promoted a broader charitable scope, they cooperated to pursue the related goals of providing charitable assistance and moral rehabilitation (Lindenmeyr 1986: 6–8). One of the products of the work relief movement was the creation of Industrial Homes, which were envisioned as a particular form of charity: they were not precisely poorhouses, but spaces that trained people to work and required them to work. By the very end of the nineteenth century, the state created an agency to supervise workhouses, thereby offering state support to this form of charity (Lindenmeyr 1986).

The state support and partnerships that religious charity had enjoyed ceased abruptly in the twentieth century with the Bolshevik Revolution that ended the reign of Russia's imperial family and led to the establishment of the Soviet Union and its communist political system. As part of the new Soviet state's efforts to eliminate the vestiges of Russia's past, political leaders sought to institute new social structures and institutions that would ensure the equal distribution of resources to all citizens. Both religion and charitable forms of assistance were eliminated, first as the state secularized associational life and then when it brought assistance services under state control, reclassified them as a form of social protection (*sotsia'lnaia zashchita*), and transformed them into an entitlement system for all Soviet citizens. In 1929, the Soviet Union formally stopped religious groups from administering charitable programs (White 1993).

Through these maneuvers, the Soviet state redefined assistance and welfare from a form of material compensation to a specific group—the poor and marginalized—within the larger population to a set of benefits that were guaranteed as basic rights of citizenship.[5] These institutional changes were accompanied by the ideological transformation of personal ethics and practices of benevolence from personally held values of compassion and giving, especially those inspired and cultivated by religious traditions, into political values and civic duties. The official elimination of "charity" included its removal from Soviet vocabulary and its revaluation as an anti-Soviet activity (Bourdeaux 1999: 187; Lindenmeyr 1998: 319). Meanwhile, voluntarism was institutionalized and turned into a public obligation (see Shlapentokh 1989: 100–101).[6]

Toward the end of the Soviet period in the 1980s, however, state assistance practices changed again, paving the way for new forms of social support to emerge in the post-Soviet period. During the 1980s, when the Soviet Union struggled with recurring economic problems and shortages of food, consumer goods, and services, the state was increasingly unable to ensure adequate welfare services for its citizens. During this same period, the Chernobyl disaster in 1986 and the Soviet state's feeble responses to provide medical, environmental, and social services to affected citizens raised widespread public concern about the potential for impending economic and moral catastrophes. These concerns spurred Soviet citizens and sympathetic foreigners to create charitable groups that could address these problems, a development that prompted observers to wonder whether these groups were genuinely altruistic or in fact represented new forms of public organizing outside those administered by the state (White 1993).[7]

Particularly notable among these new, nonstate charitable groups were religious communities that quietly began providing support to local organizations and individuals in need. These included Mother Teresa's

Missionaries of Charity, who have been credited with facilitating the emergence of Western Christian aid, especially from European Catholic and Protestant communities in the USSR (Bourdeaux 1999; White 1993). During this same period, Soviet President Mikhail Gorbachev allowed the reemergence of religious life, albeit under careful management, for the millennial celebration of Orthodox Christianity in Russia.

This initial revival of both religious life and charitable activity was soon followed by the collapse of the Soviet Union in 1991. Government officials in the newly independent Russia repealed restrictions on both religion and religious charity, enabling religious communities and assistance groups to become more active in the 1990s. This was the same moment in which the Russian state's adoption of neoliberal practices and disinvestment from social welfare created a breach to be filled by non-state-affiliated social services groups (cf. Muehlebach 2012). One consequence of this transfer of assistance to nonstate groups was that official classification and popular understanding of assistance as a right or entitlement of citizenship was replaced by a system in which assistance was either a reward for particular behaviors (for instance, political activity) or, more commonly, as compensation awarded on the basis of one's presumed need or deservingness. This shift produced a new type of welfare citizen defined by a combination of moral and material criteria. At the same time, this new welfare citizen fit neatly into Russia's new economic ideology, which valued capitalist qualities such as entrepreneurialism. In a perverse logic, Russian assistance recipients were forced to compete against one another to demonstrate who could best exemplify neediness and deservingness, whether through personal stories of suffering or displays of bodily scars.[8]

To address the gaps left by the Russian state's movement away from assistance, religious and nonreligious organizations stepped in to provide services and support state welfare agencies that had lost their funding (see Caldwell 2004). Among religious organizations, although the Russian Orthodox Church played perhaps the most important publicly symbolic role in reclaiming the field of religious activity and charity in the post-Soviet period (Hann and Goltz, eds. 2010; Mitrokhin 2004), non-Orthodox Christian religious communities were also significant actors in pursuing a double-pronged approach of religious and charitable outreach (Caldwell 2004; Elliott and Deyneka 1999; Knox 2008; Wanner 2007).

While religious and nonreligious charities alike were critical of the state's retreat from welfare provision during this period, it was not necessarily an antagonistic relationship, but rather one in which the state depended on nonstate organizations for complementary and supplementary services. As a result, despite the creation of two distinct spheres—the state and the nonstate—both have been intimately entangled with and, in many cases, mutually dependent on one another. For instance, over the past ten years as migration issues have become increasingly salient for Russia, the Christian Church of Moscow has forged a close working relationship with the International Organization for Migration (IOM) and the United Nations High Commissioner for Refugees (UNHCR). Collectively, these three organizations have worked with asylum seekers, with each group taking on a particular role in the process: the CCM provides immediate relief services such as emergency medical care, food relief, and a strong social network; the UNHCR provides legal services and protections for asylum seekers who have received certification as refugees and works with Russian authorities to ensure that refugees receive the services they are guaranteed; and the IOM provides resettlement services to officially registered refugees, helps economic migrants who decide that they no longer wish to remain in Russia but lack the resources to travel to their homelands, and works with organizations in "sending" countries to discourage would-be economic migrants from traveling to Russia in the first place. Over time, this partnership has expanded to include other organizations that address related needs such as legal advocacy, language training, or relief programs for caregivers. In such cases, no one group is responsible for the larger problem but each group takes on a small piece in coordination with the others. Through such efforts, these organizations also work closely with the Russian state, even if at times their relationships are more adversarial than cooperative.[9]

In other cases, partnerships are more surprising, as religious groups cross otherwise sharply demarcated denominational lines or join up with state and nonstate secular groups that might otherwise have very different ideological positions or histories. For instance, as the CCM-IOM-UNHCR partnership has expanded, their sphere of interactions has grown to include other secular NGOs, foreign embassies, the local police, federal migration authorities, and members of the criminal justice sector.

Partnerships with members of the law enforcement community are particularly challenging for religious organizations because they invite criticisms that churches are colluding with authorities for surveillance and punishment purposes, a damning charge that evokes Soviet days when the Russian Orthodox Church cooperated with the authorities, including the secret police (Shlapentokh 2006). At the same time, working closely with the police and federal migration services exposes religious communities and their parishioners, recipients, volunteers, and donors to potential scrutiny by these same authorities. In a context where Russian authorities have been highly critical and suspicious of NGOs and grassroots activist groups and have begun penalizing individuals suspected of being "foreign agents," such as with the implementation of the "Foreign Agents Law" over the past several years, the potential that confidential data about revenue, expenses, names, and other identifying details could be exposed is a perilous proposition for religious communities.

Despite these risks, some religious communities do work closely with law enforcement authorities on issues of mutual concern. In the instances that I have documented, clergy, other aid workers, and even recipients have expressed their desires to work with law enforcement as a way to provide additional benefits, including protection, to their recipients. For religious organizations that work with marginalized populations such as addicts, the homeless, racial minorities, or economic and political migrants, the police can be a useful source of assistance in filing police reports about acts of discrimination or violence against minority victims, resolving visa registration problems, or dealing with disputes with landlords.

Increasingly, it is the police who are reaching out to churches for assistance, namely reassuring congregants and recipients that law enforcement officers want to help them, not harm them. Pastor Mark described how officers from the local police force had contacted him because they knew that members of his community had suffered racially motivated harassment and violence. These officers wanted to bring justice to the victims and solve the crimes against them and, ultimately, bring about a decrease in racially motivated violence in the city. Another minister revealed that he had been approached by law enforcement authorities with the request that he make a pastoral visit to care for foreign migrants detained in one of the special prisons that exclusively housed foreigners, most of whom had been imprisoned for crimes such as theft, smuggling, and selling drugs. Yet another minister obliquely hinted that he and members of his congregation were occasionally asked for assistance in working with North Korean defectors and in facilitating North Korean–Russian political negotiations.

RUSSIA'S NEW CIVIL SERVANT

The clearly shared priority given to public service among Moscow's faith communities in the post-Soviet period belies crises of identity in terms of how faith communities, their projects, and the individuals who participate in these activities are defined by others. At the same time, this emphasis on public service illuminates the nature of an emerging class of civil servants in today's Russia. To most Russians, perhaps the most familiar civil servant is that of Akaky Akakievich, the antihero in Nikolai Gogol's critique of imperial bureaucracy and administration in *The Overcoat*. Single-mindedly focused on the minutiae of his job as a clerk who copies documents by hand until he indulges in a new overcoat that then disappears only to taunt and haunt him around St. Petersburg, Akaky Akakievich exemplifies the soullessness and alienation wrought by Russian civil service practices. Yet whereas Akaky Akakievich was an archetype for an entire class of bureaucrats, today's faith-inspired civil servants are focused outward and represent a much more diverse Russia in which individuals can pick and choose their own issues and strategies to address them. Moreover, in contrast to Gogol's inwardly focused civil servant, today's new breed of civil servants are inspired by an ethos of personalization and by possibilities for channeling service to the community and to a greater good into personally meaningful and socially productive ways.

The diversity of these new publicly oriented civil servants, as well as the many different motivations that inspire their actions, indicates that there is no single type of "civil servant" who can make a meaningful difference. Among Moscow's religiously affiliated assistance communities, clergy, staff, volunteers, and donors come from all demographic groups: high school and university students, middle-aged workers, and elderly pensioners; males and females; Russian citizens, foreign expatriate professionals living and working in Russia on long-term employment contracts; refugees, asylum seekers, and undocumented economic migrants; foreigners from other parts of the former Soviet Union who are permanent residents in Russia; and domestic and foreign visitors to the city who decide to combine tourism with service. While Russian is the dominant language for business transactions, the day-to-day implementation of services may take place in English, French, German, Korean, Arabic, or Swahili, among others. Today's Russian civil servant is thus international and pluralist, either by choice or by necessity.

Russian and foreign students far from home who volunteered in soup kitchens and "meals on wheels" programs described missing their grandparents and enjoying the opportunity to spend time with elderly persons. Young professionals who had moved out of their families' apartments and were now living on their own for the first time while working long hours at the office reflected that they appreciated the camaraderie of working side by side with other volunteers and recipients. In some cases, volunteer work was a logical extension of a person's professional activities, as doctors, nurses, attorneys, accountants, and journalists, among many others, felt called to use their skills to help. For physicians and nurses who told me that they had deliberately chosen employment in "helping" professions, their volunteer work was simply part of their everyday jobs, even if unpaid (cf. Malkki 2015).

Individuals who participated in these types of assistance work have used various terms to describe themselves and their activities: *volontir, volunter,* or *dobrovolets* (good-hearted or kind-hearted person). Despite a frequent criticism voiced by Western development workers and civil society proponents that Russians have lost a culture of social responsibility and need to be trained in contemporary modes of public service and voluntarism, this has not been borne out by the experiences of Moscow's religious communities.[10] Nor is it an idea that Moscow's religious communities would support. Rather, Russia's religious communities, and the assistance community more generally, are characterized by a strong voluntary ethos that has translated into robust and innovative social action in many different registers. As Julie Hemment (2012, 2015) has observed

Figure 5. Promising "emergency social assistance," this advertisement for the Russian Orthodox Church's charitable organization Miloserdie announces that "We are searching for volunteers [good-hearted people]." Copyright Melissa L. Caldwell.

in her research on political activism among Russian youth, exemplified by the pro-Putin youth group Nashi, there has been a lively resurgence of assistance work aimed at contributing to a new social order. Although Nashi's activities are focused on more conservative, nationalist social issues such as preserving "traditional" Russian and Orthodox values and communities, in the post-Soviet period Russians across the political spectrum have been actively engaged in voluntary associations, including the high-profile demonstrations in favor of LGBT rights, freedom of expression, and "democratic values" more broadly that have occurred over the past several years.

Moreover, voluntarism has been officially reinstated through the revival of Soviet-era service groups organized through neighborhood associations, work groups, and schools. Students, coworkers, and neighbors are encouraged—or compelled—to devote themselves to periodic public work such as litter pick-ups, landscaping, and other types of civic hygiene. Yet while the intent of such efforts is to increase civic engagement among citizens, the involuntary, even coercive nature of efforts irritates and even discourages individuals from participating. For instance, one friend complained that it was not her responsibility to pick up after other people who had been irresponsible with their own trash, while another friend expressed his exasperation with his employer's attempts to control what he did outside of work. Both individuals supported voluntary work in general, but felt that coerced assistance was unethical and counterproductive to cultivating a general culture of service to others.

Despite the problems associated with coerced voluntarism, themes of duty (*dolg*) and responsibility (*otvetstvennost'*) were conspicuous in volunteers' and staff's self-presentations of their efforts. Much like the Red Cross aid workers described by Liisa Malkki (2015), who felt that their work was the logical extension of their position as socially responsible global citizens, or the doctors with Médecins Sans Frontières described by Peter Redfield (2013), who claimed that they had a duty to bear witness to atrocities and thus provide assistance, volunteers with Moscow's assistance programs claimed that their skills, abilities, and even spiritual backgrounds gave them a moral imperative to help others. Some individuals expressly claimed that they felt a responsibility to serve others precisely because they were persons of faith: "I am a Christian" or "*Ia veruiushii*" (I am a believer). More commonly, however, individuals described their work in sentimental terms of personal pleasure or a sense of community with those whom they served and with their fellow volunteers, such as the Sant'Egidio volunteers who told me that they felt "like family" with their fellow volunteers and homeless recipients. Within the CCM programs, staff, volunteers, and recipients occasionally forged fictive kin relationships, calling each other by affectionate honorifics such as "Grandmother" (*babulia*), "Auntie" (*tetushka*), or "son" (*synochka*). Far more common, however, was that most individuals reflected on their activities with a simple shrug and a refusal to describe oneself at all, or if pushed, a modest murmur that one was simply being *chelovek*—a person.

THE *M* WORD

The term most notable by its absence was that of "missionary." The individuals I encountered during the course of this research, both Russian and foreign alike, have actively resisted the term "missionary," either for themselves or for others involved in social justice projects, and claimed that the "missionary" label was typically outsiders' shorthand for a narrow and flawed understanding of what it meant to be "Christian." Most notably, in a context in which religion has been understood as an ethnic quality, rather than as a necessarily spiritual affiliation (Agadjanian 2001; Caldwell 2015; see also Bakker Kellogg 2015), the figure of the "missionary" could also be interpreted as an agent of ethnic, religious, and cultural conversion.[11] Even in cases where foreigners were officially affiliated with denominational bodies outside Russia and whose official job titles included the words "missionary" or "mission," there was great reluctance to self-identify as such. "The *M* word gets negative responses," lamented one American, an ordained minister who worked closely with Russian Orthodox congregations. Another foreigner who served as pastoral staff for Russia's Salvation Army community similarly expressed her weariness at her organization constantly being lumped in the general category of "mission." As she explained, the imperative to help others is not exclusively or necessarily a Christian value but one shared by all faiths as well as a nonreligious value. A Russian Lutheran minister related that while social work could be motivated by spiritual or theological values, just as important was a nonreligious humanistic sensibility of what he called "real compassion" for others.

Rather than simply rejecting the label because of negative connotations, most of my interlocutors felt that the term was so laden with imperial and political baggage that it did not accurately reflect what they did on a daily basis, how they carried out those tasks, or their motivations for pursuing them. Most people were quick to point out their professional degrees and training in fields such as social work, counseling, medicine, business, and politics as a way to demonstrate that they were professionals (Malkki 2015) who just happened to be employed or sponsored by religious organizations.

Even individuals whose official job title was that of "missionary" insisted that although personal faith surely influenced their desire to work with others in a helping capacity, it was misleading to describe themselves or others in similar positions as "missionaries," whom they depicted as people focused explicitly on conversion, not on helping others. Even the young men from the Church of Latter Day Saints, who were posted to Moscow for their mission year and were regular volunteers in the CCM's soup kitchens, refused to describe their volunteer activities as part of their mission work but held that it was separate from their church work. One young man stated that his volunteer service was a "mission to myself," not to anyone else.

This does not mean that there were not, in fact, persons—both foreigners and Russians—actively engaged in deliberate proselytism and conversion. Aid programs like those of the Christian Church of Moscow, St. Mark's, and several Korean-Russian Christian congregations I visited regularly hosted foreign church groups that traveled to Moscow to spend a week or two on a "mission trip." Most commonly, these were groups of teenagers from American Protestant churches on an "alternative spring break," in which they visited another country in order to do faith-motivated service work as a way to reflect on and develop their own spiritual sensibilities. Christian congregations from South Korea sent regular contingents of young adults as part of their global outreach. As Sarah Chee has documented in her research among Christian social services programs in South Korea, Russia was considered a prized destination for youth mission trips. Although South Korean youth were expected to pay their own way on these trips, organizers generally offered them for free to North Korean defector youth, for whom the trips were promoted as incentives to encourage defectors' spiritual and political transformation into good Korean, and Christian, citizens (Chee 2015). One Lutheran minister commented on the complications posed by visitors whose primary objectives seemed to reflect a voyeuristic curiosity about poverty and poverty relief in Russia. He noted that it was a struggle for the church to accommodate these visitors, but he maintained that it was nevertheless ethically and spiritually important to extend kindness and hospitality to them: "We must [allow] tourists in our church."

"Mission groups" were not exclusively religious in origin, as secular or nonreligious organizations and companies coordinated "volun-tourism" trips to Russia. American university students concerned with social justice issues were frequent visitors to assistance programs, as were foreign journalists looking for a good story about Russian hardship and care. While the contributions of such visitors were occasionally helpful, other volunteers questioned their motives and dedication and even complained privately about the disruptions caused by these one-time visitors. In summer 2007, over the course of just a few weeks, one assistance program was besieged with visiting Russian and foreign journalists and aid workers who wanted to see and document the program. The tiny offices that housed the program's services were filled to capacity, and staff, recipients, and regular volunteers were forced to step over and around recording equipment or wait in the hallways and outside the building until the spaces had cleared. Staff expressed particular concern that the constant deluge of film crews and microphones that occupied valuable space in the cramped quarters and at times forced would-be patients in their medical clinic to stand outside would deter recipients from coming to the program. Privacy concerns were also an issue, and some recipients covered their heads with caps or shirts in case a television camera was pointed in their direction.

On a separate occasion later that summer, after the minister of the congregation that sponsored this program had been approached by yet one more student-focused social justice volun-tourism organization, he confessed that he was exhausted and frustrated by the repeated requests. The requests were tiring not just because they came so frequently and because he and his staff had to dedicate time to answer them and find tasks (and sometimes housing) for visitors, but because these "requests" were not necessarily framed as offers of pure altruism. Rather, they were often couched in terms of teaching students about poverty and injustice in Russia, and thus were in fact requests for him and his staff to

Figure 6. Journalists from an international news agency interview a staff member with a faith-based social services program about the organization's human rights activities. Copyright Melissa L. Caldwell.

engage in additional work that took them away from their primary focus on recipients.

These types of "missionaries," whether secular or religious, both hindered the work of aid workers and troubled the dynamics and relationships in which assistance programs were embedded. By asking aid workers to "teach" them and provide meaningful life experiences, visitors positioned themselves as recipients who were there "to be converted" to a particular social justice ideology and experience. Although occasionally experienced by aid workers as a nuisance because it required them to divert their time and energy away from the "real problems" they needed to alleviate, these demands were generally tolerated if only because they were understood to be part of the larger project of outreach and public relations on which assistance programs depended. (I am, of course, very much aware of the extent to which anthropological research resembles the dynamics of these visits by the volun-tourists I describe. I am greatly appreciative of the many people who graciously and generously allowed me, the anthropologist, to tag along with them and who answered my many questions.)

What was more problematic, and even dangerous, was that assistance workers had to ensure that visitors adhered to formal policies governing religious communities in Russia. Because of the strict rules set by the Russian government prohibiting proselytism of Russian citizens by foreigners, assistance programs had to ensure that assistance activities were completely separated from the religious activities of the programs that sponsored them. For assistance communities with foreign ties, there is even greater pressure to adhere to governmental policies against proselytism so as not to appear as foreign agents actively trying to subvert Russian society by converting Russians away from Orthodoxy. Organizations that allowed religious activities or proselytization to take place within their assistance programs could be fined, shut down, or lose their registration. Given these stakes, assistance communities have been very careful not to permit overt expressions of religiosity or proselytization to take place in their programs.

Moreover, most assistance programs followed procedures designed to prevent the intrusion of nonassistance activities and personnel into their practices, such as by preventing recipients or volunteers from selling homemade goods or distributing advertisements for local businesses. As a result, there were few, if any, opportunities for people to engage in more familiar acts of proselytism such as prayer, distributing religious literature, inviting people to religious services, or forms of witnessing or sermonizing. Those activities were largely confined to formal worship services or private encounters among religiously inclined persons themselves, not in encounters with recipients.

Dr. Matt, a physician who regularly volunteered with several assistance programs and was active in Bible studies in his own church, was adamant that while his personal faith motivated him to help others, he was very careful not to engage in any kind of religious display when he was interacting with his patients. He told me that while he was honored when other people spontaneously shared their own spiritual journeys with him, he did not initiate spiritual conversations with them.[12] So circumspect were the clergy from congregations that supported and administered assistance programs that recipients typically did not know they were ministers.

More than once, I have seen staff at various programs stop visitors who were trying to engage recipients in prayer or distribute religious materials. In a memorable case at one of the CCM's soup kitchens in the late 1990s, a student mission group from the United States was warned several times by program staff to stop praying with recipients. When the program's director discovered that several students had slipped out and made their way to administrative offices upstairs, where they were attempting to pray with people not affiliated with the program, he unceremoniously hauled them back downstairs, publicly chastised them, and then told them to leave. A normally laidback, forgiving man who many years later became a minister himself, he was uncharacteristically abrupt and angry that day. While his anger was genuine because of concerns over the potential damage caused by the students, it was also clearly a public performance to onlookers that the CCM would not tolerate violations of their policy.

Such actions did not mean that there was an absolute separation between religious and assistance encounters, but assistance providers did have to be clear about which activities were religious and which ones were charitable. Assistance programs could not make professions of faith, participation in religious activities, or membership in a religious organization a prerequisite for receiving assistance. Nor could they subject recipients to unwanted expressions of religiosity. Religious communities can, however, extend benefits to enrolled members of their own congregations or to individuals who appeal to the church or somehow engage with the religious community. At the same time, as long as there is no coercion, recipients are free to attend church-sponsored events, such as Bible studies and coffee times. An officer with the Salvation Army commented on this paradox when she gave me a tour around their building. After pointing out the facilities for social services work, she then showed me the areas where the church holds Bible studies and other worship-related events. Although the two sections were clearly separated from one another by heavy doors and hallways, she commented that occasionally recipients wandered through the building and found their way to religious gatherings. She said that while recipients were never encouraged to join in, they were always made to feel welcome if they chose to do so. For her, it was a delicate balancing act of maintaining separation while extending hospitality to those who chose, either intentionally or accidentally, to traverse the two distinct spheres.

Even as the technicalities of separation and distinction between what is religious and what is assistance can, in principle, offer a productive workaround for religious groups that want to engage in explicit proselytization activities, or at least benefit from them, they have actually proved problematic for organizations that want to focus on their assistance work. What has happened is that although religious congregations have tried to maintain clear separations between their spiritual ministries and social ministries, observers and their own congregants have not always recognized this distinction.

The experiences of the Russian Orthodox Church are a case in point. Historically, the ROC has prioritized "believers" as beneficiaries of church assistance. In a context where Orthodoxy is understood as an ethnonational quality intrinsic to Russianness (Agadjanian 2001), this label of being a "believer" does not require active membership or participation in a particular religious community or theological tradition, but stands in as an intrinsic identity quality. As such, ethnic Russians could claim that they are "believers" and hence entitled to Orthodox assistance. In some cases individual clergy and churches have adhered to more conservative understandings of this notion and have limited provisions of assistance to enrolled members of their own congregants, a move that has angered Russians who believe that the church should help anyone who requests assistance (Caldwell 2010). Clergy from other Christian congregations have related similar problems, especially when needy individuals show up at religious services in search of assistance and then become angry after being redirected to the congregation's social ministry programs. As a result of such expectations on the part of potential recipients, religious organizations must navigate a delicate public relations battle of trying to showcase their good works while safeguarding their ability to do that work.

Perhaps the strongest argument against using the label "missionary" for volunteers and staff with faith-based assistance organizations came from staff with secular assistance and development organizations in Moscow. Benjamin, the director of Oxfam's Russia division, argued passionately for a distinction between "missionaries" and "religious enthusiasts." Similarly to a Catholic priest who told me that he preferred to use the word "service" because it was an expansive term that encompassed many types of activities and motivations, Benjamin made an analogous case for the word "mission." Drawing on theories and models from professional development literature, he noted that "mission" was actually a more expansive concept that emphasized goals and objectives for social change that were not necessarily tied to religious beliefs of practices but were a universal feature of all assistance work that was intended to alleviate poverty and injustice. When I asked him if his counterparts at religious assistance programs were missionaries, he replied, "to a certain extent they are. . . . But if [you mean] a traditional Christian missionary, then no . . . but generally speaking, yes." Elaborating further, Benjamin noted that from the perspective of the Russian government and Russian citizens, the label of "missionary" was generally used to refer to the foreignness of individuals and organizations that were perceived as engaging in activities against Russia's best interests. When organizations such as the British Council, the Ford Foundation, or Soros were accused of doing something improper, he said, they were labeled "spies" and "missionaries" and then kicked out of the country.

Indeed, the language and concept of mission seemed to be more commonly used for and among individuals who were involved in otherwise secular assistance programs, most notably "development" organizations, that were deliberately pursuing projects of social change (see also Salemink 2015). When asked about the place of "mission" in Russian aid projects, Benjamin stated that contemporary development literature was filled with references to "mission," a fact that raised questions for him about whether "social developers" were, in fact, "missionaries." The extent to which the language and concepts of "mission" were becoming entrenched in social development work was evident in its institutionalization, whereby the "mission" of an organization had to be specified in terms of its goals, objectives, projected activities, tax filings, and even naming.

Drawing a distinction between "missionaries" and "religious enthusiasts," Benjamin stated that it was easy to make comparisons between social developers and religious institutions. "People are stuck to this idea of mission. . . . Are they converting people to this social development ideology? Yes, they are." Going on, he commented that in today's Russia, "business has a mission now, too—to be socially responsible . . . Russia's businesspeople talk about converting people to ethics of social responsibility in the same way as if they are converting pagans. . . . The discourses are the same, although [they are] not religious."

CIVIC RELIGION IN THE SERVICE OF THE CIVIC GOOD

Much like in the late nineteenth century, when religious charities offered Russians significant opportunities for engaging in civil society activities and for articulating and practicing new modes of citizenship, especially among middle-class women who were otherwise excluded from the public sphere, today's faith-based organizations provide opportunities for individuals to pursue projects that are not just personally meaningful but that also enable them to participate publicly in ways that shape the future of Russian life and policy.

Maria, the development director of the CCM's social services NGO, described the strengths of her organization and its supporters precisely in terms of its potential for future growth in directions not yet envisioned: "We are a growing social organization and we're growing without a predetermined form, so it can grow any way you want. You can make it your own; there are no limitations because there is no precedent." Maria's comments were echoed by those of Anna, the congregation's social ministries director, who noted that even though she did not have a real job description and so did not entirely know what she was getting into when she accepted the position, she has found that the notion of "social ministry" has evolved in many unexpected ways: "As people get on board, we are engaging a community that was previously untouched. It frees up resources we can use."

The flexibility that is a hallmark of religiously affiliated assistance organizations makes it accessible and inviting to volunteers, who are able to mobilize their own individual circumstances in ways that are advantageous to everyone. While most assistance programs rely on the regular commitments of a core group of staff and volunteers, a more general feature of assistance programs is that participants—volunteers, staff, and even clergy—move among programs according to their own personal interests as well as more practical concerns such as location, schedule, and groups of friends. For instance, the two main social clubs for foreign expatriate women in Moscow sponsor a diverse array of programs, but the women I encountered typically participated in only a handful, and their choices were largely influenced by where they lived in Moscow, where their friends volunteered, and whose driver was available to transport them. It was fairly common for small groups of friends to organize their weekly schedules around their volunteer work so that they could meet up, work together, and then leave together for lunch, another meeting, or to pick up their children from school.

Qualities of flexibility and spontaneity have been especially attractive among younger Russians, especially those in high school and university. Social media has made it easy for them to create charitable meet-ups where they can create and implement a plan quickly and with a minimum of structure and advance planning. While most projects are one-time events, with individuals gathering to collect goods for donation, distribute those goods, or advocate for a cause, more formally organized organizations also rely on these more impulsive offers to help. Sant'Egidio is a good example of a group that takes all comers and redirects their help into tangible action. Sometimes individuals show up just once, while other times a first offer to help turns into long-term volunteering.

In other cases, the format of assistance is loosely structured and contingent upon local circumstances. Moscow's street ministries are often of this sort, as staff and volunteers must constantly adjust their activities and locations to respond to a population that is always on the move. Physicians with one faith-based organization that follows a regular weekly routine of service to Moscow's homeless population also carry personal doctor's kits of supplies that they can pull out and use as needed. After many years of itinerant service in Moscow, the Salvation Army now has its own building where they provide regular and drop-in services, as well as receive and store supplies for their programs. Having their own building has not eliminated the need to provide mobile services, however, as the Salvation Army continues to organize weekly food distributions of hot meals to homeless persons who gather at local parks around the city. While the Salvation Army has a regular circuit they travel, their actual destinations on any one night depend on where their homeless recipients congregate. Even on the same night, volunteers might find themselves moving between locations as their recipients move, often in response to the presence of the police. Through both programs—one located in their building and one that moves around the city—the Salvation Army's experiences highlight the tensions and uncertainties that come with the need for flexible assistance that can accommodate changing communities and circumstances on the ground.

Ministers with several different congregations revealed that they are always expecting the unexpected and that their time is, by necessity, fluid and unstructured—a reality that is far removed from the highly structured, routinized nature of Akaky Akakievich's work. On days with regularly scheduled worship services or church activities, the time immediately preceding and following church services can be a moment where people arrive and make spontaneous requests for assistance: money, some food, a place to stay. Clergy and staff are just as likely to receive telephone calls or e-mails in the middle of the night or on their days off. Whether to hand out private contact information poses a thorny issue for clergy and staff who must weigh the need for at least a modicum of privacy and some semblance of a personal life outside of their assistance work against the possibility that someone in grave danger or need might miss out on assistance. Among clergy and staff who have decided to be available outside regular program hours, there is a sense that helping others is not something that can be planned or predicted but rather reflects the reality of human existence, which is always contingent, dynamic, and full of unanticipated possibilities.

The inherent fluidity and potentiality of faith-based organizations is not always understood as a strength, however, but can also be experienced as generating tensions and hindering effective action. Representatives from other organizations complained that lack of structure and organization was problematic because it distanced them from actual work. Allison, the American diplomat who worked in the US Embassy as a liaison between the US Embassy, the US government, and Russian assistance programs, described the larger community of assistance providers as one that was "fragmented" and characterized by "anomie." She stated that despite some important examples to the contrary—and she identified the CCM and its partners as notable examples—the majority of assistance groups moved past one another and so did not know one another. There was a strong desire for these other groups to know who else was working in the area of assistance and to share knowledge and other resources, but their efforts consequently focused primarily on meeting one another and discussing potential partnerships, rather than actually implementing those plans. This focus on meeting and planning rather than on implementation was prominent in the break-time conversations among participants at the "roundtables" organized by development organizations that I attended in 2009. Privately attendees revealed that they were both frustrated that their time was wasted by organizational meetings that never moved beyond "meet and greets," and worried that if they did not participate in these meetings they might lose out on scarce resources and access to more powerful funding agencies and governmental officials.

Such instances of fluidity and uncertainty are characteristic of a larger concern that service is at risk of being colonized by practical needs and bureaucratic approaches that threaten to reconfigure the service relationship so that the individuals who require assistance are no longer the poor and needy but the assistance providers and funders themselves. An insider in the ROC patriarchate confided that the church faces significant challenges in terms of actually doing the work that it wants to do.[13] According to this person, Orthodox priests endure tremendous demands on their time and resources to help parishioners and address the immediate needs of their churches, which make it difficult for them to undertake the social ministries that they wish to do. This is compounded by unevenness in abilities and interests among individual congregations, so that some churches were more active and successful than others. What Orthodox churches needed, the insider speculated, was a formally institutionalized system composed of regular volunteers, resources, and programs that could support and sustain church operational needs in the realms of both spiritual and social ministry. Once the institutional needs were satisfied, churches could then start building their programs and directing their focus outward.

As clergy and staff related, too often their biggest challenge was not attracting volunteers but finding competent and effective volunteers who could provide the appropriate skills. This was a theme that came up in various guises in very different contexts, ranging from clergy who endeavored to teach their congregants that regular tithing was more effective

Figure 7. Russian and foreign volunteers with a faith-based social services program load up a van with food supplies donated from a Moscow grocery store. Copyright Melissa L. Caldwell.

than periodic appeals for providing assistance and sustaining programs to program directors who struggled to teach eager volunteers and supporters best practices for effective and consistent service delivery.

The size and scope of CCM's activities brought these challenges of harnessing the energies of well-meaning volunteers into sharp relief. On days when the CCM distributed food bags to refugees, asylum seekers, and low-income students and migrants, several staff members spent the morning visiting a local superstore to pick up donated pallets of frozen meat, canned vegetables, rice, oil, and other staples. A volunteer with a car usually accompanied them in order to transport the supplies back to the program's offices. Once at the offices, the vehicle needed to be unpacked and the supplies sorted and bagged, and extras stacked neatly in the storage room.

Given the logistics of traffic in Moscow, the vehicle usually arrived shortly before the distribution began, and dozens of young men were

Figure 8. Russian and African recipients in this faith-based social services program help unload donated food supplies that will be distributed through the organization's food bags. Copyright Melissa L. Caldwell.

waiting patiently outside the building. As soon as the vehicle pulled up, the men surged forward to empty the trunk and move the food inside, where another group of men quickly opened the piles and began sorting food and filling bags. For about an hour the scene was chaotic as plastic bags and ripped pieces of paper floated around the room and littered the floor. Staff tried to shout instructions over the noise, while eager volunteers tried to be as helpful as possible. Mistakes were frequent, as some bags ended up with too many items while others had too few, or bags of rice and flour were ripped and spilled on the floor. While things were usually sorted out properly by the end, staff were clearly frustrated that their "system" for easy management of so many items was so quickly disregarded. Over many visits spanning many years, the scene never changed, and I routinely witnessed staff and trusted volunteers valiantly attempt to keep order and ensure people followed proper guidelines.

Similarly chaotic encounters among well-meaning but undisciplined volunteers were present at soup kitchens I visited. While the act of placing filled dishes and cups on a plate and delivering them to recipients seated at a table may not at first seem too complicated, soup kitchens rely on an extremely rigid and efficient protocol of service delivery in order to ensure fairness in portion control, reduce spillage, manage cost, and serve as many recipients as possible in a finite period of time. New volunteers receive detailed instructions on how to place dishes on a tray to carry as many meals as possible, where to return used dishes and trays, what kinds of substitutions were permitted, which recipients could be trusted to help themselves, and which recipients needed careful monitoring.

Over the many years I have attended the CCM's soup kitchens as ethnographic observer and volunteer, I have witnessed new volunteers expressing frustration both about the requirement to be "trained," however informally, and the complexity of actually serving meals speedily and efficiently. At the same time, exasperated soup kitchen staff and the restaurant staff who cook the food have complained about newcomers who are eager to help but do not follow the rules or try to introduce their own ideas for administering the program. Thus for social assistance programs, what is lacking is neither the concept of volunteering nor enthusiasm for volunteering, but rather their ability to find, discipline, and retain the best-suited volunteers.

While few organizations observed in this study had implemented official training programs for potential volunteers, most had some form of orientation run by officially designated orientation leaders that they requested volunteers undergo before being able to help. In very real ways, volunteers often became the first cohort of recipients, even if the services they received were professional rather than material, especially when such voluntarism orientations subsequently led to paid service opportunities either within the same organization or at other organizations.

The sense that effective assistance work increasingly required structure and planning was especially apparent in the interactions between different organizations. As I was told and shown repeatedly by individuals from multiple organizations, much of their work with other groups was directed not at aligning their respective spiritual traditions or ethical goals, but rather at achieving compatible management styles.

The need to achieve compatibility and consensus out of difference and uncertainty was clearly apparent in 2007 during the several months of preparation leading up to the formal founding of the interfaith service program described in chapter 2. Representatives from a core group of congregations and denominational development agencies—the CCM, the Russian Lutheran Church, a Catholic church, Caritas, and United Way, most notably—held frequent planning meetings. As the hosting institution that would sponsor and administer the program, the CCM took the lead in the planning meetings. The CCM's minister tirelessly called up other clergy in Moscow and met with them to gauge their interest and commitment. CCM staff worked behind the scenes to line up funders, donors, supporting welfare offices, and facilities for the program.

After several months of meetings and conversations between the CCM and representatives from Caritas and a Russian Catholic community, it seemed as if they had finally reached agreement on the number of recipients to serve and which social welfare office to approach for a list of qualified residents to invite to join the program. In the end, however, the entire collaboration unraveled when one of the Russian staff members from the Catholic group went on holiday and the other left for a new job abroad, leaving the kind but inexperienced priest unable to negotiate with the social workers, and a list of recipients never materialized. At the same time, discussions with the Lutheran Church over the plan to rent office space to house the program also fizzled out after the building manager elected to rent the dedicated offices to a real estate company. In the course of a few weeks, the entire interfaith project was almost derailed because of different bureaucratic priorities and shortcomings.

In the end, the negotiations did eventually yield a successful social services program. Nonetheless, the resulting project had clearly been affected by the differences and uncertainties among the various partners and constituencies. Not only did it take longer to complete and implement the project than had been expected, but the final group of participating members also changed to accommodate the exit of some participants and the incorporation of others. These changes entailed the reorganization of both participants' roles and responsibilities, as well as the enrolled recipient groups. Whether or not the uncertainties that were intrinsic to this project foreshadowed later issues, within five years the program had closed and many of the interfaith partnerships had been transformed or even dissolved.

In summing up the effects of the work performed by faith-based organizations and by the paid and unpaid staff who worked through these organizations, Susanna explained that the primary requirement was not proselytizing but rather simply being a Christian presence. "Sometimes we just care for people, [there are] no requirements." Susanna's words reflected a critical tension and challenge for Moscow's faith communities. On the one hand, faith communities must establish themselves as religious communities, while simultaneously demonstrating that they are more than religious, or even nonreligious. On the other hand, religiously affiliated service programs must also position themselves as organizations that are more than simply charitable initiatives that distribute money, food, clothing, and other items and instead demonstrate that they are fundamentally invested in the greater good. In reflecting on what he saw as the "social responsibility" of the church to serve society, one minister commented that it was better to do than to speak too much. He concluded by stating: "In the Bible, faith is empty [if it is just] words and without work."

Ultimately, the care work practiced by Moscow's faith communities is a form of activist social work that serves and buttresses both the Russian state and economy, even as it contests the state and other communities. Faith communities are not simply doing the bidding of the state, but are instead actively contributing to a new and different type of service economy grounded in compassion and kindness. As such, by playing with the uncertainties of the fields in which they exist and operate, faith communities open up possibilities for alternative models of civic engagement and economic development.

6 The Business of Being Kind

If the activities of Moscow's faith communities represent new approaches to public service in Russia, they have also inspired new modes of economic activity. In Russia's neoliberal reality, need, deservingness, and affect have become opportunities for political and economic entrepreneurial investment. Both within their own communities of supporters and beyond in Moscow's commercial sector, religious groups and religiously affiliated assistance programs compete and cooperate with private businesses and state agencies to promote and capitalize on the simultaneously civic and financial value of compassion. Generic appeals for donations have become more sophisticated and lucrative, as charitable organizations and donors engage one another through more commercial activities of buying and selling need and despair—a development that ironically challenges the official designation of "*nekommercheskii*" that is applied to nonprofit groups such as these.

Local newspapers have added "charity" sections with classified advertisements, often accompanied by pictures of disabled children, sad-eyed pensioners, or homeless animals, that allow potential donors to "shop" for the perfect recipient or program to support. Assistance programs that sell artwork or other items made by recipients, especially disabled veterans and children, and companies that sell commercial products for which part of the revenue is dedicated to a specific charitable project are all instances in which compassion is being transformed into tangible, material objects. Social problems and ethical responses become consumer goods that circulate within a marketplace where Russians can make choices about the values and qualities that they want to promote and consume.

Most of the faith communities that I followed offered some type of compassion commodity—greeting cards, small art prints and lithographs, small handicrafts, and children's toys—with the revenue earmarked to support the activities of their social services programs.[1] In response to repeated requests from recipients for job training opportunities, as well as personal interest in spending time in the countryside, the CCM rented a dacha (summer cottage) plot several hours outside Moscow, where they planted a small garden. On weekends, a group of recipients, primarily African migrants, and church members (Russian and non-Russian) took day trips out to tend the garden and harvest the bounty, which was available for sale on Sundays after church or through CSA (community supported agriculture) boxes. Over time, it became too challenging to coordinate the trips, and the church moved the garden to a privately owned plot in Moscow, where they have installed greenhouses and employed an asylum seeker with agricultural experience as a master gardener.

The commercial potential of compassion and assistance came through perhaps most explicitly in my encounters with staff and recipients from Russia's Oxfam programs. As several of the organization's staff and affiliates told me on different occasions, the focus of Oxfam's work in Russia departed from the organization's more traditional activities such as alleviating children's food poverty, and instead was focused on more economically oriented goals of empowering low-income women from the provinces to become entrepreneurs and small business owners. Through my friend Nadya, who worked occasionally as a consultant and interpreter for Oxfam, I met some of the women who had successfully gone through the organization's programs and created their own businesses, which were often devoted to craftwork such as embroidery or jewelry-making. Our interviews were a curious mix of personal history and sales pitch, in which the women presented their wares and tried to use their own stories about overcoming hardship to persuade Nadya and me to buy something.

Figure 9. A Moscow Protestant church created an organic garden to provide recipients with job skills, the opportunity to work outside, and the prospect of selling the produce to generate funds that are reinvested in the program. Copyright Melissa L. Caldwell.

Curiously, because these compassion commodities were meant to be commercially sold objects, rather than gifts, they were deliberately impersonal and commercial, unlike the "aid bunnies" that were made by Finnish knitters who invested a sense of themselves, including made-up personal biographies for the bunnies, into these gift-objects destined for child trauma victims (Malkki 2015).

Figure 10. A Russian woman who received small business grant money from an Oxfam entrepreneurial development program makes "compassion commodities" such as this handicraft to fund her business. Copyright Andrew G. Baker.

Reflecting broader trends of "philanthrocapitalism" and "venture philanthropy" (Adams 2013: 21) in the global humanitarian economy that some have described as being a form of "disaster capitalism" (Adams 2013) or even "disaster democracy" (Takaki Richardson 2014), over the past twenty years Russia's commercially oriented modes of compassion have not so much emerged alongside the country's postsocialist capitalist economy as they have developed as a critical niche within it. As kindness, compassion, and other forms of affect have become more than moral imperatives or cultural values, they have inspired lucrative business opportunities for new cohorts of entrepreneurs and businesses that parlay aid into a robust "compassion economy" (James 2010) with its own producers, distributors, consumers, forms of currency, and possibilities for growth. The personal appeals and simple, unsophisticated, and even haphazard appearance of many "charity" campaigns bely the robust economy of resources, labor power, and infrastructure that enables, and perhaps even necessitates, such objectives and

Figure 11. Another example of a "compassion commodity" is this key chain that was sold by a member of Moscow's deaf community to raise funds for social services projects to support deaf Muscovites. The key chain was accompanied by a piece of paper with instructions for learning the Russian alphabet in sign language. Copyright Andrew G. Baker.

activities. Food banks, clothing drives, after-school programs, sidewalk health clinics, drug and alcohol counseling, and legal aid drop-in centers are not possible without an increasingly professionalized (and licensed) work force, regular and lawful infusions and circulations of money and other material goods, reliable distribution and storage networks, and ample political capital to grease the wheels of Russia's formal and informal economies.

In many respects, although the individuals who are intended to benefit from this compassion economy may be alienated from Russia's capitalist market, the individuals who provide aid are not. In fact, Russia's compassion economy requires a robust labor force of paid and unpaid workers (see also Muehlebach 2012). Aid workers and clergy are just one tiny cohort within a much larger serving economy populated by professionals such as logistics managers, drivers, employment and human rights attorneys, accountants, janitorial staff, medical professionals, managers, grant writers, and public relations experts, among many others. This compassion economy is one in which profit and surplus are no longer fantasies but realized outcomes that in turn require ever greater cohorts of laborers, workplaces, and opportunities for producing, managing, and reinvesting the resources that circulate.

What does it mean to think of Russia's compassion economy as an economy, and most specifically a market-based economy in which the focus is not simply on sustainability but on growth, and where growth is not simply a fantasy but a reality—and often a reality that brings with it new problems? Thinking about Russia's compassion economy as part of a neoliberal market-based economy raises intriguing questions about labor, the relationship between production and consumption, and the types of material objects and immaterial qualities that circulate through this system (see also Adams 2013; James 2010; Muehlebach 2012). Can care, kindness, and compassion be the raw materials, modes of production, and even products that support not just a viable, but a generative economic system? If so, what happens when care, kindness, and compassion are both the raw materials that generate this system and the profits that emerge? Can a compassion economy be competitive, and if so, what are we to make of such activities as "competition," investment, growth, accountability, and even transparency in this context?

In her work on "affective economies," Sara Ahmed (2004: 119) has persuasively argued that emotions are not simply states of being that are internal to the person who experiences them, but rather are external qualities that move between persons and, through this circulation, produce results, including binding people to, or separating people from, one another and their communities: "emotions *do things*," she writes.[2] Drawing from both psychoanalysis and Marxist theories of circulation to think of emotions as "forms of capital," Ahmed (2004: 120) argues that emotions gain their strength and meaning through social interaction: "emotions circulate and are distributed across a social as well as psychic field." Circulation produces not just value, but surplus value.

More concretely, Vincanne Adams (2013: 11) has described the specific market of charitable goods, services, and laborers that emerged in the wake of Hurricane Katrina in Louisiana as being embedded in a "virtuous circle" characterized by assumptions that "the work of providing charity can also be profitable." This was a uniquely affect-oriented economy that "[relied] on specific kinds of suffering to generate new and quite large profits." In Italy, Andrea Muehlebach (2012: 39) has observed similar trends that have relied on the "revaluation of the marginal" to produce a system in which "the worthless of the world produce its greatest wealth." In both of these cases, Adams and Muehlebach are describing how economic systems based on suffering and sympathy—"affect economies"— develop and grow financially and institutionally out of the need to provide services to and for vulnerable and disenfranchised members of society. Affective experiences, in the form of grief, pity, or compassion, and virtue, in the form of altruistic behavior, work together as forms of capital to catalyze and propel economic processes that generate not only profits but surplus. These affective surpluses are forms of capital that must be reinvested into the system to maintain it and keep it going into the future. This productive quality of affect is what animates the faith and hope that Moscow's religiously affiliated assistance workers practice in their efforts to transform uncertainties and unknowns into possibilities.

By emphasizing the simultaneously social, psychic, *and* material dimensions of emotions, Ahmed, Adams, and Muehlebach provide compelling models for understanding the dynamics of compassion economies as they move beyond more utilitarian, albeit sentimentally inspired, modes of responding to need with donations and instead inspire and generate future growth in ways that approximate a more capitalist system of continuous profit-making and reinvestment. Above all, Ahmed's approach provokes an uncomfortable but intriguing question about the extent to which we can consider the nature of the Invisible Hand that guides compassion economies like that among Moscow's faith communities (cf. Muehlebach 2012: 26).[3]

TOWARD A MARKET ECONOMY OF SENTIMENT AND SELFLESSNESS?

The creation of a compassion economy—perhaps even a compassion industry—is not new in post-Soviet countries like Russia, but one that has been observed in many other parts of the world as intrinsic to development and humanitarian programs (e.g., Adams 2013; Bornstein 2005, 2012; Escobar 1995; James 2010; Muehlebach 2012; Redfield 2013; Rudnyckyj 2010). In the Russian case, the formal revival and reinvention of the country's compassion economy in the early 1990s resulted from the country's adoption of neoliberal economic reforms and disinvestment from social welfare. When international development programs arrived in Russia and other post-Soviet countries, they brought with them their own resources, personnel, and information and logistics systems. As a result, development and other assistance organizations generated their own thriving economy that was grounded in the circulation of global development funds and resources, as well as the creation of a professional cohort of development workers skilled in grant-writing, project management, and training (see, for instance, Phillips 2008). As Ruth Mandel (2012: 226) has noted, "civil society represented a growth industry in the development business of shaping the 'transition' from a discredited, dysfunctional socialist command economy to the neoliberal governance-driven society."

Over the past two decades, development objectives have changed, as international funders and the Russian government have adjusted their priorities about the types of "problems" that required attention—from women's issues to civil society initiatives, and from legal restructuring to human rights interventions, among others. As priorities have shifted, so have financing streams, resulting in episodic fluctuations and stoppages, which have in turn hindered long-term security or steady growth in the development field. Such changes have made it difficult for Russia's development workers to keep up with changing priorities or to reinvent themselves in order to continue winning development grants (see Hemment 2012, especially notes 24 and 31; Mandel 2012). Among my Russian friends and acquaintances, few people who were employed in the 1990s and early 2000s by development grant money have retained their positions. Most have suffered through recurring cycles of employment and unemployment, frequently resorting to patching together multiple jobs and short-term funding opportunities to support themselves and their programs. Several American acquaintances have been forced to transfer out of Russia when their programs (e.g., Peace Corps, Ford Foundation, and USAID, among others) were unexpectedly closed by the Russian government, and close Russian friends have suffered the heartbreak of seeing programs they created go from incredible successes to permanent closure.

In light of these circumstances, what makes Russia's faith-based compassion economy intriguing is its ability to weather financial cycles that have negatively affected other sectors of the country's economy. Curiously, unlike other institutions within Russia's banking, manufacturing, media, and real estate sectors, which have been hit by repeated cycles of boom and bust, resulting in breathtaking accumulations of capital and equally stunning losses, the compassion economy has remained relatively stable, even showing steady but noteworthy growth in terms of profits, surpluses, and expanding networks of production, distribution, and consumption. Judging by the successes of the network of faith communities I tracked in my research, there seems to be something slightly different among faith-based charities and their partners in terms of the kinds of economic activities they have cultivated, where self-interest has been replaced by kindness and benevolence.

In the late 1990s, one of the biggest challenges facing many churches that sponsored social ministries was ensuring a steady infusion of resources to support their recipients while also demonstrating that they had the ability to survive as institutions. Programs depend on both money and goods, for different reasons and with different values and problems ascribed to both. Both cash and material goods had the potential to be stored and used as needed, although both had different life cycles at different moments. As for cash, donations often came in different currencies, and owing to the fluctuating exchange values between the Russia ruble, American dollar, British pound, and euro, organizations had to make critical calculations to decide on the currency in which to keep their money, as well as whether to keep their money in a bank or in a safe in an office. In the 1998 economic "crisis," when the value of the Russian ruble plummeted and banks limited the amount of money that could be withdrawn (and in some cases closed altogether, causing investors to lose their savings), organizations that had placed their money in banks or kept their funds in rubles suffered devastating financial losses. Today, with official policies governing that all transactions be conducted in rubles and that receipt of foreign currency requires additional reporting procedures, organizations that receive funds from abroad face uncertainty in terms of scrutiny and their ability to access their resources. With regard to material goods, organizations must worry about expiration dates and perishability, as well as aesthetic and seasonal trends that might make particular items, such as clothing, more or less desirable and helpful. (A walk through one program's charitable clothes closet was akin to a trip a decade back in fashion time.)

Cash was especially important. Every organization that used space needed cash to pay rent and the meager salary of a director. During the 1990s, when recurring financial problems prevented many Russian government agencies and businesses from paying out salaries and pensions on a regular basis, it was not uncommon for landlords, store owners, and others to extend credit to private citizens and organizations, allowing them to defer payments for several months at a time. Because virtually everyone was affected by the uncertainties of the Russian economy, vestiges of the socialist-era sharing economy returned, binding everyone, including charitable organizations, into extensive networks of gifting and delayed reciprocity. Charities benefited from these arrangements, especially given that there was often moral outrage against business owners who demanded payments at the expense of needy recipients. When the Russian economy stabilized in the early 2000s, and salary and pension payments were regularized—and supported by greater reliance on the formal banking sector—landlords and store owners began demanding back payments and were less inclined to allow subsequent late payments. This made charities vulnerable if they did not enjoy regular, guaranteed financial support.

Programs that served homeless populations, like a sidewalk soup kitchen that operated near the then-functioning Moscow branch of Medécins Sans Frontières, depended on consistent donations of key ingredients that could be turned into meals suitable for mobile populations (soup, bread, kasha, tea), as well as disposable serving containers that could survive multiple uses and being stuffed in a rucksack. Another program that has long supported migrants needed not just material goods (clothing, hygiene kits, baby supplies) but also cash to purchase items as necessary.

As for CCM, their concerns focused on securing regular and adequate infusions of cash to support their projects, in-kind donations of food, basic hygiene supplies, and small "treats" to supplement the hot meals, food bags, and clothing that they distributed through their programs, and a cohort of reliable volunteers who could help with any task. At any given moment, the staff faced a shortfall of cash that prevented them from planning ahead more than a week or two or a deficit of volunteers who could be mobilized into service. During both especially cold or pleasant weather, it was not uncommon for nary a single volunteer to show up at the soup kitchens, leaving the director alone to serve meals to several hundred recipients. The weeks leading up to holidays were especially tense, as church staff tried to figure out how they could find small gifts to give their recipients while also ensuring that there were enough volunteers lined up to meet the increased demand from recipients.

At the church services and staff member meetings that I have attended over many years observing the CCM, prayer and faith were strategies employed just as often as cold-calling local businesses, municipal agencies, and community groups to drum up support and resources. At various moments during the time that I was following the CCM's work in the late 1990s and early 2000s, staff meetings were tense as the church's clergy and church council worried that they were only a few weeks away from having to reduce their services or even close their programs completely. The CCM's staff and beneficiaries watched carefully as other large charities in Moscow endured similar challenges and just as often lost their battles, despite their best efforts. The CCM's clergy, staff, volunteers, and beneficiaries often had a front-row seat to these challenges, as beneficiaries from other charities that had been forced to shut down turned up at the CCM's soup kitchens in the hopes of being added to their registry. While CCM staff tried valiantly to accommodate them, it was rare that they could do more than offer an occasional meal.

Nearly fifteen years later, the situation has changed significantly. The CCM has increased the number of persons that it helps on a regular basis by expanding its original programs and adding several new programs. It is tightly networked into a community of other charitable organizations as well as domestic and international funding organizations. Although it still struggles at times to keep a regular base of experienced volunteers, turnover is largely a product of the dynamic nature of the CCM congregation and community, many of whom are foreigners and Russians who move frequently for work, either to other parts of Russia or abroad, not a lack of support for the church's programs.

In many respects, one of the biggest problems facing the CCM is not one of scarcity but rather of excess. The CCM has become so well respected for the effectiveness of its charitable programs and the ethical and professional standards it sets that it enjoys regular donations of money and goods, thus forcing church staff and members of the church to consider not just how to make best use of those resources but simply how to cope with them. While instances of excess donations are not exclusive to the CCM, as is evident with the Russian Lutheran Church, which has extensively renovated its facilities and opened several new programs, or the Salvation Army that now has its own building and is expanding its programs, these developments are not typical of all assistance programs. What is significant about successful programs like the CCM is that they are known to be among the organizations best socially networked and thus most able to use donated goods and funds through their own programs or through their partnerships with other organizations. Behind the scenes, staff and clergy are regularly making telephone calls and sending e-mails to their counterparts in other programs, including at the Russian Orthodox Church, trying to redistribute resources.

For instance, after the church finally moved its main administrative offices and outreach center from the cramped confines of a converted basement under a cafeteria that served one of the church's soup kitchens and into a new building with significantly more space for meetings and program activities, excitement over the new space turned to dismay as the extra rooms were filled with donations. One room that was meant to be a small consultation room for beneficiaries to meet with health care workers and legal aid representatives was quickly filled with boxes of donated clothing. After the clothing was sorted and organized, the available space was then filled with boxes of packaged foods donated by a local food company. The consultations that were intended for this room were instead relegated to a small "break room" and took place on and around the ancient ping-pong table that occupied most of the space. The physicians and nurses that staffed the health care program complained about the intrusions of the donated goods and asserted that at the very least they needed a proper examination table to conduct gynecological exams and minor first aid procedures.

Figure 12. Labeled as *miloserdie* (charity) and "Prepackaged national/traditional meals," these bags of food supplies were donated to a Moscow faith-based social services program by the Russian Provisioning Foundation. Copyright Melissa L. Caldwell.

In 2015, when I returned for a quick visit to Moscow, I dropped in to the CCM offices to see their newly renovated facilities. Inside and outside the office for the director of the social services programs were stacks and stacks of plastic bags, filled with donations of dried pasta and other non-perishable food items. When I asked if the donations were for the CCM's food pantry, the director laughed and said that he had no idea what he was going to do with the food. He explained that they were unexpected donations that had just come in from an organization that had heard about the church's projects and thought they could use them. Although it was a sizable amount of food, there were not enough individual portions of any one type to put in the food bags, and so the CCM could not offer them to their enrolled recipients, who would complain if they did not receive their normal allotment. Once a staff member or volunteer had some free time, that person would be making calls in an attempt to redistribute the food.

What changed over the course of fifteen years to produce not only such an embarrassment of riches, but also new problems caused by these riches? Although some members of the congregation and outside observers from the larger religious and charity communities in Moscow have privately attributed the increase in donations and clear investment in the church's programs to several individual clergy or volunteers who were believed to be especially charismatic and able to attract supporters, others have suggested that these developments reflect the power of prayer, faith, and divine intervention in making these opportunities possible. Still others have suggested that these developments are more pragmatic and reflect the congregation's need to diversify into projects that are more necessary or even politically expedient in today's Russia.

None of these reasons satisfactorily explains the CCM's sustained growth over time and the ways that this congregation has been able to leverage that growth into new opportunities. And specifically, none of these explanations recognizes how donations have become investments that have produced not just social capital for donors and other supporters who can show that they made "smart" choices in backing these initiatives—including through plaques that bear their names—but also financial profits that the church has been forced to reinvest in existing or new programs. Because the church and its charities are not-for-profit entities, they cannot return profits to shareholders or otherwise spend the funds on activities not directly related to their charitable mission.

This situation is not unique to the CCM, but one experienced by other faith-based charitable groups in Moscow. Although the CCM is certainly one of the most successful and most visible of these organizations, other clergy and charity staff have had to deal with related issues of how best to make use of the resources that come their way, how to balance the concerns of donors and beneficiaries, and how to make strategic choices that support their existing services while also proactively responding to new challenges and opportunities.

Even the fact that the CCM now has an officially registered and recognized nongovernmental charitable organization with dedicated space and staff and is no longer a cluster of social ministry projects run primarily by volunteers out of their backpacks and cars attests to how Russia's legal and financial spheres have evolved so that there are formal criteria that allow "charities" to exist and operate more like corporate entities in the official economy. Other researchers have observed similar expansions, as charitably inclined individuals and groups formalize their operations, extend their services, and branch out in new directions, whether it is through the routinization of tithing, almsgiving, and donation practices (Tocheva 2011), the creation of service-learning work activities for drug addiction and HIV treatment programs (Zigon 2010), or the creation of side businesses tied to community outreach (Köllner 2011).

Another illustrative example of these developments is that of United Way Moscow. During my fieldwork in the late 1990s, I repeatedly tried to set up an appointment with the director of United Way Moscow. At that time, the office was based in an old, rundown office building on the outskirts of Moscow. No one ever answered the telephone or returned my repeated calls or e-mail requests for an appointment. When I wondered aloud to clergy and aid workers whether the office was in fact functional, I was reassured that there was, in fact, a woman who managed the office and the agency's activities. Relieved, I kept at my attempts to reach her, finally resorting to visiting the office building on the days she kept "office hours" for drop-in appointments with her agency's partners and potential partners and waiting at the front desk for her to arrive or to answer the internal telephone manned by the security guard at the front desk. She never answered. I became such a regular visitor over several months that I developed a friendly relationship with the security guard, who took pity on me and gave me a place to sit and chat with him while I waited. He confessed that he had only seen the woman once or twice and finally advised me to give up and use my time more productively than to wait for her.

Fifteen years later, at the same time that the CCM was enjoying its dramatic growth, the minister mentioned that United Way Moscow was one of their partner organizations. When I described my earlier ineffectual efforts to get in touch with United Way, he immediately offered to connect me with the new director. Within days I was on my way to a meeting with the director at the new offices, housed in a shiny new office park with other media technology and investment companies. The United Way offices were extensive and busy, as staff members scurried to meetings, compiled data and wrote reports, worked through promotional material, and managed the agency's library resources. The director and the assistant director were professionals who held graduate degrees in management and business administration and spoke perfect English. During our meeting they detailed an extensive set of projects with which their agency was involved, their short-term and long-term goals, and the challenges and opportunities they had identified in moving their organization and its partners forward. The discussion was more akin to a meeting with managers in the corporate setting and a far cry from my initial encounters (or lack thereof) with the organization. They proudly confirmed that their organization had been successful and now it was their responsibility to keep and build on the momentum.

Ultimately, such examples of growth in Russia's compassion economy illuminate what happens with a shift from an economy of scarcity to an economy of surplus or even excess. Conventionally Russia has been described as a "shortage society," given its long history of scarcities over the past several centuries. Certainly the Soviet era has been understood in terms of deprivation owing to, on the one hand, cycles of war and natural and manmade famines and, on the other, inefficient systems of production and distribution that produced recurring shortages of food and other material goods, housing, and services (see Fitzpatrick 1999). In this system, where goods and services trickled haphazardly through the official market and flowed more regularly through elaborate networks of personal contacts—i.e., friends and friends of friends—social relations replaced money as the currency that enabled the circulation of goods, and services and commodities were transformed into gifts. Accordingly, gifts enjoyed a dual life both as the social glue that bound friends, neighbors, and relatives together into overlapping relations of dependency and responsibility, and as a form of incentive or leverage that citizens used to access privileges and other favors (Ledeneva 1998).

Katherine Verdery has argued that state socialist societies are best understood as appropriational or acquisitional societies, because acquiring and controlling resources was more lucrative and generative than either production or consumption. More significantly, neither production nor consumption in either the formal or informal spheres was possible without the accumulation of material and social resources. Throughout all levels of state socialist society, individuals responded to scarcities by hoarding materials and connections and then mobilizing them when necessary (Verdery 1996). Typically derided by outsiders as corruption, this "gray" or "black" market was, in fact, the everyday reality for most Russians and other citizens of state socialist countries. To a great extent, the stability of Russia's formal economy has depended on, and perhaps even required, the constancy of this informal economy (cf. Muehlebach 2012).

So ever-present and customary was this informal economy of mutual support and exchange that it was, rather, those activities that took advantage of social relations and acquisition that were considered morally repugnant. Speculation, in the sense of taking advantage of the market for profit, was officially banned, while taking advantage of personal contacts (*blat*) was morally taboo (Ledeneva 1998). Both, however, existed as everyday realities, with citizens alternately castigating others who engaged in them while misrepresenting their own efforts to do the same. When I specifically asked individuals about whether they had engaged in *blat*, my respondents all categorically denied doing so, even as they informed me—usually in whispers—that other respondents had done so.[4] What emerged was a system of collective misrecognition in which individuals strategically navigated the intersecting domains of morality, sociality, and materiality.[5]

The morally suspect implications of "taking" rather than "giving" has also informed persistent criticisms against the Russian Orthodox Church's charitable services. Acquaintances who have been denied assistance from the ROC have complained that the church has devoted its attention to "grabbing" and hoarding resources rather than giving (see Caldwell 2010), a claim that was acknowledged but disputed by ROC staff I interviewed, who lamented the church's poor "public relations" skills for not making their work more visible. In several cases where Protestant churches I followed had partnered with Orthodox congregations for charitable projects, recipients often recognized only the work of the Protestant partners and mistakenly praised them for providing services that the ROC had, in fact, given.

While such views generally resulted from misinformation and lingering resentment against the ROC for past complicity with the Soviet state, they occasionally had just enough basis in reality. In fact, as charity staff with Orthodox groups confirmed, it was not uncommon for Orthodox congregations to privilege registered parishioners for their services—a strategic logistical practice that is common among congregations elsewhere but that Russia's Protestant congregations were generally forbidden from doing by law. In fact, as I observed, there were informal partnerships between Orthodox and non-Orthodox congregations that allowed Orthodox congregations to direct potential recipients who were not eligible for their services to Protestant congregations that could help them. During planning meetings at various charities, one of the primary topics of conversation among staff was how to work with local welfare agencies to share the load with their Orthodox counterparts. Often more visible were the actions of individual Orthodox clergy such as the ones described by Detelina Tocheva (2011), who strategically withheld certain kinds of assistance to supplicants as a way to encourage and enforce particular norms of moral and social conduct.

At a broader level, infused in this focus on state socialist citizens' acquisitional activities has been a theme of pessimism, even desperation. Even as anthropologists and others have attempted to present state socialist citizens as empowered social actors who were strategically navigating and manipulating the structures of their daily lives to their own benefit, this approach nonetheless casts these activities as responses to the system—even survival strategies (Caldwell 2004; Humphrey 1995; Shevchenko 2008). Moreover, accounts of the gift-giving activities that comprised socialist exchange practices have examined acts of giving and receiving in terms of mutual interdependencies that set up unequal hierarchies of need and value (Ledeneva 1998; Patico 2005). Ultimately, these perspectives have foregrounded giving in its relation to taking—either as hoarding social and material capital that can be given at a later time or as accepting those forms of capital and the strings they bring with them. Neither giving nor taking is a debt-free activity.

This preoccupation with taking may, however, misrecognize a more profound and productive aspect of Russian exchange relations—namely the difference between gifting and giving. In practice, gifting obscures the redistributive dimension through a collective fiction that emphasizes a spontaneous generosity and de-emphasizes reciprocity. Yet even though reciprocity is never mentioned, it is always expected. By contrast, giving as it is performed in Russian compassion economies is in fact a form of investment that is deliberately and publicly intentional: it is meant to produce concrete results, not just to sustain the assistance system, but also, and more importantly, to generate revenue and even profit that can, in turn, catalyze future development. While both gifting and giving relationships entail a temporality of futurity and open-endedness, gifting is oriented to repeating cycles of prestation and receiving that position participants in never-ending cycles of obligation and indebtedness, so that gift exchanges are never closed. By contrast, giving implies a futurity of growth where returns are redirected away from the initial giver and into future opportunities that will, in turn, fuel further future opportunities. As such, giving is a future-oriented act of aspiration and optimism that is more akin to arbitrage systems in high finance in which the endpoint is never known but always anticipated or desired (Miyazaki 2003, 2006). Within compassion economies, giving is a form of faith-full speculation in which the goal is to produce possibilities (see also Adams 2013; Mattingly 2010).

This does not mean that compassionate givers do not benefit from "returns" in the form of public recognition for their work, expressions of gratitude, a sense of personal satisfaction, or even expectations that program staff provide reports about how donations have been used. In fact, givers of charitable donations also engage in acts of misrecognizing the social and moral importance of reciprocity as a form of return, even as they deny that they expect returns. Virtually all of the individuals interviewed in the course of this research claimed that although they appreciated knowing that their efforts were productive, very few explicitly said that recognition of any sort was a motivating factor in why they gave of their time. For most respondents, a consistent theme was that giving was the "right thing" to do and expectations of receiving something in return were not necessary, perhaps even inappropriate. These disavowals of the need to be recognized for their donations are not any different from the disavowals made by individuals engaged in gifting relations with relatives and friends but who nonetheless expect accountability in some foreseeable future. But in the case of compassionate giving, the important point is that participants do not also expect that the cycle of donation is closed but continues on into the future, far beyond oneself or one's own expectations. This is not a cycle of imagined closure but one of an assumed unending but uncertain movement of potentiality into an unknown future.

At the same time, in more concrete terms, givers did not expect to receive a tangible return-gift in the form of profits, material objects, or even favors, because those would have to be deducted from the overall revenue of the program. In effect, what donors and supporters were doing was investing seed money into programs in order to inspire and enable future developments. This reorientation to the generative capacity of giving conveys qualities of hope and optimism that are lacking in the more desperate qualities evoked by the emphasis on acquisition as the precursor to gifting. This represents a profound shift in how charitable aid has been experienced in Moscow over the past two decades. While many aid workers would certainly acknowledge that there have been times when they have despaired of being able to raise sufficient resources to continue their projects and have had to plead for support, there remains a sense of optimism that circumstances will improve, accompanied by concrete results that prove success and future growth.

CULTIVATING KIND BUSINESSES

What, then, does an economy of compassion or kindness look like? How does it work? When my Russian acquaintances have described "compassion" as part of their own experiences with offering and receiving care, they have typically invoked mutually shared emotional experiences such as love and friendship—a perspective that resonates with Russian terms for compassion, empathy, and sympathy, as discussed in chapter 3. By drawing on such concepts in their reflections, assistance providers and recipients emphasized understandings of social assistance as personal, existential, and even spiritual experiences of social intimacy. In contrast, Russians have described "business," especially its neoliberal capitalist variants, in terms such as impersonal, selfish, and even immoral. Even as Russia's new capitalist economy has become normalized, there remains a sense that business and the new cult of money and the predictability and routinization of transactional behaviors have displaced the more familiar and morally superior intimacies and contingencies of social relations (Lemon 1998; Lindquist 2005), while the privileged position afforded to sufferers (Ries 1997) has been taken over by those who have demonstrated their successes in the new Russia (Patico 2005; Ries 2002).

In the first decade of the post-Soviet transition these distinctions between compassion and business raised concerns that intrinsic qualities of Russianness were under threat and disappearing. Citizens were angered by the consequences of corporate reorganizations that pushed many people out of work and by the lack of regulations on banking and real estate that have cost many citizens their life savings. Citizens also associated capitalism with increasing crime rates and social problems such as drug use, prostitution, homelessness, and abandonment of the most vulnerable members of society. A frequent lament that I encountered during my research in the 1990s was that the younger generation was becoming too focused on making money and consumerism and they were abandoning their responsibilities to their family and to society in favor of their own interests. Such fears have not necessarily come to pass, but the underlying concern with the value of distinguishing between business and compassion is significant and has had repercussions on how aid workers have presented themselves and their activities.

In the late 1990s, the manager of a large cafeteria that had won the contract to provide meals for one of the CCM's soup kitchens attracted scrutiny when church staff compared their accounting records against her books and the roster of beneficiaries compiled by the local welfare office. During the initial negotiations over the contract, the manager had emphasized that compassion was an important value to her because of her religious background. In a meeting that I attended, the manager reiterated this point and described how she had been a secret Christian during the Soviet era, when religious activity was officially forbidden. As the manager pulled from beneath her blouse a large cross that was hanging around her neck, she showed it to the CCM's clergy and staff and assured them that her faith and ethical commitment to helping the disadvantaged meant that she would always do right by them and their beneficiaries. "You can entrust them to me," she said.[6]

Scarcely a year later, CCM staff discovered that under the auspices of her own "charitable program," the woman had been adding her employees to the registry so that they could receive free meals paid for by the church. After several fruitless attempts by the CCM's staff to rectify the situation and force the manager to reimburse the church and remove her staff from their rosters, they parted ways. When I later discussed the situation with a pensioner who was both an activist for the elderly and veterans at the local welfare office and a recipient in the CCM soup kitchen program, my friend criticized the cafeteria manager for her unethical behavior. When I reminded my friend that the manager had presented herself as a Christian businesswoman, my friend tartly responded that the manager was "a good businesswoman, but not a good Christian."

This sense that business and compassion were not fully compatible appeared again fifteen years later in my meeting with the United Way director. By way of conversation, I asked her how she came to be involved in charity work and, given the extensive work she did supporting charitable initiatives, why she found this work important. To my surprise, the United Way director responded that she was not a particularly compassionate person. "I am not a soft-hearted person who is interested in listening to other people's problems," she said. But she was, she asserted, a very good manager. Believing that her particular strength was in managing people who were compassionate to others, she was inspired by the logics of management and bookkeeping and found the small, personalized nature of nonprofits a good place to put those interests in practice. That her agency helped people in need was a nice benefit, but it was secondary to the professional satisfaction and growth that she had achieved.

The perceived disconnect between business and compassion also appeared in the accounts of disillusionment relayed by charity workers who had been disappointed to find that not everyone felt or practiced a moral imperative to be kind and help others. The CCM's experience with the dishonest cafeteria manager was not an isolated occurrence, as I heard accounts from staff at other programs of substandard or botched services and even outright fraud by contractors who had promised to provide services but then either failed to follow through or used the presumed trust of compassion work to hide illicit or immoral activities. Food relief programs were commonly misled—and overcharged—by cafeterias that promised to provide high-quality food but instead served unappealing, watery, and tasteless dishes. Staff with several other food aid programs and health care programs in Moscow described experiences with contracted service providers who had won over a charity by presenting themselves as caring and compassionate members of the community and then cheated the charities by overcharging for services and channeling resources to their own family members and employees. Ten years after the CCM was forced to part ways with the cafeteria director who had been a good businesswoman but not a good Christian, the church found itself in a similar situation when a larger church that had been contracted as a landlord to provide space and utilities for the CCM's medical facility reneged on its agreement by unexpectedly renting out the space to local businesses and forcing the charity to go elsewhere.

The apparent uncertainties and incompatibilities that were believed to exist between compassion and business extend to the nature of assistance work itself. In Russia as elsewhere around the world, both providers and recipients of care have expressed concerns that the movement of compassion work into the commercial sphere might critically change the nature of compassion and the effectiveness of compassion work, often in unexpected ways that are both positive and negative. These concerns resonate with issues raised by observers and practitioners of care work, who point out that as care becomes professionalized and outsourced, such as with nannies, housekeepers, hospice workers, paid staff in charitable programs, and other persons who provide care work, new hierarchies, dependencies, and degrees of intimacy are created (Carse 2005; Clark 1997; Muehlebach 2012).

When care work becomes commercialized, compassion shifts registers from an affective relationship to a structural relationship (e.g., Anderson 2000; Benda-Beckmann and Benda-Beckmann 2000: 15; Constable 1997; Hochschild 1983, 2000; Read and Thelen 2007), a shift that prompted Susan Arpett Long (2002: 2) to question whether "providing care [is] the same as caring." The introduction of hierarchies and asymmetries through distancing, then, moves away from Russian concepts of

compassion and mutual assistance that emphasize symmetrical, recipro-
cal, and mutual relationships of shared affect and experience.

Such apprehensions about distance and depersonalization have not
necessarily been borne out in practice, however. In fact, while there have
certainly been incompatibilities between compassion and business, more
striking are instances of the inverse: the ethics of shared suffering and the
imperative to help others has traveled from care work to business. Here it
is the negative qualities of business that have been tamed and redeemed
by compassion. In this context of public discontent with the asymmetries
produced by capitalism, the corporatization of compassion provides a
powerful alternative that is grounded in ethics of egalitarianism and
mutuality (see Carse 2005). Increasingly there are not just overlaps but
interconnections between charities and businesses, thus blurring the lines
between the nonprofit and for-profit worlds in intriguing ways.

As noted at the beginning of this chapter, charitable activities are
becoming increasingly more prominent and active in Moscow's business
market, both as service providers that are operating alongside, and sometimes competing with, other businesses such as health care providers,
clothing shops, and schools, and as employers that provide competitive
wages and professional development opportunities, including networking. In terms of employment, funding, and organizational business strategies, Moscow's compassion industry shares similarities with other types of
assistance industries, most notably the NGOs and development agencies
that sprouted in Russia in the early to mid-1990s. Small charities that
previously relied solely on volunteer labor and were often administered
from volunteers' kitchens and living rooms are now hiring paid staff to
maintain recipient lists; track donors and their donations; handle the
logistics of storing, dispensing, and disposing of in-kind donations of
food, clothing, medical supplies, and other materials; and even to manage
teams of volunteers.

In some cases, charities are creating ranks of paid staff, thus transforming unremunerated "volunteer" labor into a different form of remuner-
ated, but still individually initiated and ostensibly "volunteer" labor.
Although most staff are not compensated beyond a small stipend that
supplements other sources of income, this salary brings with it responsibilities in terms of the hours they must spend every week engaged in this

work, the types of work they do, their attire, and how they interact with other staff, recipients, and donors. While charities see this compensation as both a reward for hard work and an incentive to retain reliable workers, the professionalization of voluntarism risks undermining the motivations of volunteers who find themselves increasingly bound by formal responsibilities to do the work they would have otherwise done for personal reasons. As a case in point, I discovered that it was often difficult to meet staff from faith-based charities during or after worship services for the churches that employed them or for which they were regular volunteers. I had assumed that those times would be a logical place to meet, but I learned that often Sundays were their only "downtimes" from their jobs or regular volunteer work. While some individuals did other things instead of going to church (sleeping in, watching television, visiting friends), others attended different churches in order to have some distance from their work and their recipients.[7]

Increasingly, however, nonprofit organizations find themselves pushed into the realm of small businesses as they are subjected to the same official regulations governing labor, workplace safety, and financial reporting. Charities and other nonprofits are increasingly bound by official regulations that require them to keep careful records and official ledgers of their "profits," "expenses," and "inventories," as well as the "work" hours and activities of their volunteers. In some cases, volunteers must be licensed and complete formal training courses, and their facilities must pass official inspections for electricity and sanitation. Staff at one charity described the complicated process by which they had to modify the accounting system they had used to satisfy their funding organization to one that could document and track the various figures required by the Russian government. In the new system, it was not simply revenue in and revenue out that mattered, but detailed accounting of the origins of those deposits and the disposition of those funds, among many other details.

Even as practitioners recognize the extent to which compassion work is being corporatized, not all organizations have successfully made the transition. Nina, the director of the patriarchate's development office, complained that it was often difficult to administer charitable programs both because there was a shortage of trained staff and because of difficulties in accessing the necessary supplies and funds to run even a small program.

As she noted during our conversation in 2009, at that time the Russian government "did not liberate donors to determine where their taxes go," meaning that the state ultimately decided how taxes and other revenues were allocated, with the result that charitable initiatives were frequently overlooked.

Just as significant was that for many years Russian tax laws did not reward donors with reductions in their taxes, so that there was no incentive for businesses to give except for personal connections. Nina commented that any organization needs money and skills in order to administer programs. Often church-related organizations cannot do this, she said, especially because church programs depend on large numbers of volunteers and there is often high turnover. Rather, what organizations need are official staff members who are legally responsible for the activities, although this was usually not possible for churches. "Last year we hosted a group of German visitors who wanted to see our programs," she recalled. "They asked us why we were involved in so many activities rather than focusing our attentions more narrowly and efficiently." Continuing, Nina stated, "Our weak point is [public relations]. Sometimes we are too Christian." By way of explanation, she commented that recent trends in social media were problematic for her church's ability to market itself and its activities. This inability to promote a coherent and compelling message about the church's projects and objectives meant that the church failed to attract attention— and resources—from donors and volunteers and to generate goodwill among the general public.

Nina did not see the Christian focus of her denomination's projects as the problem; rather it was that Christian organizations were not necessarily skilled at navigating the contemporary world of branding and communication. "The church is not so proactive" about advertising, she said. Yet even if the church had the resources to expand in this area, she reflected, there was a disconnect between the desires of the mass media on the one hand and the church's needs and the public's interests on the other. In contrast to the mass media's desire to focus on controversies and what she called "hidden debates," the general public was tired of scandals, she said. As a result, the church did not benefit from such inflammatory stories.

Thus for Nina, despite the very important and good work that her denomination and its charitable initiatives was able to do—running hospitals, orphanages, hospice programs, and elder care programs, among many others—there were clear indications that models and practices from the business world were necessary and expected for charitable organizations, and long-term success depended on whether organizations could make this transition. In fact, despite Nina's lament that the ROC was not PR-savvy, the church did rely on contacts with other denominations to publicize their work and combat negative perceptions, such as Susanna, who counted among her tasks as liaison to the ROC the need to educate Russians about the church's activities and its impact in Russian society.

Nevertheless, at the same time as charities and nonprofit organizations are looking more like businesses, more and more companies are resembling charities as they promote forms of corporate social responsibility, both to encourage their employees to engage in public service and to make use of new tax credits for charitable donations of soon-to-expire stock and excess revenues. Some companies have even created specialized roles—both paid and unpaid—for facilitators who coordinate the company's charitable activities, initiate charitable programs, recruit employees for charitable work, and act as liaisons with staff from charities and other nonprofit programs. The commercial possibilities of compassion were highlighted during one of many conversations with Benjamin, Oxfam's Russia director. As a career administrator who had advanced professional degrees in development and nonprofit management, Benjamin had a broad perspective regarding both his own organization and the larger field of charity and development, both in Russia and internationally. On this occasion, as we discussed the simultaneously practical and philosophical dimensions of Oxfam's work, Benjamin noted that the emphasis on social development among organizations such as Oxfam was being adopted in the commercial sector, as businesses realized the moral and financial value of social responsibility. Benjamin described the growing impetus for social responsibility among Russia's businesses by referencing a quote from a previous director: "Mission is first and profit is next." Continuing, he described socially responsible business owners as part of a new breed of social entrepreneurs who cared about both mission and profit and were actively reworking Russia's economic world.[8]

Companies that publicly donate goods, services, and funds to charitable programs can rebrand themselves as responsible and compassionate members of the community and thus capitalize on the goodwill generated by these efforts. The promotion of these businesses as more attuned to the needs and interests of the local community translates into images of these companies as more reliable, trustworthy, and rewarding. One chain of coffeehouses in Moscow has particularly benefited by opening their facilities to local nonprofit, civic causes and distributing fresh bread and other fresh foods to a network of food banks. These efforts have generated a loyal group of regular customers who direct their business—and that of their own employers, friends, and other contacts—to these coffeehouses. A printing company in Moscow has enjoyed similar successes following a manager's offer to make at a significantly discounted price the necessary business cards, posters, and other brochures for a large local charity. By coincidence the charity director was at the same time working with a friend who was organizing a charitable art show to benefit a women's organization that was a major donor to many Moscow charities. After the charity director told her friend about the printing shop manager's offer, the second woman negotiated with the print shop to produce the artwork for her project. Even as the print shop likely lost some revenue from supporting two charitable initiatives, it also secured at least two new clients for regular future needs.

These developments also coincide with more explicit partnerships between charities, development organizations, informal networks of private citizens, and corporate donors. Corporate and nonprofit entities join forces to host black-tie benefit events that bring together Moscow's financial and business elite with the city's social workers and even recipients. While CEOs and other businesspeople make deals, volunteers and staff from charities circulate among them, asking for donations. Raffles to benefit the featured charity also become opportunities for local companies to get free advertising, as the gifts typically involve an advance look at high-end goods and services that have not yet hit the local shops.

Although there are no precise figures about the financial impact of Moscow's compassion industry, its growing role and visibility are apparent in deals such as these. When I was scheduling interviews with staff and volunteers from assistance programs, I was intrigued at the regularity with which my interlocutors invited me to meet them at a coffeehouse or restaurant that was supporting the programs in which they were involved.

Several people volunteered that they had chosen those sites precisely because they wanted to pay them back for their generosity.

THE LIMITS OF KINDNESS

Yet even as these ventures into the compassion sphere can be advantageous for local businesses, the commercialization of nonprofits can create unexpected challenges. Staff and volunteers with nonprofits complain that the greater oversight required for monitoring the flow of resources, labor, and recipients forces them to spend more time dealing with flow charts, files, and bookkeeping ledgers and less time with the people they want to help. Volunteers who formerly enjoyed the one-on-one intimacies of meeting with recipients and getting to know their families and circumstances now find themselves scheduling endless meetings with donors, attorneys, accountants, politicians, and other government officials. The director of donations for one Moscow charity complained that she found herself constantly haggling with potential donors as if she was in the market. Another volunteer who acted as a facilitator between corporate donors and charitable recipients described how her role had shifted so that she was often approached not as someone who could make things happen between prospective donors and clients, but rather as someone who could make a company's "problems" go away—that is, she could dispose of their leftover and expired stock so that they would not have to deal with the hassle.

The burdens placed on the affective dimensions of social relationships by activities more familiar to the business world—accountability, negotiations, and scrutiny of fair and appropriate allocation of resources—are acutely felt by assistance workers who have to screen potential recipients for services. Because of the need to follow eligibility requirements for programs, assistance workers often must prioritize "objective" criteria such as income levels, housing circumstances, and employment records rather than sitting down and getting to know the "real lives" of their clients. One of the points of contention raised by the doctors who participated in the Aga Khan's 2009 roundtable focusing on charitable medical care was that the formalized nature of their work often prevented them from treating their patients as human beings and forced them instead to see their patients as figures in a ledger and as a string of numbers on an identity card.

In several of the soup kitchens I have followed over the years, charity staff recognized most recipients by face and automatically checked their program identification numbers off the check-in list before the recipients could even present their registration cards. In most programs that I visited, check-in rosters were organized by recipients' registration numbers, not by their names, most likely to speed up the check-in process. This also helped volunteers who were not fully fluent or literate in Russian and unfamiliar with Russian naming conventions. When I asked staff about the names of particular recipients, especially people who came regularly and I wanted to invite to an interview, the staff members rarely knew their names. To their credit, the staff members I knew best expressed embarrassment and frustration that although they knew intimate details about recipients' lives from daily conversations, because it was numbers written down on their paperwork, and not names, it was the numbers they had memorized. At the same time, I discovered that often recipients did not know the names of the staff, preferring instead to call them by endearments and applying the one or two names they did know to all of the staff and volunteers. In some ways, the relationships forged through these identification numbers were more intimate than knowing actual names, and certainly more productive for accomplishing the purposes of the encounters.

In one medical clinic, when a new physician took over the supervision of the consultations, he was surprised to discover that the previous physician and nurses had rarely used any form of record-keeping. Rather, they relied on personal memory and extensive conversations with patients. But as the program expanded to accommodate a growing number of patients, the incoming physician was forced to implement more formal record-keeping measures in order to track patients' progress and medical supplies. The physician reflected that he became a physician primarily to work one-on-one with patients in ways that emphasized and enabled mutual empathy. For him, the record-keeping and charts were a necessary evil to help him and the other medical providers do their jobs more effectively by giving them more detailed information that would in turn facilitate even closer relationships between doctors and patients.

Even the format of the new patient charts promoted this ideal of a more personal relationship: rather than asking a series of questions that patients were required to answer in writing, the charts included an outline of the body, and patients were encourage to draw in their own experiences (broken arm or cuts), questions, or any other details. The physicians and nurses could then talk more directly to their patients and move directly from the paperwork to their bodies, mediated by personal questioning. This method also meant that physicians and patients were not immediately separated from one another by other barriers such as language differences or literacy issues.

The paradoxical distance and intimacy made possible through bureaucratic procedures became especially apparent in the encounters between staff and volunteers in a Moscow faith-based NGO that helps minorities, especially applicants for political asylum and victims of human trafficking and race-related hate crimes. While staff have significant discretion to provide medical, legal, and social services to anyone they believe deserves it, they are severely constrained in the types of services they can provide to asylum petitioners, owing to the fact that they must follow the legal criteria for asylum petitions set down by national and international laws. In many cases, staff who are vetting applications get to know their applicants extremely well and develop close, emotional connections with them. Staff explain that knowing intimate details about applicants' experiences as victims of attacks, rape, attempted murder, and extreme poverty forges a deep emotional bond where they come to care about their clients as real people and even in affective terms of friendship.

The degree to which staff and recipients felt that the formulaic, bureaucratic application procedures could facilitate more intimate, and even affective, relationships became clear in two cases from summer 2009. In one case, the three women who processed case files for the NGO came to know a young woman from Ghana very well, by virtue of repeated meetings and discussing deeply personal details about her family life and living situations. The four women began meeting outside of the official meeting times, passing on paperwork or sharing a quick coffee. When the woman received approval to be resettled in the United States, the staff members worried that the woman would feel alone in her new home, and they kept in frequent contact with her for several months to make sure that she was settling in smoothly. They even made sure to enlist friends who lived in the woman's new hometown and asked them to call and check on her. The second case was similar, and involved a man who was resettled to another part of the United States at roughly the same time. Staff members, volunteers, and fellow recipients back in Russia kept in touch with him to follow his settling-in process and to offer assistance in whatever ways they could. The role of social media such as Facebook is not incidental in facilitating not just these feelings of "friendship" but also the ability for people to stay in touch and remain aware of people's personal lives.

Nevertheless, by virtue of being in a structural position of having to make determinations of eligibility that are set by external bureaucratic requirements and investigation techniques, staff risk losing that emotional closeness with their applicants. In one encounter that was typical of the many I observed, several staff members sat through a lengthy interview with an applicant whom they had known for some time. The man detailed the abuses he and his family had suffered as ethnic minorities in his home country and the severe deprivations they were enduring as refugees in Russia. He provided photographs and other personal documents attesting to his family's hardships. Despite these forms of evidence and despite the staff members' great affection for the man, they were forced to deny his application because his circumstances did not meet the requirements set forth by the resettlement agency.

The end of the otherwise gentle and supportive hour-long meeting degenerated into hostility as the frustrated applicant shouted that the staff were horrible, evil people. The director of the program was visibly shaking as she struggled to maintain her composure and reassert the official reasons they were forced to deny his petition. After the man finally left, she broke down in tears and lamented that such encounters left her emotionally and spiritually drained because she empathized with him and wanted so badly to help him but her hands were tied. Like her coworkers, she considered giving up the position because the structural requirements forced her to disengage from the very people she wanted to help. At the same time, it is important to note that the distancing that is part of these bureaucratic encounters cuts both ways, as the requirements of assistance programs often force recipients to create fictionalized personas and occupy roles of subordination.

Such "gatekeeping" efforts are neither new nor unusual among non-profit assistance programs that cannot simply help everyone in need but must carefully and responsibly use their limited resources and thus make decisions that seem to run counter to the imperative to care for others. But participants in the charitable projects I have studied seemed to be particularly frustrated by the gap between what they wanted to do and what the circumstances allowed. Here, however, it was not an absence of compassion but the absence of material resources or options that they found most problematic. Repeatedly, individuals from many different types of charitable programs explained to me that sometimes the only option available to them was to "be with" a person who needed help—in other words, to comfort through accompaniment and by acknowledging a shared presence in that particular moment. From my observations in screening interviews and from conversations with aid applicants and beneficiaries, it seemed as if receiving compassion was for them, too, often just as important, if not more so, than receiving material resources.

While the asylum petitioner described above was clearly angry about what he perceived as a failure to receive formal recognition of his problems and thus eligibility for refugee status, his outburst was unusual. Many other petitioners left their interview appointments far more resigned about being turned down and instead walked into the community room where they could spend time in the company of other petitioners and volunteers. In several instances, individuals who had been attending the charity's outreach programs for many months or even years and were well known to the programs staff and volunteers declined to apply for the asylum process or other programs. This left volunteers and staff puzzled as to why such persons would not avail themselves of the chance to get more assistance, but from the perspective of the potential applicants it was perhaps better to have themselves known and acknowledged through personal encounters, rather than having to be put through the ordeals of a bureaucratic procedure.

THE BURDEN OF EXCESS GENEROSITY

When the Sant'Egidio volunteers I followed made their rounds of the local streets, searching for homeless persons who might be in need of a hot meal, the volunteers spent more of their time socializing with their homeless acquaintances than actually handing out food. Several individuals refused the food, explaining that they simply wanted to chat and catch up with the volunteers. When we returned to the chapel where volunteers had earlier prepared the meals to deposit our containers and leftovers, it was evident that the volunteers I had followed had not experienced anything unique, as other volunteers returned sandwiches, soup, and beverages that they had not been able to pass on to people in need of them. The leftovers that Sant'Egidio's volunteers returned to the chapel illuminate another challenge facing charities and one that helps show the particularities of this compassion economy. Although the goal of compassion economies is that they be self-sustaining, the reality is that either charitable ventures fail to generate sufficient resources—material or labor—or they generate too much. Although excess can in some instances be caused by poor planning and incorrect estimates of need, it can also be the result of successful planning. And the excesses produced by success have profound implications for the compassion economy.

As became apparent within the Moscow charitable communities that I followed, both success and enthusiasm can generate profits and eventually lead to excess revenue. At different times, the CCM's charities found themselves overwhelmed with donations of food, clothing, and other goods. Once the CCM ran out of storage room at its outreach facilities, it filled its rented storage space beneath one of the cafeterias contracted for the food relief program. After the standing freezers and storage rooms were filled, CCM staff resorted to lining pallets of food along the walls in the hallways, making it difficult for anyone—charity or cafeteria staff alike—to move and complete their tasks. After it seemed as if the donations had stabilized, giving staff a chance to work through the existing stockpiles and create room for more, another round of unexpected and generous donations came in. At that point, the staff resorted to asking members of the church congregation and other volunteers if excess food goods could be stored in their apartments and garages. While this created logistical problems later, as charity staff were forced to drive around Moscow to collect those items, the directors felt that they could not turn down the offers of food.

Other charitable organizations described problems with managing the enthusiasms and desires of volunteers that might exceed the opportunities and spaces available. There is an unevenness in the flow of work as sometimes there are too few volunteers to carry out tasks, while at other times there are too many. The challenge for directors is to manage volunteers so everyone feels welcome and needed, while parceling out tasks in such a way as not to overwhelm recipients.

Boredom and a sense of not being useful can impede the smooth flow of charitable activity. This is especially the case among individuals who are new to voluntarism. Among the cohort of "experienced volunteers"—typically nonworking spouses of expatriate businessmen, most of whom are North American and European wives who fill their days with charitable activities—this is usually not a problem, as they are familiar with the ebbs and flows of volunteering and combine their volunteer work with socializing and either fill gaps in work with chats with other volunteers or have other volunteer activities for which they can leave.

By contrast, individuals who are new to volunteering might have expectations that they can immediately jump in and do what they see as "important" work. Ministers with several congregations confessed that one of the biggest challenges they faced was in teaching their congregants how to serve by focusing on the recipients' needs and not their own interests. In different ways, almost all of these ministers referenced the legacy of Soviet socialism, where voluntarism had been transformed into a coerced activity of work to support the public and, by extension, the state. Now, these ministers reflected, it was necessary to teach volunteers how to serve without expecting anything in return, either in the form of gratitude from the people they were helping or in the form of recognition from authorities. Moreover, it was necessary to cultivate a sense of regularity among volunteers, so that they saw service as a regular part of their daily lives. Finding ways to keep volunteers engaged and channel their enthusiasm, even on days when their labor was not needed, was a difficult task.

Some clergy and charity directors worried that it was in fact an overabundance of enthusiasm from volunteers that posed a greater threat to the stability of their programs. Father Paul commented that one of his biggest problems in overseeing the charitable activities of his large, liberally progressive, and socially active congregation was dealing with "compassion fatigue." He explained that he frequently encountered congregants who were "burned out" from taking on too many activities and were neglecting their own interests and needs (cf. Adams 2013: 179; Elisha

2011: 154). He had counseled numerous congregants—especially married couples—who were experiencing family problems that were, he felt, caused by overinvolvement in outside charity activities. From his perspective, he felt that it was imperative that volunteers not become so invested in the lives and needs of other people that they overlooked their own families, enabling small familial problems to fester into larger ones. He argued that although Moscow's city officials greatly appreciated that there were many volunteer opportunities that made it easier for people to become involved in social action, the city's desire to harness this labor power put him at odds with the needs of his own parishioners. Consequently, he had to balance the importance of encouraging his congregation to be active in projects benefiting the local community against his responsibility to advocate to his parishioners the necessity to "love yourself."

A minister at another congregation explained that one of his biggest challenges was curbing the enthusiasm of one of his most financially generous congregants. The man, a wealthy businessman, wanted very much to help by giving money and sharing his networks. Although the congregant had had some good ideas, he quickly moved from workable concepts to complicated plans that were far from feasible. In one instance, his desire to find a way to support homeless people evolved into a grand scheme for the church to purchase clusters of apartments and turn them into low-income transitional housing and, by extension, transform the church into a landlord. The minister felt that part of his job was to help guide the other man in ways that made the best use of his particular gifts—spiritual, social, and even financial—but also were appropriate and productive to the larger needs of the congregation and its charitable projects. More rarely, charities have had to deal with surplus funds, but that, too, was a realistic possibility. In such cases an especially strong appeal resulted in a greater-than-expected intake of funds, or multiple grant proposals were funded—or even overfunded, when only one or none were expected. While receiving multiple grants was an unexpected blessing, such rare occasions were problematic because funding agencies typically attached deadlines by which the funds had to be used. Thus grant recipients had to find creative ways to use the funds, rather than losing them altogether.

Whether it comes in the form of material goods, cash, or labor power, surplus is a double-edged sword, because while the surplus is useful and a marker of success, it cannot be easily disposed of in the same way that surplus can in a conventional capitalist economy. Because compassion economies are not meant to generate profit, surpluses cannot be divvied up to shareholders, added to the salaries of directors and managers, or used to purchase nonessential equipment. Rather, surpluses must be absorbed or reinvested within the system in order to benefit recipients and the programs. In other words, surpluses are active entities that require movement. They cannot be held in reserve for too long without being made static. Moreover, putting surpluses into savings or growing a program to expand services or the types of available programs risks diluting the image and philosophy of a particular charity and offending donors and beneficiaries.

Ultimately, despite the fact that within Moscow's compassion economy it is faith, as expressed through acts of kindness and generosity, that mobilizes both abstract hopes and dreams and material commodities into possibilities, practitioners are well aware of the problems wrought by generosity. Not only must they navigate and deflect donors' conditions or priorities, but they must also find strategies for investing that generosity. These acts of negotiation are fraught with financial, social, and ethical uncertainties, especially in moments when aid workers struggle with instances in which there is more kindness than need. As a result, their roles shift from being that of being prudent caretakers and investors of kindness to being gatekeepers and even rejecters of generosity. When generosity becomes a burden, it further prompts them to consider the potential failings of their efforts to do good. This is a topic that I take up in the next chapter.

7 The Deficits of Generosity

In spring 2010, my fieldwork took an unexpected turn when I arrived in Moscow for a short trip that coincided with a long-planned fund-raising event held by one of the programs at the center of this book. The event took place during a black-tie gala dinner-dance for participants in a city-wide amateur athletics league. While the majority of participants belonged to Moscow's expatriate community—primarily European, North American, and Australian executives and professionals—there was a sizable contingent of Russian members, most of whom were highly paid directors and managers at large international firms in Moscow. The dinner-dance was an annual event to celebrate the end of the athletics league's season and award prizes to the teams and their players. The minister of one of the churches most active in Moscow's charitable sector had played on one of the teams, and the organizer of the league suggested that perhaps the church could hold a fund-raising raffle during the event to support their programs.

In the months leading up to the event, the church's development director, social ministry outreach director, and volunteer coordinator placed endless telephone calls and sent countless e-mails to all of their contacts and their contacts' contacts, trying to recruit them and solicit donations

for the raffle. By the week leading up to the festivities, they had accumu-
lated an impressive assortment of desirable gifts. Corporate and private
donors had offered bottles of rare wine and whisky, luxury spa packages,
dinners at five-star restaurants, weekend hotel packages, and even airline
tickets for the raffle. More donations arrived on the night of the event, as
guests dropped off ornately wrapped packages at the hostess table outside
the banquet hall. Rumors circulated that perhaps a global mobile technology company would donate a not-yet-released smartphone or that a luxury car company might give away a new vehicle.

I arrived in the last frantic days before the event, as the three directors
dashed around Moscow, trying to find rolls of raffle tickets, gift bags, and
wrapping paper. There were ongoing discussions about the best ways to
create a buzz of anticipation among raffle ticket buyers and how to persuade guests to buy as many tickets as possible. The donations were valued and revalued in attempts to create a logical sequence for handing
them out in a way that would build to the most exciting and desirable gift.
Which was more desirable and valuable: a several hundred dollar gift cer-
tificate to an exclusive shop, a private dinner at one of Moscow's most
exclusive restaurants, or two free airplane tickets?

In the midst of this last-minute planning, the emcee for the evening
called repeatedly. A roguish Australian man with a reputation for a wander-
ing eye and roving hands, the emcee treated the charity's staff members—all
foreign professional women in their twenties—with a mixture of disdain for
their youth and unwanted romantic advances. In his phone calls he issued
an endless list of suggestions and instructions for details ranging from how
they should be dressed, the scripts they would collectively use to announce
the raffle and the gifts, and even when and how to present and award the
donated gifts. The phone calls and demands became so frequent and so
outrageous that eventually the women stopped answering his calls, even
while worrying that doing so might jeopardize their relationship with him
and the gala's event planners.

On the night of the event, I accompanied the three staff members and
two high-school-aged daughters of a regular volunteer and supporter of the
church's charities to the raffle. We dressed in cocktail dresses to blend in
with the formally attired guests, and donned sparkly neon-colored
Halloween wigs to make us recognizable as the raffle ticket sellers. During

the cocktail hour and dinner, we circulated around the room, explaining the charity's projects and selling tickets. As the evening went on and the alcohol flowed freely, the guests became increasingly inebriated, some to the point that they could barely stand unassisted. With this increased intoxication came increased ticket sales, and we nearly ran out of raffle tickets to sell. After the raffle ticket sale ended and it was time to draw the winning tickets, the emcee gathered us up on stage and introduced us to the audience, leering at each of us and placing his arm around our waists (his attempts to do so with me failed miserably). He then whispered reminders to each of us about how we were supposed to prance about the stage to show off the gifts and present them to the winners.

The raffle was hugely successful for the charity, raising far more money than anyone had dreamed of, including spontaneous donations of hundreds of dollars in cash in some instances, and generating enthusiasm and promises of in-kind assistance from individuals with connections in food and consumer goods companies. For all intents and purposes, this was a significant gain for the church's charity, both financially and socially.

Obscured by the overall successes and excitement of the evening, however, were more troubling issues that began percolating with the emcee's incessant telephone calls in the days leading up to the event and then solidified during the night's festivities. Throughout the evening at the gala, each woman had to fend off flirtatious advances from intoxicated male guests and the emcee. But those same flirtations often produced greater, unsolicited donations. As guests—both male and female—became more intoxicated, they became looser with their wallets. The charity's staff were greatly disturbed at how they were caught up in a game of salesmanship in which they were selling not only the charity's projects but also themselves as objects of desire and then benefiting from the generosity of people who were perhaps not sober enough to be making sound financial decisions.

As a side note, I will attest that of all the unusual situations I have experienced during twenty years of fieldwork, these interactions with the emcee and other guests were perhaps among the most challenging and ethically problematic. Like my female colleagues, I found myself struggling to reconcile my responsibility to sell tickets against my adamant conviction that I would not play along with the expectations of the host and other similarly inclined guests.[1] Yet beyond the specifics of these misogynist encounters, the overall events of that evening were methodologically and ethnographically revealing, in that these encounters made possible particular questions and insights that might not have been evident otherwise. As I was nearly of the same age and of the same professional status as many of the other guests (ironically, being a professor in the University of California system was treated as morally equal, or even superior, to holding an MBA or JD and directing a company), my conversations with them about ticket selling often turned into discussions about sexism among Moscow's business and expatriate communities, guests' views on the need for charity and the role of religious communities in providing assistance in Moscow, and the moral responsibility of Russian businesses—including international corporations—to be good neighbors and good citizens.

Both during that evening and in the days following, the ethical and practical issues of the event were recurring topics of conversation among the three directors. Had they successfully shielded the female high school students from these more adult situations while benefiting from the young women's sincere desire to help the charity? Could the behaviors of other guests at the gala have any negative effects on the reputation of the church and its charity? Although the charity needed the funds, was it appropriate to flirt with or otherwise chat up a guest (male or female) in order to smooth the way for a donation? Most importantly, was it appropriate to benefit from the generosity of a drunken guest who might not be making decisions with a clear head? Who had taken advantage of whom in that situation: had they taken advantage of a vulnerable, albeit financially secure person in order to benefit another person who was financially and socially vulnerable? And if so, which was the more ethically right position: to protect a drunken rich person or to protect a poor person?

What the charity's staff found themselves unexpectedly confronting were profound questions about the unexpected uncertainties and even dangers caused by generosity and excess, which led them to question whether there were instances in which it was better to refuse gifts and offers of help that were sincerely given, even if problematically performed. Ultimately, for the charity's staff, it was an issue of who would suffer the most if they either accepted problematic assistance or rejected it.

Despite the fact that giving is fundamental to assistance and care encounters, a reality noted by Erica Bornstein's comment (2012: 15) that the contemporary focus on assistance reveals that "Giving may well be an ethos of our time," it is far from a straightforward activity. In particular, the disposition of gifts has proven to be especially tricky, both for those who are engaged in acts of giving and for those who study them. Giving within a framework of assistance typically requires rules—either implicit or explicit—about propriety, most notably both appropriate forms of gifts and appropriate beneficiaries. In both cases, issues relating to need and deservingness come into play, sometimes complementarily and sometimes at odds with one another, as markers to designate those who are appropriate recipients and what types of gifts are most appropriate. Decisions about whether to offer aid in the form of money, loans, food, nonfood material goods, shelter, education, advice, or other intangible forms of support are ultimately all decisions about what types of gifts are most expedient, ethical, or culturally appropriate in a particular context. They are also decisions about whether an aid recipient is worthy of that particular gift. Within assistance encounters, acts of providing support do important work by reifying and affirming needs, needy populations, and appropriate directionalities of assistance (Fassin 2012; Feldman 2007; Redfield 2013; Ticktin 2011). Offering assistance is thus an activity saturated with power, as funders, donors, and aid workers are the individuals who control the circumstances under which aid is given and to whom. At the same time, those who control and administer the provision of assistance also control the terms of the events and experiences that precipitate need and determinations of who qualifies for assistance (Fassin and Rechtman 2009; Redfield 2005).

These rules about proper gifts and beneficiaries also entail norms about the proper directionalities through which assistance flows. Typically, assistance providers, donors, funders, and even public observers are concerned with whether gifts reach their intended beneficiaries or become redirected to secondary or even tertiary beneficiaries, or are removed from the formal channels altogether, as often happens (e.g., Adams 2013; Redfield 2013: 90–97), including in the immediate post-Soviet context where Western aid was rerouted, sometimes into private pockets (e.g., Wedel 1998). Drawing from his work with Medécins Sans Frontières,

Peter Redfield (2013: 94) has observed that "to follow a donation from solicitation to use . . . reveals an ethical maze rather than a straight line." Rules about proper directionalities are also infused with expectations about what recipients do with the gifts they have received (see Redfield 2013): have they used them appropriately or have they misused them, such as occurs with anxieties about welfare fraud and demands to drug-test welfare recipients in the United States, as well as with more general concerns about "compliance" and "accountability" that often inform treatment programs for homeless persons, the unemployed, and people suffering from addictions, among others (Garcia 2010; Lyon-Callo 2004). Perhaps just as important are concerns with how recipients have responded to the gift-giver: have they demonstrated an appropriate degree of humility, gratitude, or responsibility?

Within anthropological concerns about gift-giving, it is this moment of response to the initial gift that has provoked the most debate, especially in terms of whether recipients are compelled to reciprocate in some fashion and how those acts of return are performed and experienced (Douglas 1990; Mauss 1990). Such discussions raise concerns about whether expectations of reciprocity or return might violate the spirit of the gift by introducing forms of coercion into the encounter. This attention to the potentially coercive nature of gift-giving reveals important questions about the motivations and attitudes of both givers and recipients and the ways in which an ethos of gift-giving creates certain conditions and expectations in daily life (see Bornstein 2012; Muehlebach 2012: vii–viii). Although recipients can reject a gift, acts of refusal disrupt the presumed directionalities and sociality of the interaction, further highlighting the inequalities embedded within gift-giving relationships. This focus on the relationship between giving and receiving, regardless of whether gifts are returned or redirected, foregrounds the power dynamic that exists between the giver and the recipient, with the giver sitting in the position of presumed power by expecting to have some say in the disposition of the gift and the recipient always being in a subordinate and potentially subversive position.

The value placed on both gifting and giving that has long shaped Russian social practices of assistance has assumed new significance in post-Soviet formal assistance encounters as the more fluid, intangible, and even deliberately ambiguous dimensions of Russian practices of providing assistance have been drawn into the formal accountability logics that govern international assistance practices and dictate appropriate pathways for the disposition of resources (Redfield 2013). This shift, on the one hand, is an exercise in both economic and cultural translation in which assistance workers must reconcile different, and often conflicting, logics of assistance into a single institutional system—what James (2010) would call a clash between competing forms of bureaucraft. Staff from Russian assistance organizations especially lament the challenges of translating Russian bookkeeping practices, which can range from nonexistent to unbelievably arcane, often handwritten in fading ledger books, into Western bookkeeping practices that require different columns, data, and even computer software packages. On the other hand, these are processes that intentionally expose the mythologies of misrecognition surrounding gift-giving by publicly—and legally—turning gifts into commodities that must be acknowledged, classified, and financially valued by participants. This is especially challenging in the Russian context where the cultural norms governing mutual support and friendship require that givers and recipients do not publicly recognize gifts or gifting encounters, especially when money changes hands (Lemon 1998).

Through this emphasis on accountability, foreign donors and funders to Russian programs demand assurances that their resources are reaching actual recipients who are genuinely in need and deserving of assistance. Like aid workers elsewhere in the world, Russia's assistance workers must cultivate and present real individuals with real lives and real narratives so that donors can imagine that their resources will have a specific and concrete destination and impact. Assistance providers have noted with distaste the ethical issues related to demands for producing accounts of their recipients that verge into the realm of poverty or misery porn. In 2009, an affectionate encounter between a white volunteer and the young child of a Nigerian assistance recipient that was captured by a visiting film crew to one charity's medical clinic was soon circulating through the international media in a story about white-on-black racism in Russia. At the same time, donors frequently want more than worthy recipients: they want grateful recipients. Moscow-based aid workers have grumbled about the challenges of communicating gratitude on the part of recipients to donors, particularly when recipients may not be particularly happy to be receiving assistance, even if it is necessary, or when recipients approach assistance as something to which they are entitled rather than as something for which they must demonstrate need and deservingness.

Assistance groups are caught in a paradox. Because few organizations possess their own resources to redistribute, most rely on donations of funds, goods, and services from others. As a result, although the public identity and role of assistance organizations is that of a giver, in actuality they are mediators who must first take or receive before they can give. Assistance groups are thereby placed in the difficult position of being represented and imagined as aid providers, or at the very least as brokers who put donors and recipients into assistance relationships and as the channels through which these movements of assistance flow. When public expectations cast assistance organizations as active givers, their own role as recipients dependent on others is disguised.

More significantly, when assistance organizations assume or are assigned the moral and legal responsibility to help others, their ability to turn down resources becomes problematic. One of the difficult realities of assistance work is that aid is always and necessarily partial and incomplete (Cabot 2014: 73; Redfield 2013). Although the goals of assistance are ostensibly to improve the circumstances of recipients, and even of all those who need or request assistance (e.g., Farmer 2003), those who provide assistance must make strategic choices about which programs and individuals to support at any one moment. Such decisions can be both practical and philosophical, but the reality is that unequal or partial distributions can further victimize potential recipients (James 2010), thus furthering the sense that assistance encounters always proceed from deficit.[2]

Less attention has been paid to what is perhaps a more intriguing and challenging issue: what refusals of assistance might reveal about assistance practices, particularly in circumstances in which it is not a shortage of resources but rather a sufficiency or even surplus of resources that is at stake. Over the course of my fieldwork in Moscow, assistance communities have increasingly grappled with decisions about turning down resources and opportunities and the practical and ethical implications of these refusals for themselves, the individuals and institutions they are trying to cultivate as supporters and donors, and ultimately for the people they are trying to help. Such incidents provoke intriguing questions about the consequences when assistance organizations and potential recipients turn down resources and services or deny them to others who need them.

THE ART OF REFUSING

In spring 2007, Bettina, the wife of a European diplomat stationed in Russia, received an urgent telephone call from a Russian acquaintance who worked in the Moscow management office of a global home furnishings company. Such calls were not unusual for Bettina. During the several years that Bettina had lived in Moscow, she had volunteered her time and services to a variety of philanthropic associations in Russia, gaining a reputation as someone who could match donors and recipients. Through these activities, Bettina had cultivated an extraordinarily rich network of contacts with individuals affiliated with Russian and non-Russian businesses, funding organizations, and social services programs. An outgoing, charismatic woman, Bettina easily and frequently persuaded her contacts to donate their services, funds, or surplus goods to the charities she supported. For instance, one food relief organization regularly received a large weekly donation of yogurt and milk from a major Russian dairy company and a significant financial contribution from one of the foreign embassies in Moscow, all courtesy of Bettina. When this aid program needed additional food or hygiene items for emergency food bags or for holiday gifts, Bettina did not hesitate to ask her contact at the dairy to increase their contribution, before moving on to other contacts at other companies in the address book she kept with her. She was also generous with her networks and passed on contacts' information to acquaintances affiliated with other aid programs. Yet this relationship was not simply unidirectional. At the same time that aid programs approached Bettina for help finding benefactors, potential donors also contacted her to help them dispose of surpluses or match up donated goods and services with the most appropriate and needy recipients.

On this particular day, Bettina's contact at the home goods company was calling with an incredible offer: one hundred unused, brand-new baby cribs, complete with mattresses and bed linens, in pristine condition, and free to a good home. The manager explained that the company had discontinued this style of baby cribs and now the local store could no longer sell the cribs. The manager was looking to unload the cribs by giving them to needy recipients. As an extra bonus, the manager promised that the company would deliver the cribs, put them together, and show the recipients how to operate the cribs, all for free. All Bettina had to do was find a recipient.

Because of her long-term volunteer work with several Moscow-area baby houses and orphanages, Bettina was confident that she would be able to locate homes for the free cribs quickly, and she immediately began working through her lengthy list of contacts with local children's hospitals, baby houses, and orphanages. Her enthusiasm quickly turned to dismay, however, as every telephone call that she made went nowhere. Bettina was repeatedly turned down by baby house and orphanage directors who refused to accept the donated cribs. The most frequent reason given to her by directors she or her friends called was that they were afraid that the brand-new cribs were more dangerous, less hygienic, and less efficient than the existing equipment in the orphanages. (Bettina's contact at the company subsequently disputed these claims, citing the fact that their products were certified as exceeding the international regulatory requirements for health and safety.)

These excuses were met with skepticism by Bettina and the several friends who were helping her make telephone calls. Like Bettina, her friends were regular volunteers in Moscow's baby houses and orphanages, and each had extensive firsthand knowledge of the frequently decrepit and meager conditions of these settings and expressed disbelief over the repeated rejections. When Bettina described the events to me, she and the friend who was with her that day speculated that the orphanage directors were either noncaring and lazy, or, more likely, worried by the potential political implications of accepting such an offer. Bettina and her friend suspected that for the orphanage directors, accepting gifts like these from a larger foreign corporation could send an unintended message about the inadequacies of the Russian government to care for its littlest and most vulnerable citizens. Eventually, Bettina's persistence paid off, and several orphanage directors whom she knew well grudgingly agreed to accept a few cribs.

Bettina's experiences with trying to distribute donated cribs resonated with those described by other potential donors and intermediaries who have been frustrated in their efforts to help others. Oksana works as a case manager for a Moscow-based nonprofit organization that supports HIV-prevention and AIDS-treatment programs throughout Russia with funding, medical supplies, and various outreach materials, including prevention and treatment education. One of the tasks of Oksana's organization is to direct and monitor the flow of funds and resources from Russian and foreign donors to Russian social services programs that provide medical treatment, counseling services, and public outreach. As Oksana explained, devastating funding cuts to public health and welfare services in Russia over the past two decades have left governmental agencies and hospitals ill equipped to provide health care services. Hence, the most active programs in this field are private charities, mostly affiliated with religious communities (a point also mentioned by Nina, the development director for the patriarchate). Although these charities typically operate independently of local agencies, they have collaborative relationships with social workers and physicians who refer clients and provide advice and administrative assistance for working within local legal and bureaucratic structures. Because of Russian legal codes, medical assistance typically flows through official channels rather than directly to local organizations. Hence, Oksana's organization worked in close partnership with local officials rather than around them.

In describing the activities of her organization, Oksana and her American colleague Michele recounted the challenges of brokering partnerships between donors and funders, on the one hand, and the local officials who would receive and then redistribute the resources, on the other.[3] Particularly frustrating to them was that despite the intense and growing need for HIV-prevention and AIDS-treatment services, local government officials were often reluctant to accept assistance that they might then, in turn, have to distribute to local non-Orthodox Christian faith-based charities. Because local Russian Orthodox and Muslim clergy involved in the project were concerned by the presumed immorality of HIV and AIDS, they questioned whether items such as condoms might encourage immoral sexual behavior. Additionally, the moral pressures exerted by these clergy extended to views that more progressive Protestant congregations might also promote immoral behaviors, such as homosexuality or sexual intercourse outside marriage.[4] As a result, local officials were constrained in terms of working with only these Orthodox and Muslim groups and in accepting only resources that they could then pass on to Orthodox and Muslim communities.

There were two complications to this, however, as these local practices frequently violated the nondiscrimination policies enacted by the American funders. First, the official nondiscrimination policies set out by American funders, including the US government, required local officials to work with all eligible service providers, regardless of religious orientation. Second, anti-homosexuality sentiments held by some clergy and congregants from the local Orthodox and Muslim communities meant that HIV-prevention and AIDS-treatment programs were not necessarily provided to all eligible recipients. Echoing a claim that I heard from other assistance providers who engaged in HIV, hepatitis, and addiction treatment programs, Oksana explained that in the morality logic promoted by the Russian Orthodox Church and Muslim communities, HIV and hepatitis were believed to be exclusive to same-sex sexual contact. As a result, sex workers, intravenous drug users, and unsuspecting partners of or children born to individuals with HIV or hepatitis were automatically excluded from these programs. Oksana's organization thereby found itself in a catch-22 in which it had resources to distribute but no receiving agency that would accept and distribute them. In recounting these challenges, Oksana, like her counterparts I interviewed in other programs, described the decision-making processes of their potential partners in terms of apathy, ignorance, and even meanness. More than one irritated assistance provider asked rhetorically why religious belief should be allowed to interfere with the need to help people in need.

These frustrations with perceived apathy, ignorance, and meanness on the part of reluctant assistance providers were not limited to the moral politics of official institutional partnerships but also cropped up in people's more personal encounters when trying to make donations. During the course of our conversation, Oksana's perception that assistance programs were marked by a pernicious quality of apathy became much more pronounced, as she linked her professional efforts to find willing recipients with a recent personal attempt to make a donation to a local charity. When Oksana and her son relocated to Moscow for her job, they purged their wardrobes of outdated and unworn clothing. Oksana decided to donate the clothing to a church in her home city so that the items could be redistributed to the less fortunate in the community. Yet Oksana's efforts to donate the clothing were stymied at every turn. Oksana recounted how she and her son drove to every Orthodox church in the medium-sized city (population 250,000) in an effort to give away the clothing. At each church they visited, they were turned away by church staff whose behavior ranged from disinterest to outright hostile refusal of the gifts.

In desperation, Oksana and her son eventually tried the lone Catholic church in the area. She recalled that when they arrived at the church's entrance, they were greeted warmly by church staff, who were very clearly in the midst of a group meal. When Oksana and her son apologized for disturbing their meal and said that they could return at a later time, the church staff refused to let them depart and invited them inside. According to Oksana, the behavior of the Catholic church staff was radically different from their Orthodox counterparts: the clergy and laypersons who were present not only cheerfully and gladly accepted their gift of clothing, but they also asked for Oksana's name and that of her son in order to recognize and thank them on a publicly displayed plaque acknowledging donors. Oksana claimed that she and her son declined the generous offer, because, as she put it, they simply did what compassionate people should do and so they did not want or need public acknowledgment of their actions.

When Oksana recounted these events later, she expressed her confusion and frustration with the Orthodox churches she had contacted. Through her work with the nonprofit organization, and her regular participation in her own Orthodox parish, Oksana knew that Orthodox churches sponsored a variety of social services programs for Russia's poor and disenfranchised. As Oksana pointed out, it was public knowledge in Russia that there were many homeless people who needed clothing and other forms of assistance, and churches were constantly asking for help for their assistance programs. What she experienced, however, was that despite these public pleas for assistance, individual Orthodox churches refused to accept the help they were offered. By contrast, it was the Catholic church, a denomination long at odds with Russia's Orthodox hierarchy and in legal limbo with the Russian state, that had graciously welcomed her and her gifts. She claimed that she was so impressed with the attitudes of the Catholic members that had she not already been an Orthodox believer, she would have converted to Catholicism.

At roughly the same time that Oksana was experiencing difficulties in trying to fulfill her charitable impulses both at home and at work, similar problems cropped up in the efforts of the CCM, the Russian Lutheran Church, Caritas, and its partner organizations to create the interfaith social services program that has been described previously. Although some of the problems in launching that initiative resulted from different skill sets and priorities of participants, one of the most significant problems emerged when Caritas staff attempted to enroll recipients in the program.

After participating groups in the consortium had secured guaranteed funding, material support, space, and volunteer labor, the last thing that was needed was a list of recipients to enroll in the program. In recent years as state and municipal funding for social welfare services had dwindled, single mothers and their children had emerged as one of the populations most in need of assistance and most likely to be overlooked by private charities. Social workers from the local city welfare offices who were consulted reported that single mothers were especially vulnerable because of a lack of enforcement of child support laws and challenges faced by mothers to balance employment with child care and school commitments. Consequently, they advised the interfaith group to focus on this community by providing a daily food program, school supplies, holiday parties, and other services as needed. Given this advice, Caritas's social workers were confident they could mobilize their long-standing contacts within the local social welfare offices and government agencies to generate a list of needy families. Working through the local official channels also had a potentially secondary importance in ensuring the public and legal legitimacy of this venture. Yet despite repeated assurances that a list would be forthcoming, and despite repeated telephone calls and e-mails from Caritas staff, months went by without anyone from the local welfare offices or government agencies responding with a list of names. Instead, Caritas staff heard constant excuses as to why a list was not yet available: one person was on vacation, another person was on a business trip, or yet another person did not have access to the official roster.

Ultimately, after many months of inaction, Caritas and its partner organizations were forced to look elsewhere, outside official channels, for recipients. Staff members with the various partner organizations were at a loss for trying to explain why potential partners might turn down what were ostensibly freely given and needed services. Several expressed their dismay by speculating that local social workers and officials were perhaps more apathetic than they had first appeared.

Several months later, the realities of refusal as an intrinsic element of assistance projects appeared again during a different series of events involving clergy affiliated with this interfaith partnership. The first set of events occurred during the Christmas winter appeal by Moscow's Salvation Army congregation. As part of its outreach services to Moscow's homeless population, the Salvation Army was collecting blankets, mittens, socks, and food. Several Moscow churches supported this initiative by asking their congregations to donate items. One church served as a collection point, and for the several weeks that the appeal was in operation, congregants neatly stacked the donated items along the walls of the church sanctuary. When the minister of the church announced the appeal every week during services, he also explicitly reminded congregants of the precise parameters of the donations: blankets, mittens, and socks must be brand-new, unused, and clean; for food, only nonperishable canned food items could be accepted. The minister repeatedly warned congregants that perishable items, foods wrapped only in plastic or cloth, other uncanned goods, and used or dirty blankets, socks, and mittens would be discarded. Despite his pointed and frequent entreaties, every week inappropriate items were left. Whereas food items were thrown away immediately, lest they attract rodents, it was unclear what became of the unusable blankets and clothing. In private, the minister commented on how difficult it was for him to tell generous individuals not only that their gifts were inappropriate, but also that they would be thrown away without being used. For him, discouraging people's impulse to help was at odds with the need to make them feel good about contributing to a cause beyond themselves.

The second set of events entailed analogous difficulties with unusable gifts, but on a much larger scale and with different issues of usability. Over the past ten years, the Christian Church of Moscow has developed an impressive network of donors from the area's food corporations, restaurants, supermarkets, and medical providers. At any given moment, the congregation's basement storage space at one of the restaurants that hosted its daily soup kitchen was piled from floor to ceiling with cases of yogurt, canned vegetables, boxes of instant noodle soups, and a freezer filled with frozen chickens.

Over time, this generosity has become something of a burden on the congregation. Despite increasing the size of the food bags they distributed and the number of recipients they were serving, the congregation could not keep up with the amount of food and other supplies they were receiving. As their storage spaced filled up with stock, staff began searching for volunteers willing to donate another resource: extra space in their homes, garages, and even offices. This then necessitated finding individuals who could donate their cars to transport the goods across the city for storage and later for distribution. The huge quantities of donated food were matched by the amounts of gently used clothing, and household goods that other donors began offering to support the church's refugee outreach program. Eventually, church staff began searching for other organizations to whom they could offload some of their donated items. In some cases, excess snacks were redirected out of the charitable programs and instead to church fellowship events, and church members quietly perused the shelves overflowing with donated clothing, taking things for themselves or their children and making space for new items that were dropped off.

Yet even these efforts became insufficient for keeping up with the huge quantities of goods that were donated. As church staff debated whether they should decline donations temporarily until they were able to work through their stock, the minister worried that by turning down donations, they would offend potential givers and risk forfeiting any future donations. In the end, the minister decided that it was far better to continue accepting donations, even with the additional complications and potential for being unable to distribute them effectively.

Although this strategy proved somewhat manageable for the church, as staff were able to persuade more congregants and friends to provide space in their closets and garages, and to locate other charities that were willing to accept surpluses, the church was soon confronted with another, even more challenging dilemma. Toward the end of the global swine flu epidemic in 2010, the CCM was approached by a Western embassy with an offer of H1N1 vaccinations for the church's free medical clinic. Given that the clinic's clients were low-income migrants and refugees who either lived in overcrowded apartments and dormitory rooms crammed with multiple occupants or were homeless and were thus at greatest risk of catching and carrying the virus, church staff felt certain that the unexpected gift would be enormously valuable for their clients.

It was only later that they realized the unimagined implications of the donation: first, the church had to accept the entire amount of the vaccines, but by the time the supplies arrived, the epidemic was already waning and there was limited need for the vaccine; second, the vaccines could only be dispensed by state-licensed physicians, which meant that the church had to hire licensed Russian physicians rather than relying on the voluntary services of the nurses and foreign physicians who worked in their clinic; and third, the church could not dispose of unused vaccines without following special procedures.[5] Consequently, church staff found themselves in the difficult position of being unable to refuse the vaccines because they were worried that to do so would be more problematic than accepting the donation.

Although these examples have focused on refusals at the level of organizations when they are shifting between requesting, offering, and accepting assistance, incidences of resources being declined by individual recipients in assistance programs were surprisingly common. As I discovered by sitting through many shifts at the check-in tables at soup kitchens, food banks, and medical aid programs, it was not uncommon for enrolled recipients to fail to show up for appointments to receive services or to show up but decline some or all of the services offered. In food aid programs where I have observed, I frequently witnessed recipients pawing through food bags and removing items that they did not like. One soup kitchen program had an unofficial system by which recipients could make "exchanges" among particular food items: extra bread in place of an entrée, or only soup in lieu of other items. On occasions when the cafeteria ran out of a desirable item or when the soup kitchen staff decided to stop exchanges after too many recipients were requesting substitutions, recipients elected not to take anything.

Refusals were also seasonal, with summer being noticeably lighter in requests for assistance than winter. Among food aid programs, staff generally expected lower turnouts during summer, as many recipients had access to supplemental food sources via relatives, friends, and neighbors with access to summer cottage gardens, or on days with inclement weather when elderly and disabled recipients found it challenging to navigate city streets (Caldwell 2004). Programs that served migrants often experienced higher turnout on days with bad weather, as recipients wanted to find a place that was dry and warm. Those same programs also experienced lower turnout during summer, when it was common for migrants to travel outside of Moscow for work at summertime resorts. Recipients and aid workers alike generally explained these cycles of accepting and refusing assistance as normal and expected elements in the aid dynamic, as individuals' circumstances and need for assistance change over time.

More intriguing were instances when recipients turned down forms of assistance that they had gone to great lengths to access. This occurred with applicants to asylum and resettlement programs who had spent considerable amounts of time, energy, and money trying to navigate the bureaucratic procedures and prove themselves and finally had received official recognition of their status, only to turn down or never activate the formal status and benefits they had finally been awarded.[6] For aid workers who had expended considerable efforts and called in personal favors of their own to help these individuals receive these benefits, their refusals were not only puzzling but even distressing. Although precise reasons for why specific individuals turned down assistance were difficult to determine, some aid workers had their own theories. In some cases, aid workers speculated that recipients had decided to pursue a different course of action. In other cases, aid workers surmised that individuals felt uncomfortable receiving aid publicly. In still other cases, aid workers later learned that recipients had realized that although receiving formal status as "refugees" or gaining eligibility for resettlement had certain advantages, it also brought requirements and constraints that were less desirable. For instance, official refugee status and resettlement eligibility included limits on income and assigned housing that individuals were unwilling to accept.

In different ways, these acts of refusal reveal the uncertainties and complexities yielded by generosity. Rather than addressing, resolving, or eliminating problems, excess compassion can produce its own problems, both logistical and ethical. One of the consequences of redistributions of excess goods is that some organizations become "dumping grounds" for other people's undesirable castoffs. This places these receiving organizations in the position of having to decide when to move donations out of

the networks of the compassion economy and into the trash. Such occurrences also risk devaluing organizations that are deemed "not good
enough" for more desirable items. These concerns extend to individual
recipients who must struggle with whether to accept aid that they do not
want. Such negotiations illuminate the precarious position of recipients
within power structures: under what conditions are recipients allowed to
be fully empowered agents who can decide what they want and what they
need? In this vicious, virtuous circle, how do aid workers and their recipients understand their different roles as well as their responsibilities to one
another, and even their sense of rightness and compassion when they have
to make difficult decisions about refusing assistance?

WHEN "NO" IS THE BEST PRACTICE

Locating precise reasons for why local officials, organizations, or recipients turn down assistance is not easily determined. In some instances,
reasons seem obvious, such as when resources are given with strings
attached, as in the case of American donor and funder practices for
HIV/AIDS programs that required local intermediaries to adhere to policies of nondiscrimination that violated local sentiment and realities. In
other instances, the aid that is given must be rejected because it is not
proper for the circumstances, such as with the Salvation Army's Christmas
appeal in which clergy were forced to monitor and reject food and other
items that could not be stored. In still other cases, refusing aid helps an
organization or community promote larger symbolic values by allowing
them to "save face" and not be forced to present themselves and their constituencies as needy, disenfranchised, or dependent on assistance, especially foreign assistance. Critics have suggested that this was one of the
reasons behind the actions of the Russian government to expel such
organizations as the Peace Corps and Medécins Sans Frontières, among
others, over the past two decades.

The consequences of refusing donations are multiple. Some organizations risk losing their credibility as reliable and compassionate service
providers among both donors and recipients if they continually turn down
donations of otherwise serviceable and necessary resources. As Russia's

Orthodox Church has discovered, citizens are critical when church officials decide to refuse donations, limit assistance provision, and turn down requests for help. Despite the reality that churches may be physically incapable of responding to every potential donation or request for assistance, Russians interpret these refusals as evidence of the ROC's immorality and illegality (Caldwell 2009).

In addition to concerns with public image, aid workers must also consider how turning down gifts might affect their own volunteers and staff. For the minister whose congregation was in danger of becoming too successful at providing services, which in turn attracted additional donations from donors who wanted to support programs that had the best track record and greatest accountability, he worried that his congregation was continually losing its spiritual focus by instead having to expand its outreach services and find additional trustworthy charities to receive their surplus supplies, just so the church could maintain its reputation with donors. Even as the minister recognized this quandary, he maintained that that challenge might, in fact, be a catalyst for pushing his congregants to deepen their own personal spirituality by forcing them to look harder for ways to help even more people in need. For him, turning down donations meant turning down an opportunity for his congregants to grow in their personal faith by trying to find ways to extend their outreach to others. Another clergy member who had opened his home and allowed people in need to stay with him, both short-term and long-term, worried that even though it was challenging never to have a moment of true privacy, he would lose his own moral compass and spiritual core if he ever asked guests to leave or refused them his hospitality.

The very dynamics of refusals are revealing in terms of the expectations and obligations that circulate through humanitarian economies. Although both aid workers and recipients may idealize a system in which there are always sufficient and appropriate resources to reach all who are in need, achieving a balance between supply and need is difficult. What instances such as those described above suggest is that perhaps deficiencies and stinginess are not, in fact, always the most critical problems, and instead it may be that generosity is the problem. Generosity can produce its own deficits and shortcomings that may be more difficult to accommodate and resolve. Thus, while there are rules and conventions governing practices of giving to ensure fairness, it may be that it is the receiving side of humanitarian partnerships that is the least predictable, and therefore the most tenuous and fragile.

This sense that receiving is far more emotionally and logistically fraught than giving appeared vividly in the comments of Pastor Georg, a Russian Lutheran minister. In his position with the diocese of his denomination, Pastor Georg had extensive experience working with a number of charitable programs in Moscow and strong views about the problems involved with refusals of assistance. By way of explanation, Pastor Georg commented that one of his challenges was trying to help fellow Russians recognize the difference between taking and receiving. Pastor Georg perceived "taking" as an activity that required little thought or attention and was more akin to "grabbing" anything that came available, regardless of whether it was useful or needed. In contrast, he identified "receiving" as a more deliberate and thoughtful activity that involved attention to the circumstances under which something was needed and given, as well as consideration of proper use and disposal. What he had seen most often, he remarked, was the former and not the latter.

This perspective resonated with the views of other assistance providers and recipients who have been critical of recipients' behaviors at distribution events. In the late 1990s, a Russian friend who was an activist for low-income families invited several staff from one of the assistance programs with which she volunteered and me to an International Women's Day celebration. After the concert, the organizers handed out free boxes of candy, while another local organization offered women's clothing (it was unclear if the clothing was for sale or a give-away). Both sets of tables were flooded with women energetically reaching in to grab items that they then either stuffed in a bag or threw back on the table before grabbing something else. Shaking her head in dismay, my friend complained that the women demonstrated a lack of propriety. At another assistance program I visited regularly, I have observed staff scold recipients for trying to take extras. On more than one occasion, staff (both Russian and non-Russian) later expressed to me their views that such behaviors were endemic among assistance recipients.

Although perspectives such as these are troubling for what they reveal about attitudes among some participants in the assistance world on both

sides of the encounter, Pastor Georg's analytical distinction between taking and receiving offers a helpful starting point for understanding the
place of refusals as deliberate and considered acts themselves, rather than
as moments of inaction or apathy. Refusing becomes a practical mode
through which potential recipients, who may be either intermediaries or
final beneficiaries, view and experience the continued trajectory and ultimate disposal of resources. As such, receiving may not be the ultimate goal
or even endpoint of humanitarian assistance interactions, and refusals
offer opportunities for rethinking not simply the uncertainties inherent in
assistance encounters, but more importantly the opportunities and potentialities that are made possible through assistance.

BEING MERCIFUL WHILE SAYING NO

In the late 2000s, the CCM was approached about starting a new program
that brought the complexities and ambiguities of refusal into sharp relief,
at times straining the faith of the church's staff, congregants, and recipients. For almost twenty years, the church had quietly worked with African
students, refugees, and other migrants, providing them with food, clothing, and legal aid contacts. Because of the considerable trust and goodwill
the church enjoyed among this community, as well as the church's close ties
with other congregations and programs that supported Russia's migrant
communities, it had been approached by the key international agencies
that work with asylum seekers and asked to provide information and
screening services for their asylum programs. The church's minister and
several staff members had undergone rigorous trainings sponsored by the
United Nations High Commissioner for Refugees (UNHCR), International
Organization for Migration (IOM), and various Russian and international
diplomatic and legal agencies, and they were knowledgeable about the official criteria for granting official refugee status and eligibility for resettlement, the types of documentation that were required for applications, and
what they could and could not say in their conversations with potential and
actual applicants.

These developments coincided with the CCM's creation of an officially
recognized and registered NGO that would actually administer this work,

maintaining a sharp institutional and legal division between the CCM's religious and secular activities. The CCM's NGO would also be held accountable for maintaining neutrality in its asylum processing activities and adhering to the strict policies and procedures set out by federal and international law. As a result of this added responsibility, the church's social ministries had expanded beyond social services to include an explicit human rights dimension, and the church became sought after for advisory consultations with federal and international agencies on matters pertaining to political and economic migration from the Global South, xenophobia, and discrimination.[7]

In 2007, shortly after the CCM had begun this new venture, Pastor Mark invited me to accompany him for several screening interviews. By way of invitation, Pastor Mark confessed that he was stymied by the particularities of one case, and he asked for my help as both an anthropologist and a woman. The applicant was an African female university student. In her application for refugee status and resettlement, she had written that when she returned home, she would be forced to undergo genital modification. The minister and his male staff members were understandably uncomfortable, not only because they would have to question the woman about very sensitive matters, but because they felt that they did not know enough about how this particular case of genital modification should be viewed against the official criteria set out in the official requirements. They thought that I, as an anthropologist, might be able to help interpret the cultural implications of the case.

The interviews were held in the congregation's social ministry offices, housed in the basement of an apartment building where one of their soup kitchens was based. I had been in those offices many times before to meet with the church secretary, soup kitchen staff, African students, and Russian recipients. The offices had long been a safe place for members of the congregation and social services programs to gather together, use the small library and ping-pong table, attend English lessons and job training programs, and participate in formal and informal church activities such as catechetical training or Bible study lessons. On this day, however, the offices were being used for the screening interviews and evaluations. In the small room occupied by the ping-pong table, the minister, the director of the social services programs, and several other staff and volunteers with the asylum project were reviewing files and meeting with applicants for refugee certification and resettlement.

As the conversation unfolded, another female volunteer and I took the lead in asking delicate questions about the nature and circumstances of the proposed bodily modifications. The young woman repeatedly stated that she did not want to be forced to undergo these modifications, before revealing, in her words, that not only was it a relatively less intrusive form of female circumcision (as far as these things go), but that it was only because she was the oldest child in her lineage and had succeeded her father in a chiefly political system. She explained that because she had inherited her father's political and economic position and resources, she also had to assume his role as the "patriarch" of the community. One of the consequences of this was that she had to take on the male roles and responsibilities of this position—which included being circumcised. The young woman asserted that although she was not particularly bothered by taking on her father's role, she did not want to be circumcised, and she felt that this was sufficient grounds to let her avoid that responsibility.

Although female genital modification was a recognized reason for granting asylum, this particular set of circumstances did not meet the criteria set out by the governing bodies. After conferring about the criteria and the particular details of the woman's application, our small screening team regretfully told her that she did not fit the requirements for asylum and her case would not be forwarded. Angrily, the woman demanded that her case be reconsidered, before she was politely but firmly escorted out.

Afterwards, the other members of the screening committee reviewed the case. What was especially evident in their discussion was a shared feeling of dismay and frustration about being unable to help the woman in some meaningful way. As their individual comments revealed, the different members of the screening committee found it difficult to balance their responsibility to follow the regulations that were given to them by the official organizations that made the final determinations against a sense that they should be compassionate people to their fellow human beings. Above all, they struggled to reconcile their roles in the nonreligious sphere of social justice with their personal beliefs about an appropriately faith-driven, or even Christian, way to treat other people. From legal and pragmatic standpoints the committee was not convinced that the woman faced a greater-than-normal danger if she returned home, especially because she would be returning by choice to take up a position of great prestige and power. At the same time, how could they condone an activity that would bring her pain and suffering? Which was the lesser sin: rejecting her application because it did not fit criteria set by the authorities, or accepting her application but at the risk of showing the authorities that the committee could not follow policy, thereby damaging their reputation for objectivity and fairness and ultimately losing the ability to assist asylum seekers altogether? How could they continue to be a community that promoted and practiced compassion and social justice if they occasionally had to engage in actions that were potentially harmful?

Such conundrums about greater goods and lesser evils became ever more frequent and significant as the CCM took ever more active and public roles in Moscow's human rights world. In summer 2009, Pastor Mark received a series of strange international telephone calls in the middle of the night. Pastor Mark was accustomed to desperate pleas for help from foreigners who had turned up in Russia and needed assistance. But this was a very different phone call that disturbed him in a way that did not usually happen. The caller identified himself as an African living in Germany, and told Pastor Mark that he was worried about his sister, who had recently arrived in Russia from Sierra Leone and had lost her documents when she was robbed at a Moscow train station. Could someone from Pastor Mark's church or its affiliated NGO help his sister get her documents and assist her on her way on to Germany? he asked. Over the next few hours, the same man called Pastor Mark several times, each time being more demanding for assistance and reporting that his sister was more and more distraught. Pastor Mark regretfully told the man that he could not provide assistance at that moment, and advised the man to tell his sister to come to the NGO's office first thing in the morning and the staff would see what they could do.

The next morning, I was at the program's offices when the woman arrived, accompanied by two large, imposing African men. After Matthew, the Kenyan office manager who answered the door, showed the woman and two men to a waiting area, he confided to the NGO's staff that something about this did not feel right. Upon visiting with the threesome for a few minutes, Pastor Mark, Matthew, and the other staff members agreed that something was wrong. The woman appeared frightened, and there were no apparent cues that she knew the men who had accompanied her. Rather, they seemed to be chaperoning her, rather than escorting and helping her. This became more evident when Matthew attempted to separate the men and the woman and direct them to different rooms. Whether it was appointments with applicants to the asylum / resettlement screening process or meetings with recipients for their medical and other social services programs, the church's policy was to meet with applicants individually. When Matthew informed the woman and the two men of this policy, the men became visibly displeased and insisted that they remain with her. But Pastor Mark and Matthew were adamant. The young woman seemed apathetic.

During her meeting with the NGO's staff, the woman repeated the same story: she had arrived at a Moscow train station and then someone had stolen her documents. She could not, or would not, explain which train station or how someone had come to steal her documents. The details about her brother in Germany changed: he was at different moments a brother, an uncle, a friend. All she wanted or needed were new documents and money to travel to Germany. In the waiting area, the two men were making similar requests; all they needed were new documents and money to help her travel. Given the circumstances, the NGO staff and Pastor Mark were quite certain that she was being trafficked; this was a familiar story. Repeatedly in the privacy of the screening room, they advised her that while they could not provide her with new documents or travel money, they could help her in other ways. They could make her safe. They could help her contact the proper authorities. They could advocate for her. But she would have to help them help her. The young woman apathetically declined. She said that she knew some other people from Sierra Leone in a town several hours outside Moscow. She would go there, she said. And then she left.

Afterwards, Pastor Mark and his staff reviewed the events repeatedly, rehashing the conversations, the strange details, their many efforts to try to make her feel comfortable in opening up to them and asking for help, and the responses of the woman and the two men. The CCM staff lamented that although they wanted to help her and that they were absolutely certain that she was in trouble, they could not help her. What they wanted to do was make an intervention, and they each took turns fantasizing aloud about how they could have pulled it off and whisked her away from the burly men.[8]

Several weeks later, I joined a series of formal asylum screenings conducted in the NGO's offices. In this case, two young twin brothers from Cameroon were being interviewed. Barely teenagers, the boys were identical except for the massive scar that cut across the face of one. They were interviewed separately, and the staff and I reviewed their files, both individually and together, before the interviews started. Both young men had been conscripted as child soldiers, and their claims for asylum were based on that detail. Yet shortly after they had been conscripted, they were separated, with each brother taken by a different commander. At some point during the fighting, as the various factions had changed positions and allegiances, the two brothers had been on opposing sides. After they both escaped, they found each other and made their way to Russia. While both young men had compelling stories and legitimate details to back up their claims of deprivation and being forced to fight (scars, specific details, some supporting documents), the problem was that one brother had been given a position of privilege by his commander, and in that position he had been forced to commit crimes against the group to which his brother belonged. In other words, according to the requirements for asylum set out by the UNHCR, one brother was officially a victim while the other could technically be branded a perpetrator, despite his age and the fact that he had been coerced into servitude.

After interviewing both brothers, the NGO staff met and discussed the two cases. Their immediate task was to determine whether they felt either or both young men warranted being moved further along in the screening process. They were deeply upset by the possibility that only one young man would be authorized to move on, because both brothers clearly had been traumatized and victimized and they only had each other for support. In the end, the staff decided to recommend both brothers for further screening, and then they met with the two young men and described the next stage of the process. Carefully working around the official policies dictating what screeners could and could not tell the young men about the process, the NGO staff found ways to counsel them on how to tell their stories and how to reconcile strategically the differences between their experiences through explanations. This skirted the line of what was permissible in their duties, but the NGO staff explained later that clearly there was a need here to treat the young men with compassion and ensure that they both had an equal chance at asylum. As the staff explained at different stages, their credibility with the asylum and resettlement authorities depended on their ability to be fair and to uphold the regulations. Adhering too loosely to the regulations could endanger their ability to provide this important service of treating applicants humanely and compassionately. Yet the staff felt that in this case, the consequences of rejecting one brother and not the other were too dire to contemplate, and they felt that it was better to risk being reprimanded for being too lenient.

A few days later, the staff struggled directly with the consequences of refusal, when they turned down another applicant. A Sierra Leonean man in his thirties arrived at the NGO's office, dressed neatly in shirt and tie and carrying a briefcase. According to his case file, he was claiming asylum for himself and his family as political refugees. He had written that he had been involved in a pro-democracy political party that had been oppressed during the civil war and its aftermath. He and his family had escaped and made their way to Russia. At the outset of the interview, before the staff members had had much of an opportunity to ask the preliminary questions they needed to verify information and set the scene for the types of information that should—and should not—be provided, the man opened his briefcase and began pulling out materials: clippings of newspaper articles, handwritten letters, handmade political materials, and CDs with television news programs. He ignored the staff members' instructions to answer only their questions, and instead he provided a long narrative about his activities and said that it was all documented on the materials that he pushed across the table. The staff members tried to stop him, saying that they could not accept supplemental material like that and that the material was not relevant to his case. But the man refused to listen, and a shouting match ensued. Eventually, Matthew, the office manager, forcibly escorted the man to the door. With raised voice, the man accused the staff members of being hypocrites and of not being serious about their desire to help people who were in need.

After the man left, the staff members and Matthew were visibly shaken. They conferred with one another and explained that while they believed the man and wanted to help him, he had provided too much information. By carefully saving all of those documents—materials that would have been unavailable in Russia but that he could only have brought with him—it appeared that he had strategically planned to request asylum before he had even left Sierra Leone for Russia. In other words, because the man had been so proactive and provided too much information, it gave the resettlement agency too much knowledge that they could then track down and verify (or not) his claims. He had volunteered an excess of data, which was more problematic than a shortage of data, because it gave the government bodies that did the final vetting too much information to use against their official checklist of which details "counted" and which ones did not.[9] More problematic was that because the man possessed this much material, the resettlement agency would likely believe that he was a person with the means to gather and preserve this information and thus was not a true "victim." Had the man been more reticent about the information he shared, the staff could have worked with him to navigate the system through partial information and prevarications. But because there were no unknowns that they could work around or fill in with guesses and hunches, they had no choice but to turn him down. In this case, the staff members were constrained by the circumstances in which they—and the applicant—were caught, and they were forced to refuse his application. As they debated the circumstances, the staff members struggled with trying to reconcile the fact that although they could not help this one man, this was to them clearly a case in which accepting his case file and putting it forward would likely limit their ability to help others in the future.

For assistance workers like these individuals whom I encountered in Russia, refusals were not something that most expected to do, and certainly not something they wanted to do. Having to turn down assistance to others, especially to people who were clearly in need of that assistance, challenged their most deeply held values about social justice. In some cases, volunteers and staff members violated formal policies in an effort not to refuse services; in other cases, volunteers and staff who found it too emotionally difficult to deny assistance simply stopped volunteering or found other venues where they could provide the assistance they felt was necessary. Several ministers confided that at different times they had to counsel their staff, volunteers, and even parishioners to take a break from their work out of concerns that those individuals were at risk of losing objectivity and of suffering emotional distress from having to make refusals.

Even though making difficult decisions about refusing assistance to recipients was an ordinary part of service work, these realities revealed the limits of compassion. Assistance providers and recipients grappled with the fact that compassion is never totalizing or neutral, but always partial and embedded within hierarchical systems of value, where the ideal of helping everyone is always an illusion. The shortcomings of generosity also reveal the uncertainties intrinsic to faith as a practice of social justice. Incidences of refusal prompted some individuals to contemplate whether they were being tested spiritually: how could they learn to discern rightness in situations where there were multiple possibilities and how could they be compassionate even when having to deny assistance? For others, these cases signaled deeper crises of faith, both spiritual and secular. How could a personal belief in a just and merciful God, or in a more generically secular utopian vision of a world of equality and goodness, be reconciled with a real-world reality that inequalities would persist and that they would be unable to solve them?

These were the uncertainties that faced Moscow's assistance workers on a daily basis. Yet at the same time, what kept assistance workers going was a sense that they had been entrusted with a sacred responsibility to be stewards of their community. As such, despite the difficulties that came with the responsibility to weigh and negotiate competing needs, interests, and concerns, it was their duty as stewards to make those decisions as lovingly and ethically as possible, rather than simply leaving people in need— their fellow humans—to the impersonal and inhumane machinations of an unjust, uncivil world. In this vein, it was faith's generative capacity to produce possibilities, even if they were not yet or not fully knowable or imagined, that propelled people to keep trying to help others.

8 Conclusion

PRECARIOUS FAITH

Within Moscow's faith communities, despite principled stances and the conviction that action can ameliorate suffering and make the world a better place, individuals struggle to address and make sense of the uncertainties and inconsistencies that they witness on a daily basis. For some individuals, these uncertainties play out in their efforts to reconcile disparities between what they are able to do and what they wish they could do. For other individuals, the struggles entail reconciling their responsibilities to their fellow humans with those that they feel toward their country. Two Salvation Army officers discussed the challenges they faced in trying to fix problems while remaining respectful of larger political ideologies. Captain Anton stated:

> President Medvedev [in 2009] gave a speech . . . where he said that Russians need to take risks with their freedoms. That is a scary thing to do. We have [Salvation Army] officers who do not challenge our administration because it is scary. But that is the point. We have to take risks. For us, we can't be disobedient to the government, which would be illegal, but we have to be willing in some places to be countercultural, especially in how we respond to bribery and corruption. By standing against those things it can take longer for us to accomplish our goals, but we have to stand against them.

Continuing this thread, his colleague Captain Aleksandra added:

> There are changes in our approaches here in Russia, depending on the leader. It has been problematic for some people. Because of the risks the Army has taken in the past and our involvement with human rights work, our name was in the paper too much. But we try to stay within the bounds of the law. We intercede for the disenfranchised who have no voice and we do it in a way that does not blame the government. We are working alongside the government and working with the government.

For still others, these struggles have been matters of religious identity and practice, a theme identified by Pastor Mark in his reflections on the decisions made by different religious communities about whether and when to reveal their social justice activities. He commented: "If we ever have to compromise or second-guess our goals in order not to appear religious, then we are doing it wrong. We are saying that God cannot protect us. The challenge, then, is one of honesty. How do you maintain an obvious and visible Christian presence but do it in such a way that people do not react . . . to it?"

Over the many years that I have been doing research among Moscow's assistance providers, I have been deeply moved and impressed by the ways in which members of this community creatively respond to inequality, change, the unknown, and the unknowable with the sincere if often elusive goal of bringing about the most good for the most people and strive to allow everyone to maintain a shared experience of humanness and humaneness. Every day assistance providers grapple with questions such as, Is it better to provide a hot meal or a listening ear? Which is the greater, more immediate need: to provide a place for someone to stay or to hear and acknowledge their story? What happens if they bend the rules for one person? Is it appropriate or necessary to force someone to accept assistance they do not want? Is it appropriate to reject offers of assistance because they might come with too many obligations? And who is the "master" they are serving: their fellow humans, a divine entity, or a state that is alternately hostile and welcoming, and dismissive of and dependent on their work?

Theirs is not an easy job, and even the most kindhearted, genial persons have each had moments of regret, anger, and even despair. Repeatedly, clergy, staff, and volunteers alike have confided that they never truly know if they have done the right thing or whether their efforts will effect real results. One minister agonized for days over whether a spontaneous decision to give cash to someone who approached him at church was appropriate. Another spent many of our conversations worrying about whether government authorities would find fault with his congregation's social justice work and whether it was too dangerous for him to talk to me, even in the privacy of his home. Still others worry about what will happen in the future to the people for whom they have cared, both materially and personally. At the same time that there have been many success stories, too often, despite the best efforts of many people, there are also devastating failures. Successful programs have closed, partnerships ended, and too many recipients and aid partners moved away, disappeared, or even died. The ever-changing political situation within Russia, marked by continuing attacks on minorities, LGBT activists, disability rights supporters, and many others, proves to be dispiriting to many.

Within these circumstances, it is understandable that Moscow's aid workers worry not simply that goodness might not prevail, but that their own sense of conviction and faith might be a secondary casualty. Despite optimistic assertions to the contrary, both faith and the affective economy it fuels are fragile and tenuous. The border zones where faith is enacted as a form of both personal and public engagement are also spaces of uncertainty, contradiction, and the unknown.

Yet even as the precariousness and uncertainty of faith and its affective economy can be disheartening and threaten to derail and undo the very important work that Moscow's assistance providers are doing, they are also, ironically, resources on which assistance providers can draw to respond to the messiness and exceptions of assistance work, while striving to protect and maintain the dignity of the people they help and the humaneness of the encounters. The joint ventures of the CCM and its partners into more explicit human rights reporting and advocacy illuminate these problems and tensions well. Members of this cooperative network—both those who seek assistance and those who provide it in various guises (clergy, attorneys, physicians, journalists, social workers, and frontline providers of material assistance)—have struggled to meet and work with one another through the processes of documenting abuses, requesting political asylum, asserting legal claims, and ensuring basic material provisions. These are emotionally fraught encounters, as potential recipients share—sometimes willingly and sometimes under duress—stories of unfathomable hardships and trauma, and program staff must make hard decisions about whether to believe these stories and how to make a personal connection of empathy even when they are unable to provide the assistance that is so desperately needed.

In such complex encounters between providers and recipients, a delicate poetics arises as to the amount and types of information that are revealed, solicited, and imagined and how that information facilitates or impedes certain types of intimacies and advocacy. At the same time, because assistance workers must mediate relationships among petitioners, Russian legal authorities, and international migration agencies, they must find ways to translate personal accounts of suffering and need into the bureaucratic structures and expectations of those larger, more impersonal systems. It is not uncommon for assistance workers to be the bearers of bad news regarding decisions made by agencies and officials higher in the decision-making process as well as the advocates who attempt to appeal and intercede for their applicants.

These are the realities of the divide that exists when members of this community are compelled to emphasize one part of the social services, social justice, or human rights approach over another. Either they are asked to address the "rights" or "justice" parts—that is, in trying to adhere to official policies about laws, rights, and advocacy in order to ensure fairness—or they must focus on the "human" or "social" parts by trying to recognize that the people they are trying to help are real people with real problems and real needs in front of them, even if human rights policies and practices cannot accommodate that humanness.

These uncertainties and tensions are not always reductively unproductive but can also represent opportunities for civic engagement in multiple registers from the most inwardly personal to the most outwardly public. Much like humanitarian and social assistance programs elsewhere in the world, in Russia the federal and international policies that formalize the structures and rules of social justice programs have instead created inconsistencies in criteria for eligibility and implementation of assistance. As a result, welfare, social justice, and human rights projects and the laws that enable and regulate them are often marked by contradictions in terms of classifications of need, identity categories, forms of assistance, and compliance requirements. Assistance providers can play on distinctions among charity, NGO, and congregation in order to provide different forms of assistance—material, social, emotional, or spiritual. They can also strategically engage donors' expectations and desires in ways that maximize the potential of gifts while minimizing the effects on programs and recipients. And they can always invoke and call on the presumed morality and sanctity of their status as either religious or social justice institutions to provide sanctuary for those in need. Uncertainty, speculation, and equivocation are thus among the most powerful resources available to aid workers and their recipients.

The multiple negotiations that occur in the border zones of uncertainty and precarity that bring together assistance workers, the people they help, and the larger institutions and structures that govern them produce multiple intimacies and distances—often in ways that are at odds with or are unexpected in the assistance encounter. This is the space of the "somewhere" that exists between social and justice, social and service, human and rights. Within the faith-based context, assistance encounters are not fully oriented either to the objective pole of human rights or to the subjective pole of compassion and empathy. This space in-between exemplifies what Didier Fassin (2012: 1–3) has described as the tension or even paradox of "humanitarian governance": the tensions between reason and affect, and even between values and affects. It is also the space that Michael Jackson (2012) has described as being "between one and one another": that is, the intersubjective moment or state that exists in the interplay between the self and the other, between acting and being acted upon. It is above all a border zone where uncertainty and precarity produce social ties of dependency, responsibility, and trust (see also Allison 2013; Cabot n.d.). Both individuals and communities come to be made— and come to be made meaningful—in these encounters, a point illuminated by Judith Butler's (n.d.) suggestion that "precariousness implies living socially, that is, the fact that one's life is always in some sense in the hands of the other" (see also Allison 2013; Cabot n.d.). Perhaps most tellingly, as revealed by the experiences of the aid workers described here, this precariousness is also the in-betweenness of knowing what is right and doing what is right.

In this space in-between, what constitutes "human" or even "humane"? In many respects, the "human" part of this comes through in efforts to maintain some form of intimacy and distance simultaneously. Difference between individuals cannot be completely effaced, because complete intimacy is itself problematic. But there cannot be an absolute chasm between the two sides, because moving through the daily realities of the assistance system requires engagement and some form of give-and-take to meet one another somewhere in the middle for a shared journey to an unknown future.

FAITH, INTIMACY, AND COMPASSION

It is in these moments of acknowledging and engaging the spaces of in-betweenness that faith-based actors work most profoundly and productively. And it is in these spaces that the generative capacity of faith becomes most distinctive and powerful. But it is also where the limits of the state and the possibilities of the civic both become more apparent.

As something external to any one individual but rather an affective quality that is put into social worlds and social dynamics and so circulates between people, faith operates with and through individuals but also independently of them. It encourages and fosters possibilities and a sense of optimism. This is not to suggest that faith provides deniability or allows individuals to distance themselves from bad decisions or a sense of helplessness. Rather, faith operates in a different register and bigger sphere of interaction where chance and possibility can be reworked as part of a greater good. Faith's own internal dynamics as it circulates among individuals and between circumstances impels its forward momentum and reproducing nature. In contrast to development paradigms that are intended to fix problems and cease existence, practices of faith are meant to keep going into an unknown future, even if problems of the here and now are resolved.

More importantly, because faith exists outside any one individual it also is what protects the simultaneity of distance and intimacy between fellow inhabitants of the faith-based world. This keeps assistance workers from falling into what Robbins (2013) has identified as the trap of associating too closely with the suffering subject and thus confusing the Self and the Other. It also applies to assistance providers who might be at risk of presuming similarities between their own perspectives and those of their counterparts. For Robbins, the bigger question is whether imagined sameness might undo and dissolve the unique particularities of what it means to be human. As the quality that moves between individuals, faith maintains a distinction between individuals; it keeps them separate even as it binds them together in a shared project, a shared journey.

Consequently, faith-based approaches preserve the gaps and uncertainties that exist between real people and the real situations they inhabit, while allowing possibilities for bridging, mediating, and working with and within these gaps. As the experiences of the people described here reveal, there were many moments in which individuals found that simply being able to engage with one another as real people with flaws and partially known identities but without needing to deal with certainty and structure is the best and most effective strategy. This was an approach that I heard repeatedly, sometimes as a last resort but sometimes as an overture. Assistance workers described the power of simply giving someone a smile or listening to their stories, no matter how preposterous, or even simply "walking with" another person for a few steps on an unknown journey. It was equally clear that often aid applicants showed up at aid centers without any real expectations for assistance but simply invoked need as an opportunity to initiate a visit and conversation.

There is an irony here, however, because religious organizations are often depicted as being conservative, inflexible, and even separate from the concerns of civic life. But is this really accurate? Is it possible that religiously based organizations might be able to deal with uncertainty more flexibly and effectively than their nonreligious counterparts? This might be the case. When staff members at the CCM complained that they did not like being bureaucrats and wanted instead to be compassionate individuals to the people they tried to help, they echoed a view I heard repeatedly from individuals who chose to work with religiously based aid organizations. These individuals claimed that they came to these organizations because they believed that religious groups were already focusing on the person, not on a case file. At the same time, the emphasis on a secular or universal humanism offered possibilities for a pluralism of perspectives and experiences, making way for people from very diverse places within Russian society to find points of convergence.

Perhaps more important was that because the fight that religious groups were undertaking was not one that was finite or had a foreseeable endpoint, it could complement the state's own future-oriented visions and needs. Because faith is an ongoing project, it is oriented to a future far beyond what any one person could envision or hope to attain, despite the shared commitment to finding ways to achieve real change in the here and now. As Pastor Mark commented, he recognized in this the story of Jesus and his efforts to heal people. By way of explanation, Pastor Mark noted that Jesus never healed people so that they could resume their old lives, but instead he healed them so that they could have new lives that were transformed. As a result, according to this logic, social ministries needed to derive from the idea of the transformation of the person—physical and spiritual. Ultimately, it is not just about making life better on this earth but also about focusing on an eternal life that begins here on this earth. Bridging this world and the next was similarly part of Father Valerii's statement that the role of the church was "to make Christ present in the world." The church remains sacred when it takes care of other people (*zabotit' liudem,* literally "are troubled/concerned by people"). Social service, he reflected, was a way to show a love of God and love to others. "God is ground zero for *miloserdie* [i.e., charity, mercy]," he concluded.

In circumstances such as the ones that Moscow's faith-based assistance workers confront on a daily basis, faith is a risky proposition. Real life is filled with injustices that cannot always be solved, and real people have flaws and flawed lives that do not always or easily meet the practical realities of assistance or the ideological goals of social justice. But faith—just like love, friendship, compassion, and care—is always propositional and reveals possibilities more than actualities. It is by believing in faith, and more importantly by putting faith into action, that members of Moscow's faith-based assistance world are trying to make the world, both this one and the next, a little better for everyone. As Father Thomas reflected, "My deepest intuition is that I am dealing with something bigger and deeper."

Notes

1. COMPASSION

1. Moscow's metro dogs have been immortalized in numerous media accounts. See, for example, Marquardt, Blakemore, and Eichenholz 2010.

2. Local outrage intensified when subsequent investigation revealed that the attacker was in fact an affluent young woman who worked in the high fashion industry. Residents were shocked and angered at what they perceived as the ultimate example of the decline of Russians' morals, especially among the country's emerging upper- and upper-middle-class young people.

3. Although I do not have figures for how many people identified themselves as atheists or agnostics, the subject came up with surprising frequency in conversations when I inquired about people's own religious backgrounds. When I raised the issue of agnosticism with one Protestant minister, her response was revealing: she said that in her liberally progressive denomination, a thoughtfully spiritual person should be agnostic.

4. Chapter X of the 1936 Soviet Constitution (see also Buckley and Donahue 2000: 253).

5. See, for example, Caldwell 2004, Höjdestrand 2009, and Stephenson 2006 for details on this early period of charity in post-Soviet Russia.

6. For other accounts of post-Soviet faith-based activity, see Köllner 2013, Tocheva 2011, and Zigon 2010.

7. For an inside look at a St. Petersburg–based Russian Orthodox addiction treatment program, its methods, and how patients understood "success," see Zigon 2011.

8. I am deliberately not citing actual media accounts because those articles explicitly identify these communities by name, which might put them at risk of retribution for some of the views and activities described in this book.

9. For recent accounts of the effects of this "Foreign Agents Law," see reports by Amnesty International (2015) and Human Rights Watch (2016).

10. See Jeavons 1994 for an illuminating analysis of religious, primarily Christian, institutions from the perspective of organizational and management studies.

11. I will note that I remain skeptical that the pension levels have been raised sufficiently, given the fact that social workers and social services providers continue to report need among elderly Muscovites. I have, however, been assured by several elderly friends that it is true. Perhaps the most compelling example of the greater incomes of at least some of Moscow's elderly is that of a friend who was a longtime activist for pensioners and dependent on a church-run soup kitchen. She not only assured me that pensions had been raised, but then showed off all of her recent purchases that she had made as a newly empowered consumer: clothing, jewelry, television, video cassettes, and a refrigerator, among other items.

12. In his analysis of religious philanthropic organizations, Jeavons (1994: 50) argues that one of the distinctive features of Christian approaches to service work is the recognition that there are numerous examples in the New Testament indicating that although "efforts to do good may have unintended consequences—sometimes not helpful—and may not achieve all that had been hoped, they will 'work for good' . . . no loving act is lost ever from the sight of God."

13. See also Comaroff and Comaroff's (2000: 295–310) invocation of "efforts to enlist divine help" in the "occult economies" they have described.

14. Vincanne Adams (2013) has described similar outsourcing of the labor of care onto individuals as a new form of citizenship in her ethnography of post–Hurricane Katrina recovery in the United States.

15. For accounts of this research on changing consumer practices, see Caldwell 2002, 2004.

16. For the case of the International Red Cross, Liisa Malkki (2015) makes a similar observation about aid work as a professional occupation. I discuss the professionalization of aid work in Moscow later in the book.

17. The Gülen movement is an international faith-based group founded by Fethullah Gülen and associated with Turkish-Muslim identity. The group presents itself as a nonpolitical educational and cultural group that draws from Islamic values of compassion and care. Critics, however, have questioned the group's motives and tactics.

18. See Baggett's (2000) discussion about the secular nature of Habitat for Humanity.

19. See Köllner 2013 for a discussion of the role of private donors in support-ing Orthodox Christian religious redevelopment in Russia.

2. FAITH IN A SECULAR HUMANISM

1. When I first began following the CCM in the mid-1990s, the church's min-isters at that time actively encouraged and facilitated "church exchanges," espe-cially with local Orthodox communities. At some point those formal exchanges became less frequent until they were revived by the new minister. Thus, although the new minister did initiate a new set of activities for a new congregation, that type of religious exchange was neither novel nor unique.

2. This was a common practice at most of the Protestant and Catholic services that I attended in Russia, as congregants from the same religion but different theological or regional backgrounds followed different traditions. For instance, progressive Protestants were more likely to use gender-inclusive language; and Lutherans, Anglicans, and Catholics tended to reference a single Christian church with "one holy catholic church," while Baptists and evangelical Christians used various alternatives in order to avoid suggestions that they were aligned with Catholicism.

3. See Scott Kenworthy's discussion (2008) of this issue with regard to the Russian Orthodox Church.

4. For a different religious context, Miller and Yamamori (2007: 4) also write: "Progressive Pentecostals . . . are attempting to build from the ground up an alternative social reality." See also Elisha 2011 and Engelke 2007.

5. See Stephenson's (2006) discussion of Soviet and post-Soviet attitudes about the immorality of homelessness. Homeless people are often officially labeled with moralizing terms such as "parasite" and "criminal," because they are presumed to violate social norms about proper residence and labor patterns.

3. PRACTICAL LOVE

1. For a related discussion within the framework of humanitarianism, see Redfield and Bornstein 2010.

2. See Muehlebach's (2012: 20–30) fascinating and insightful discussion of Adam Smith's ideas about fellow-feeling being lodged in the human breast and about the implied laissez-faire, self-activating, and autonomously regulatory qualities ascribed to compassion in the neoliberal world order.

3. Even in English, there are disagreements about whether the three terms sympathy, compassion, and empathy are coterminous or different. Those disa-greements extend to how and whether the Russian terms translate directly into

analogous English terms. I have chosen to use what is usually considered to be the more expansive and productive term "compassion" in this book and in my work more generally.

4. For accounts of walking, standing, and riding as social and even political experiences in Russia, see Caldwell 2009. Lemon's (2009) account of how public transport, especially riding the metro to the last stop, became a conduit for the flow of information and political activity during the 1991 putsch is especially fascinating. See also Richardson's (2008) ethnography of a walking club in Odessa and how members walk the city to map and experience its multiple histories.

5. See the Statement of Community as represented on the Sant'Egidio website, www.santegidio.org/pageID/2/langID/en/THE-COMMUNITY.html (last accessed 13 June 2016). Sant'Egidio's Moscow volunteers referenced these ideals in their conversations with me, even though most of the individuals I interviewed were not Catholic but were Anglican, Orthodox, and from other Protestant Christian groups.

6. This perspective of the need to recognize and celebrate human difference, as articulated by Paulina and others, is reminiscent of Amartya Sen's point in *Inequality Reexamined* (1995) that overcoming and eliminating differences does not, in fact, produce equality or justice.

4. DEVELOPING FAITH IN A MORE CIVIL SOCIETY

1. As Arturo Escobar (1995: 12) has observed, "development" does not necessarily address a set of obvious, "real" problems so much as it invents the very interests and needs (i.e., "problems") that are to be addressed (see also Mitchell 2002: 210).

2. See, for example, Creed and Wedel 1997; Field and Twigg 2000; Wedel 1998; White 1993. Neither Wedel's book (1998) on Western aid to Russia and Eastern Europe nor Field and Twigg's edited volume (2000) on the decay of social welfare systems in the post-Soviet period mention the work of religious organizations at all. Although White (1993) does mention religious groups briefly in her research on the emergence of charities in late-Soviet and early post-Soviet Russia, her focus is overwhelmingly on nonreligious groups.

3. This disavowal of the extensive role played by religiously affiliated assistance organizations is also in sharp contrast to accounts of development in other parts of the world that have invoked more inclusive notions of development that not only include both secular and religious organizations but also trouble presumed distinctions between them (Bornstein 2005; Elyachar 2005; Fountain, Bush, and Feener 2015; Rudnyckyj 2010). In their introduction to an edited volume on the relationship between religion and development in Asian contexts, Bush, Fountain, and Feener (2015) see the current interest among scholars, poli-

ticians, and development practitioners in the intersection between religion and development as having emerged only in the last ten years.

4. Although religious organizations were not the only programs to do this type of outreach, it is notable that they have typically coupled these projects explicitly with commentaries on social decline. In addition, while profit- and investment-focused economics and business trainings have been part of "spiritual economies" among Christian and non-Christian communities throughout the world, including in the former Soviet Union, they were not formal or visible components of the communities that I followed. For more on various permutations of the twinning of spiritual and economic profit-making, see also Lindquist 2005; Rudnyckyj 2010; Wanner 2007; Zigon 2011.

5. The multiple directionalities at work in the movement of persons, resources, and ideologies through transnational religious communities complicate the West-to-East political, economic, and moral trajectories that are instantiated in these dominant discourses (Creed and Wedel 1997; Verdery 2002; Wedel 1998; cf. Escobar 1995: 9), by presenting alternative versions of East-to-West, South-to-North, and internal modes of assistance and care (see also Caldwell 2015).

6. A related issue is that assertions that faith-based programs are not truly "development" organizations but are instead forms of charity or humanitarianism rest on a misunderstanding of the temporal dimensions of assistance. Notably, "charities" or "humanitarian" ventures are presumed to provide only short-term emergency assistance, a perspective that ignores the longer and deeper ethics and practices of benevolence and compassion that circulate throughout and sustain all assistance activities (Allahyari 2000; Poppendieck 1998). Moreover, the association of "charity" with "temporary" assistance belies the temporalities embedded in all forms of assistance that are contingent on the priorities of funders (see also Malkki 1995). As the cases in this book reveal, faith-based programs were able to evade the challenges of funders that were constantly changing their priorities.

7. Alison was a career diplomat whose political views were generally at the liberal end of the spectrum.

8. Sampson (1996: 129) reports that church-related organizations were deliberately excluded from the "development" category in Eastern Europe.

9. For additional anthropological analyses of the politics of development, see Ferguson 1994 and Fisher 2007.

10. See Phillips's (2008: 1) excellent discussion of what she calls "the politics of differentiation," especially in terms of how issues and participants in Ukraine have been variously defined and redefined through development processes.

11. For other accounts of this dizzying set of terms, see Abramson 1999; Aksartova 2009; Hemment 2004; Phillips 2008; Slocum 2009.

12. See, for example, Hemment 2007; Phillips 2008; Rivkin-Fish 2005; Urban 2010.

13. Analysts of post-Soviet development have similarly struggled to classify the work of religiously affiliated organizations, with most responses electing to qualify them as religious activities. Yet one of the inconvenient truths presented by religiously affiliated organizations is that they remind observers that even ostensibly secular and objective development organizations have their qualities of missionary zeal (Mandel 2012: 231; Salemink 2015: 41; Stirrat 2008: 232).

14. Russian Federation, Federal Law, No. 125-FZ of 26 September 1997, "On the Freedom of Conscience and Religious Associations [*O svobode soveste i o religioznykh ob'editneniiakh*]," at legistlationline.org/topics/country/7/topic/1 (last accessed 2 March 2012; site discontinued).

15. For cases in other parts of the formerly Soviet/socialist world, see Coles 2007; Hann 1996; Sampson 1996; Urban 2010; Wedel 1998.

16. For instances of these spatializing logics in a postsocialist context, see Phillips 2008: 20 and Wedel 1998.

17. For a treatment of the "Third Sector" among development programs oriented to women's issues in Russia, see Hemment 2004.

18. From a different perspective drawn from careful analysis of the political philosophies underlying different theories of "civil society," Urban (2010) makes a similar point and persuasively argues that Western models of civil society were based on a flawed notion of social capital that is not representative of Russian social life.

19. For similar accounts, see Abramson 1999; Coles 2007; Hemment 2007; Phillips 2008; Sampson 1996; Wedel 1998.

20. The information about AKDN provided at the roundtable was limited. For more detailed information about this organization and its projects, see their website at www.akdn.org (last accessed 13 June 2016).

5. LIVING A LIFE OF SERVICE

1. In using "civic religion" I am inspired by Bellah's (1967) notion of "civil religion" as derived from American political life and Rousseau's ideas about the "social contract."

2. Khodarkovsky (1996: 272) describes these processes of expansion and incorporation as "manifest religious destiny."

3. Religion's role as a conduit for state governance was solidified in the eighteenth century, when "the Synod officially became a part of the government" (Khodarkovsky 1996: 281–82).

4. In the seventeenth century, prior to the reign of Peter I, the church was concerned with the lack of charitable institutions to help those in need; yet even the church's call for more poorhouses was intended to put people to work (Kaiser 1998: 129).

5. Adriana Petryna (2002) has used the phrase "biological citizenship" to describe how Soviet authorities reduced civic identities to the essential biological qualities of individuals. Benefits were then distributed according to these biological qualities of citizenship.

6. The so-called *subbotniki* (Saturday) workers are perhaps the most familiar of these "voluntary" workers who engaged in construction, maintenance of community buildings, litter collection, public gardening, and other civic initiatives (see Shlapentokh 1989: 100–101).

7. As some observers have noted, the surge in charitable activity by religious groups at this time prompted Soviet citizens to compare the abilities of faith communities and the Communist Party to provide assistance. See Bourdeaux 1999: 189; Lindenmeyr 1998.

8. I have described elsewhere (Caldwell 2004) how elderly applicants to a Moscow food assistance program in the late 1990s attempted to convince social workers to enroll them by lifting up their clothes to show scars and other physical evidence that could be interpreted as proof of their difficult situations.

9. Russia's experience with political and economic migrants seeking status as "refugees" is similar in many ways with that of European countries, especially Greece, both in terms of the social and moral dimensions as well as with regard to the specific legal procedures and practices that asylum seekers, advocates, and officials must follow. For a detailed ethnographic study of asylum processes and assistance programs in Greece, see Cabot 2014.

10. See Hemment 2012 and 2015 for a thorough discussion and critique of Western models and perspectives on the inadequacies of Russian voluntarism practices, as well as the long history of voluntarism in Russia.

11. It is worth noting that even though this model of ethnic/religious identity positions the Russian Orthodox Church as the victim or object of imperial efforts by other religious communities, the church has long been an imperial agent of religious conversion within and beyond the borders of Russia.

12. Some of his colleagues, however, were not so confident about his ability to keep the two realms separate, as I learned in private conversations.

13. I am deliberately not identifying this person's position because the person was expressing a personal view that may not have been sanctioned by church officials, including this person's supervisors.

6. THE BUSINESS OF BEING KIND

1. For a fascinating account of the role of compassion commodities, both those sold for profit and those produced as gifts to circulate through global humanitarian networks, see Liisa Malkki's (2015) ethnography of the Finnish Red Cross,

especially the phenomenon of the legions of Finnish knitters who produced "aid bunnies."

2. Although in this particular essay (2004), Ahmed is focusing on the emotion of hate in order to make sense of discrimination, her larger points about the productive and generative work done by emotions is insightful for disentangling emotional activity from psychological states that are internal and unique to a particular individual. She effectively pushes emotions out of the individual and shows how they exist within social fields.

3. The generative nature of faith-based compassion economies is at odds with the paradoxical nature of development economies more generally. Within the logic of development, programs are successful when they put themselves out of business by solving the problems that they are meant to combat. Thus, there is a presumed endpoint. This is similar to the logics of humanitarian aid that is meant to solve an immediate problem and then turn to other problems, often elsewhere (e.g., Redfield 2013).

4. For a revealing case of a feud within the CCM soup kitchens in which a personal disagreement turned especially acrimonious when participants accused each other of practicing *blat*, see Caldwell (2004: 92–98).

5. Russian cultural practices of misrecognizing economic activities for moral reasons also extends to gift-giving more generally (Patico 2005) and how people touch, use, and circulate money (Lemon 1998).

6. This played on a double meaning of trust, whereby the cafeteria manager encouraged the church to place both their trust and their recipients in her care.

7. The need for emotional and social distance from volunteer "jobs" was especially tricky for clergy, who were in many ways always "on call" for emergencies. Individual clergy handled this differently: on rare occasions some were fully "on call," especially those individuals who occasionally provided a place to stay for recipients, while others were diligent about turning off their mobile phones and not checking e-mail or responding to requests during their free time.

8. Benjamin claimed that these "social entrepreneurs" were required to spend at least two-thirds of their revenues on this type of socially responsible "mission" work. Although I could not confirm this claim independently, it does provide insight into one model for an appropriate balance between revenue and charitable assistance.

7. THE DEFICITS OF GENEROSITY

1. Given the responses of the emcee to my refusals to play the game his way, it was clear that he was also puzzled. Although the fact that I was older than the other women, married, and not a longtime resident of Moscow (and Moscow's

expatriate community) sheltered me from some of the most lecherous behavior directed at the other women, it did not protect me entirely. What I discovered, however, was that I found kindred spirits among other professional women around my age who were just as disgusted as I was about the behavior of some men, which opened up fascinating conversations about gender and sexism among expatriate men.

2. See Redfield's (2013) account of Médecins Sans Frontières and their struggle to balance making strategic choices against the realities of not being able to help everyone who needs assistance (2013). These realities reveal the problems with activist stances that insist that everyone in need can and should always be assisted (e.g., Farmer 2003).

3. Oksana and Michele claimed that in the field of HIV / AIDS prevention and drug treatment, development programs deliberately encourage Orthodox, Christian, and Muslim congregations to work together, even though in some cases these collaborations take place informally and out of public view.

4. These views were expressed publicly by Metropolitan Hilarion in his address to the 2013 "Interfaith Dialogue," when he claimed the special role of the Russian Orthodox Church in fighting immoral behaviors such as homosexuality and other sexual improprieties.

5. Russian laws require foreign physicians to undergo a lengthy and detailed licensing process for certification. Few foreign physicians are able to pass the stringent requirements, thereby preventing most North American and West European physicians from practicing medicine outside either consultative services or in private clinics for foreigners. While I cannot comment on the licensing process, foreign physicians I have interviewed complain that the process is nonsensical given that West European and North American medical training is far more extensive and lengthy than that in Russia. To these individuals, the licensing process is merely a tactic to maintain an exclusively Russian medical system.

6. Heath Cabot (2014) describes similar occurrences among asylum seekers in Greece who stand in line but never avail themselves of services.

7. For more detailed discussion of the work and procedures of organizations that work with asylum seekers, especially the legal dimensions of these activities, see Cabot 2014.

8. By 2015, the CCM's NGO had developed formal procedures for assisting potential victims of human trafficking. Placed discreetly around their social services offices, on announcement boards, and in restrooms were notes with information about services and resources available to people who needed them, including instructions on how to ask for help privately.

9. One of the realities of the bureaucratization of the asylum vetting process is that there is a database of details that are used to determine a person's eligibility to be classified as a "refugee" and their suitability for resettlement. These criteria

are not absolute but change frequently, as global political circumstances change. As a result, details that might count in one moment might not in another. Recipients and assistance providers, then, are caught in the midst of this shifting field of criteria and requirements, constantly struggling to figure out how and when to evaluate the details presented to them.

References

Abramson, David M. 1999. "A Critical Look at NGOs and Civil Society as Means to an End in Uzbekistan." *Human Organization* 58(3): 240–50.

Adams, Vincanne. 2013. *Markets of Sorrow, Labors of Faith: New Orleans in the Wake of Katrina.* Durham, NC: Duke University Press.

Agadjanian, Alexander. 2001. "Revising Pandora's Gifts: Religious and National Identity in the Post-Soviet Societal Fabric." *Europe-Asia Studies* 53(3): 473–88.

Agamben, Giorgio. 1998. *Homo Sacer: Sovereign Power and Bare Life.* Translated by Daniel Heller-Roazen. Stanford, CA: Stanford University Press.

Ahmed, Sara. 2004. "Affective Economies." *Social Text* 22(2): 117–39.

Aksartova, Sada. 2009. "Promoting Civil Society or Diffusing NGOs? U.S. Donors in the Former Soviet Union." In *Globalization, Philanthropy, and Civil Society: Projecting Institutional Logics Abroad,* ed. David C. Hammack and Steven Heydemann, 160–91. Bloomington: Indiana University Press.

Allahyari, Rebecca Anne. 2000. *Visions of Charity: Volunteer Workers and Moral Community.* Berkeley: University of California Press.

Allison, Anne. 2013. *Precarious Japan.* Durham, NC: Duke University Press.

Amnesty International. 2015. "Russia Begins Blacklisting 'Undesirable' Organizations." July 28, 2015. www.amnesty.org/en/latest/news/2015/07/russia-begins-blacklisting-undesirable-organizations/ (last accessed 14 June 2016).

Anderson, Bridget. 2000. *Doing the Dirty Work? The Global Politics of Domestic Labor.* London: Zed Books.

Asad, Talal. 2003. *Formations of the Secular: Christianity, Islam, Modernity.* Stanford, CA: Stanford University Press.

Baggett, Jerome. 2000. *Habitat for Humanity: Building Private Homes, Building Public Religion.* Philadelphia: Temple University Press.

Bakker Kellogg, Sarah. 2015. "Ritual Sounds, Political Echoes: Vocal Agency and the Sensory Cultures of Secularism in the Dutch Syriac Diaspora." *American Ethnologist* 42(3): 431–45.

Bane, Mary Jo, and Lawrence M. Mead. 2003. *Lifting Up the Poor: A Dialogue on Religion, Poverty and Welfare Reform.* Washington, DC: Brookings Institution Press.

Bellah, Robert N. 1967. "Civil Religion in America." *Daedalus* 96(1): 1–21.

Benda-Beckmann, Franz v., and Keeba v. Benda-Beckmann. 2000. "Coping with Insecurity." In *Coping with Insecurity: An "Underall" Perspective on Social Security in the Third World,* ed. Franz von Benda-Beckmann, Keebet von Benda-Beckmann, and Hans Marks, 7–31. Indonesia Pustaka Pelajar; Netherlands: Focaal Foundation.

Berger, Peter. 2013. "The Challenge of Pluralism." Keynote Address, Interfaith Dialogue, "Multiple Traditions, Multiple Transitions, Multiple Modernities," Dialog-Europe-Russia, Vienna.

Berger, Peter, and Richard John Neuhaus. 1977. *To Empower People: The Role of Mediating Structures in Public Policy.* Washington, DC: American Enterprise Institute for Public Policy Research.

Berger, Peter, Grace Davie, and Effie Fokas. 2008. *Religious America, Secular Europe? A Theme and Variations.* Aldershot, Hampshire (UK): Ashgate.

Bernstein, Anya. 2013. "An Inadvertent Sacrifice: Body Politics and Sovereign Power in the Pussy Riot Affair." *Critical Inquiry* 40(1): 220–41.

Bornstein, Erica. 2012. *Disquieting Gifts: Humanitarianism in New Delhi.* Stanford, CA: Stanford University Press.

———. 2005. *The Spirit of Development: Protestant NGOs, Morality, and Economics in Zimbabwe.* Stanford, CA: Stanford University Press.

Bornstein, Erica, and Peter Redfield. 2010. *Forces of Compassion: Humanitarianism between Ethics and Politics.* Santa Fe, NM: School for Advanced Research Press.

Bosch, David J. 2001. *Transforming Mission: Paradigm Shifts in Theology of Mission.* Maryknoll, NY: Orbis Books.

Bourdeaux, Michael. 1999. "The Quality of Mercy: A Once-Only Opportunity." In *Proselytism and Orthodoxy in Russia: The New War for Souls,* ed. John Witte Jr. and Michael Bourdeaux, 185–96. Maryknoll, NY: Orbis Books.

Bourgois, Philippe, and Jeffrey Schonberg. 2009. *Righteous Dopefiend.* Berkeley: University of California Press.

Brown, Peter. 2005. "Remembering the Poor and the Aesthetics of Society."
Journal of Interdisciplinary History 35(3): 513–22.

Buckley, Cynthia, and Dennis Donahue. 2000. "Promises to Keep: Pension
Provision in the Russian Federation." In *Russia's Torn Safety Nets: Health
and Social Welfare during the Transition,* ed. Mark G. Field and Judyth L.
Twigg, 251–70. New York: St. Martin's Press.

Butler, Judith. N.d. "Precariousness and Grievability: When Is Life Grievable?"
Verso Books Blog. Posted November 16, 2015, www.versobooks.com/blogs
/2339-judith-butler-precariousness-and-grievability-when-is-life-grievable.

Cabot, Heath. 2014. *On the Doorstep of Europe: Asylum and Citizenship in
Greece.* Philadelphia: University of Pennsylvania Press.

———. N.d. "'Contagious Solidarity': Reconfiguring Care and Citizenship in
Greece's Social Clinics." Unpublished manuscript.

Caldwell, Melissa L. 2015. "Remaking the Russian State from the East: The
Role of Asian Christians as Civic Activists." In *Religion and the Politics of
Development,* ed. Philip Fountain, Robin Bush, and R. Michael Feener,
201–23. New York: Palgrave Macmillan.

———. 2011. "Assistance Migrants in Russia: Upsetting the Hierarchies of
Transitional Development." In *Global Connections and Emerging Inequalities
in Europe: Perspectives on Poverty and Transnational Migration,* ed.
Deema Kaneff and Frances Pine, 145–62. London: Anthem Press.

———. 2010. "The Russian Orthodox Church, the Provision of Social Welfare,
and Changing Ethics of Benevolence." In *Eastern Christianities in Anthropological Perspective: Eastern Christianities in Anthropological Perspective,*
ed. Chris Hann and Hermann Goltz, 329–50. Berkeley: University of
California Press.

———. 2009. "Moscow Encounters: Ethnography in a Global Urban Village." In
Urban Life: Readings in the Anthropology of the City, ed. George Gmelch,
Robert V. Kemper, and Walter P. Zenner, 55–71. Long Grove, IL: Waveland
Press.

———. 2008. "Social Welfare and Christian Welfare: Who Gets Saved in
Post-Soviet Russian Charity Work?" In *Religion, Morality, and Community
in Post-Soviet Societies,* ed. Catherine Wanner and Mark Steinberg, 179–214.
Washington, DC: Woodrow Wilson Center Press.

———. 2007. "Elder Care in the New Russia: The Changing Face of Compassionate
Social Security." *Focaal* 50: 66–85.

———. 2005. "A New Role for Religion in Russia's New Consumer Age: The
Case of Moscow." *Religion, State and Society* 33(1): 19–34.

———. 2004. *Not by Bread Alone: Social Support in the New Russia.* Berkeley:
University of California Press.

———. 2003. "Race and Social Relations: Crossing Borders in a Moscow Food
Aid Program." In *Social Networks in Movement: Time, Interaction, and*

Interethnic Spaces in Central Eastern Eurasia, ed. D. Torsello and M. Pappová, 255–73. Dunajská Streda, Slovakia: Lilium Aurum.

Cannell, Fenella. 2006. "Introduction: The Anthropology of Christianity." In *The Anthropology of Christianity,* ed. Fenella Cannell, 1–50. Durham, NC: Duke University Press.

Carse, Alisa L. 2005. "The Moral Contours of Empathy." *Ethical Theory and Moral Practice* 8(1/2): 169–95.

Caton, Steven C. 2006. "Coetzee, Agamben, and the Passion of Abu Ghraib." *American Anthropologist* 108(1): 114–23.

Chang, Hung-kuang, and Elizabeth Hsu. 2006. "Taiwan Makes Donation for Russians in Remote Areas." Central News Agency website, Taipei. Last accessed January 26, 2006.

Chaplin, Vsevolod. 2006. "Post-Soviet Countries: The Need for New Morals in Economy." *Ecumenical Review* 58(1): 99–101.

Chee, Sarah Eunkyung. 2015. "Borders of Belonging: Nationalism, North Korean Defectors, and the Spiritual Project for a Unified Korea." Unpublished PhD dissertation, University of California, Santa Cruz.

Clark, Candace. 1997. *Misery and Company: Sympathy in Everyday Life.* Chicago: University of Chicago Press.

Cnaan, Ram A., with Stephanie C. Boddie, Femida Handy, Gaynor Yancey, and Richard Schneider. 2002. *The Invisible Caring Hand: American Congregations and the Provision of Welfare.* New York: New York University Press.

Cnaan, Ram A., with Robert J. Wineburg and Stephanie C. Boddie. 1999. *The Newer Deal: Social Work and Religion in Partnership.* New York: Columbia University Press.

Coleman, Heather J. 2005. *Russian Baptists and Spiritual Revolution, 1905–1929.* Bloomington: Indiana University Press.

Coleman, Simon. 2006. "Materializing the Self: Words and Gifts in the Construction of Charismatic Protestant Identity." In *The Anthropology of Christianity,* ed. Fenella Cannell, 163–84. Durham, NC: Duke University Press.

Coles, Kimberley. 2007. *Democratic Designs: International Intervention and Electoral Practices in Postwar Bosnia-Herzegovina.* Ann Arbor: University of Michigan Press.

Comaroff, Jean, and John L. Comaroff, eds. 2001. *Millennial Capitalism and the Culture of Neoliberalism.* Durham, NC: Duke University Press.

———. 2000. "Millennial Capitalism: First Thoughts on a Second Coming." *Public Culture* 12(2): 291–343.

Constable, Nicole. 1997. *Maid to Order in Hong Kong: Stories of Filipina Workers.* Ithaca, NY: Cornell University Press.

Creed, Gerald W., and Janine R. Wedel. 1997. "Second Thoughts from the Second World: Interpreting Aid in Post-Communist Eastern Europe." *Human Organization* 56(3): 253–64.

De León, Jason. 2015. *The Land of Open Graves: Living and Dying on the Migrant Trail.* Berkeley: University of California Press.

Desjarlais, Robert. 1997. *Shelter Blues: Sanity and Selfhood among the Homeless.* Philadelphia: University of Pennsylvania Press.

Dinello, Natalia P. 1994. "Religious and National Identity of Russians." In *Politics and Religion in Central and Eastern Europe: Traditions and Transitions,* ed. William H. Swatos, Jr., 83–99. Westport, CT: Praeger.

Dionne, Jr., E. J., and Ming Hsu Chen. 2001. "When the Sacred Meets the Civic: An Introduction." In *Sacred Places, Civic Purposes: Should Government Help Faith-Based Charity,* ed. E. J. Dionne, Jr., and Ming Hsu Chen, 1–16. Washington, DC: Brookings Institution Press.

Douglas, Mary. 1990. "Foreword: No Free Gifts." In *The Gift: The Form and Reason for Exchange in Archaic Societies,* by Marcel Mauss, xii–xviii. Translated by W. D. Halls. London: Routledge.

Dumon, W. A. 1983. "Effects of Undocumented Migration for Individuals Concerned." *International Migration* 21(2): 218–99.

Dunn, Elizabeth Cullen. 2012. "The Chaos of Humanitarian Aid: Adhocracy in the Republic of Georgia." *Humanity* 3(1): 1–23.

EBRD (European Bank of Reconstruction and Development). 2004. "TAM /BAS Donors: Japan." www.ebird.com/apply/tambas/donors/japan.htm. Last accessed December 3, 2007.

EBRD (European Bank of Reconstruction and Development). 2007. "Japan Donor Information."

Elisha, Omri. 2011. *Moral Ambition: Mobilization and Social Outreach in Evangelical Megachurches.* Berkeley: University of California Press.

———. 2008. "Moral Ambitions of Grace: The Paradox of Compassion and Accountability in Evangelical Faith-Based Activism." *Cultural Anthropology* 23(1): 154–89.

Elliott, Mark, and Anita Deyneka. 1999. "Protestant Missionaries in the Former Soviet Union." In *Proselytism and Orthodoxy in Russia: The New War for Souls,* ed. John Witte Jr. and Michael Bourdeaux, 197–223. Maryknoll, NY: Orbis Books.

Elyachar, Julia. 2005. *Markets of Dispossession: NGOs, Economic Development, and the State in Cairo.* Durham, NC: Duke University Press.

Engelhardt, Jeffers. 2010. "The Acoustics and Geopolitics of Orthodox Practices in the Estonian-Russian Border Region." In *Eastern Christianities in Anthropological Perspective: Eastern Christianities in Anthropological Perspective,* ed. Chris Hann and Hermann Goltz, 101–23. Berkeley: University of California Press.

Engelke, Matthew. 2007. *A Problem of Presence: Beyond Scripture in an African Church*. Berkeley: University of California Press.

Escobar, Arturo. 1995. *Encountering Development: The Making and Unmaking of the Third World*. Princeton, NJ: Princeton University Press.

Farmer, Paul. 2003. *Pathologies of Power: Health, Human Rights, and the New War on the Poor*. Berkeley: University of California Press.

Fassin, Didier. 2012. *Humanitarian Reason: A Moral History of the Present*. Berkeley: University of California Press.

Fassin, Didier, and Richard Rechtman. 2009. *The Empire of Trauma: An Inquiry into the Condition of Victimhood*. Princeton, NJ: Princeton University Press.

Feldman, Ilana. 2007. "Difficult Distinctions: Refugee Law, Humanitarian Practice, and Political Identification in Gaza." *Cultural Anthropology* 22(1): 129–69.

Ferguson, James. 1994. *The Anti-Politics Machine: "Development," Depoliticization, and Bureaucratic Power in Lesotho*. Minneapolis: University of Minnesota Press.

Field, Mark G., and Judyth L. Twigg, eds. 2000. *Russia's Torn Safety Nets: Health and Social Welfare during the Transition*. New York: St. Martin's Press.

Fisher, William F. 1997. "Doing Good? The Politics and Antipolitics of NGO Practices." *Annual Review of Anthropology* 26: 439–64.

Fitzpatrick, Sheila. 1999. *Everyday Stalinism: Ordinary Life in Extraordinary Times, Soviet Russia in the 1930s*. New York: Oxford University Press.

Fountain, Philip, Robin Bush, and R. Michael Feener. 2015. "Religion and the Politics of Development." In *Religion and the Politics of Development*, ed. Philip Fountain, Robin Bush, and R. Michael Feener, 11–34. New York: Palgrave Macmillan.

———, eds. 2015. *Religion and the Politics of Development*. New York: Palgrave Macmillan.

Garcia, Angela. 2010. *The Pastoral Clinic: Addiction and Dispossession among the Rio Grande*. Berkeley: University of California Press.

Garrard, John, and Carol Garrard. 2008. *Russian Orthodoxy Resurgent: Faith and Power in the New Russia*. Princeton, NJ: Princeton University Press.

Gubi, Peter Madsen, ed. 2015. *Spiritual Accompaniment and Counselling: Journeying with Psyche and Soul*. London: Jessica Kingsley.

Habermas, Jürgen. 1987. *The Theory of Communicative Action*, vol. 2: *Lifeworld and System: A Critique of Functionalist Reason*. Translated by Thomas McCarthy. Boston: Beacon Press.

Halpern, Jodi. 2001. *From Detached Concern to Empathy: Humanizing Medical Practice*. Oxford: Oxford University Press.

Hann, Chris. 1996. "Introduction: Political Society and Civil Anthropology." In *Civil Society: Challenging Western Models*, ed. Chris Hann and Elizabeth Dunn, 1–26. London: Routledge.

Hann, Chris, and Hermann Goltz, eds. 2010. *Eastern Christianities in Anthropological Perspective.* Berkeley: University of California Press.

Hemment, Julie. 2015. *Youth Politics in Putin's Russia: Producing Patriots and Entrepreneurs.* Bloomington: Indiana University Press.

———. 2012. "Nashi, Youth Voluntarism, and Potemkin NGOs: Making Sense of Civil Society in Post-Soviet Russia." *Slavic Review* 71(2): 234–60.

———. 2007. *Empowering Women in Russia: Activism, Aid, and NGOs.* Bloomington: Indiana University Press.

———. 2004. "The Riddle of the Third Sector: Civil Society, International Aid, and NGOs in Russia." *Anthropological Quarterly* 77(2): 215–41.

Hochschild, Arlie Russell. 2000. "Global Care Chains and Emotional Surplus Value." In *On the Edge: Living with Global Capitalism,* ed. Will Hutton and Anthony Giddens, 130–46. London: Jonathan Cape.

———. 1983. *The Managed Heart: Commercialization of Human Feeling.* Berkeley: University of California Press.

Höjdestrand, Tova. 2009. *Needed by Nobody: Homelessness and Humanness in Post-Socialist Russia.* Ithaca, NY: Cornell University Press.

Hollan, Douglas. 2008. "Being There: On the Imaginative Aspects of Understanding Others and Being Understood." *Ethos* 36(4): 475–89.

Hollan, Douglas, and C. Jason Throop. 2008. "Whatever Happened to Empathy? Introduction." *Ethos* 36(4): 385–401.

Holmes, Seth M. 2013. *Fresh Fruit, Broken Bodies: Migrant Farmworkers in the United States.* Berkeley: University of California Press.

Hondagneu-Sotelo, Pierrette. 2008. *God's Heart Has No Borders: How Religious Activists Are Working for Immigrant Rights.* Berkeley: University of California Press.

Human Rights Watch. 2016. "Russia: Government against Rights Groups." June 10, 2016. www.hrw.org/russia-government-against-rights-groups-battle-chronicle (last accessed 14 June 2016).

Humphrey, Caroline. 1995. "Creating a Culture of Disillusionment: Consumption in Moscow, a Chronicle of Changing Times." In *Worlds Apart: Modernity through the Prism of the Local,* ed. Daniel Miller, 43–68. London: Routledge.

Jackson, Michael. 2012. *Between One and One Another.* Berkeley: University of California Press.

James, Erica Caple. 2010. *Democratic Insecurities: Violence, Trauma, and Intervention in Haiti.* Berkeley: University of California Press.

Jeavons, Thomas H. 1994. *When the Bottom Line Is Faithfulness: Management of Christian Service Organizations.* Bloomington: Indiana University Press.

Kaiser, Daniel H. 2004. "Testamentary Charity in Early Modern Russia: Trends and Motivations." *Journal of Modern History* 76: 1–28.

———. 2003. "'Whose Wife Will Be at the Resurrection? Marriage and Remarriage in Early Modern Russia." *Slavic Review* 62(2): 302–23.

———. 1998. "The Poor and Disabled in Early Eighteenth-Century Russian Towns." *Journal of Social History* 32(1): 125–55.

Kelly, Tobias. 2013. "A Life Less Miserable?" *HAU: Journal of Ethnographic Theory* 3(1): 213–16.

Kemp, Ross. N.d. "Ross Kemp on Gangs." Available at www.youtube.com /watch?v = LI4Q4RhvGNk (accessed 4 September 2008).

Kenworthy, Scott M. 2008. "To Save the World or to Renounce It: Modes of Moral Action in Russian Orthodoxy." In *Religion, Morality, and Community in Post-Soviet Societies,* ed. Catherine Wanner and Mark Steinberg, 21–54. Washington, DC: Woodrow Wilson Center Press.

Khodarkovsky, Michael. 1999. "Of Christianity, Enlightenment, and Colonialism: Russia in the North Caucasus, 1550–1800." *Journal of Modern History* 71(2): 394–430.

———. 1996. "'Not by Word Alone': Missionary Policies and Religious Conversion in Early Modern Russia." *Comparative Studies in Society and History* 38(2): 267–93.

Kivelson, Valerie. 2006. *Cartographies of Tsardom: The Land and Its Meanings in Seventeenth-Century Russia.* Ithaca, NY: Cornell University Press.

———. 1999. "'The Souls of the Righteous in a Bright Place': Landscape and Orthodoxy in Seventeenth-Century Russian Maps." *Russian Review* 58(1): 1–25.

Kleinman, Arthur. 1997. "'Everything that Really Matters': Social Suffering, Subjectivity, and the Remaking of Human Experience in a Disordering World." *Harvard Theological Review* 90(3): 315–35.

Knox, Zoe. 2008. "Religious Freedom in Russia: The Putin Years." In *Religion, Morality, and Community in Post-Soviet Societies,* ed. Mark D. Steinberg and Catherine Wanner, 281–314. Washington, DC: Woodrow Wilson Center Press; Bloomington: Indiana University Press.

———. 2005. *Russian Society and the Orthodox Church: Religion in Russia after Communism.* New York: RoutledgeCurzon.

Köllner, Tobias. 2013. *Practising without Belonging?: Entrepreneurship, Morality, and Religion in Contemporary Russia.* Halle, Germany: Max Planck Institute for Social Anthropology.

———. 2011. "Built with Gold or Tears? Moral Discourses on Church Construction and the Role of Entrepreneurial Donations." In *Multiple Moralities and Religions in Post-Soviet Russia,* ed. Jarrett Zigon, 191–213. New York: Berghahn Books.

Kornai, János. 2001. "The Borderline between the Spheres of Authority of the Citizen and the State: Recommendations for the Hungarian Health Reform." In *Reforming the State: Fiscal and Welfare Reform in Post-Socialist Countries,* ed. János Kornai, Stephan Haggard, and Robert R. Kaufman, 181–209. Cambridge: Cambridge University Press.

———. 1997. *Struggle and Hope: Essays on Stabilization and Reform in a Post-Socialist Economy.* Northhampton, MA: Edward Elgar.

Krainova, Natalya. 2009. "City Starts Razing Cherkizovsky." *Moscow Times,* August 19, no. 4213:3.

Kundera, Milan. 1984. *The Unbearable Lightness of Being.* Translated by Michael Henry Helm. New York: HarperCollins.

Ledeneva, Alena V. 1998. *Russia's Economy of Favours: Blat, Networking, and Informal Exchange.* Cambridge: Cambridge University Press.

Lemon, Alaina. 1998. "'Your Eyes Are Green Like Dollars': Counterfeit Cash, National Substance, and Currency Apartheid in 1990s Russia." *Cultural Anthropology* 13(1): 22–55.

Lindenmeyr, Adele. 1998. "From Repression to Revival: Philanthropy in Twentieth-Century Russia." In *Philanthropy in the World's Traditions,* ed. Warren F. Ilcham, Stanley N. Katz, and Edward L. Queen II, 310–31. Bloomington: Indiana University Press.

———. 1996. *Poverty Is Not a Vice: Charity, Society and the State in Imperial Russia.* Princeton, NJ: Princeton University Press.

———. 1993. "Public Life, Private Virtues: Women in Russian Charity, 1762–1914." *Signs* 1(3): 562–91.

———. 1986. "Charity and the Problem of Unemployment: Industrial Homes in Late Imperial Russia." *Russian Review* 45(1): 1–22.

Lindquist, Galina. 2006. *Conjuring Hope: Healing and Magic in Contemporary Russia.* New York: Berghahn Books.

Livshin, Alexander. 2006. "Russian Philanthropy Now Making a Difference." *East-West Church and Ministry Report* 14(4): 4–8.

Long, Susan Arpett. 2000. "Introduction." In *Caring for the Elderly in Japan and the US: Practices and Policies,* ed. Susan Arpett Long, 1–15. London: Routledge.

Luehrmann, Sonja. 2011. *Secularism Soviet Style: Teaching Atheism and Religion in a Volga Republic.* Bloomington: Indiana University Press.

Lutz, Catherine A. 1988. *Unnatural Emotions: Everyday Sentiments on a Micronesian Atoll and Their Challenge to Western Theory.* Chicago: University of Chicago Press.

Lyon-Callo, Vincent. 2004. *Inequality, Poverty, and Neoliberal Governance: Activist Ethnography in the Homeless Sheltering Industry.* Ontario: Broadview Press.

Malkki, Liisa. 2015. *The Need to Help: The Domestic Arts of International Humanitarianism.* Durham, NC: Duke University Press.

———. 1995. *Purity and Exile: Violence and National Cosmology among Hutu Refugees in Tanzania.* Chicago: University of Chicago Press.

Mandel, Ruth. 2012. "Introduction: Transition to Where? Developing Post-Soviet Space." *Slavic Review* 71(2): 223–33.

Marquardt, Alex, Bill Blakemore, and Ross Eichenholz. 2010. "Stray Dogs Master Complex Moscow Subway System." *ABC News*, March 19. http://abcnews.go.com/International/Technology/stray-dogs-master-complex-moscow-subway-system/story?id = 10145833 (last accessed 14 June 2016).

Mattingly, Cheryl. 2010. *The Paradox of Hope: Journeys through a Clinical Borderland*. Berkeley: University of California Press.

Mauss, Marcel. 1990. *The Gift: The Form and Reason for Exchange in Archaic Societies*. Translated by W. D. Halls. London: Routledge.

Metropolitan Hilarion of Volokolamsk. 2013. "Church, Society, and State in Russia: Ways of Cooperation." Keynote Address, Interfaith Dialogue, "Multiple Traditions, Multiple Transitions, Multiple Modernities," Dialog-Europe-Russia, Vienna.

Miller, Donald E., and Tetsunao Yamamori. 2007. *Global Pentecostalism: The New Face of Christian Social Engagement*. Berkeley: University of California Press.

Mitchell, Timothy. 2002. *Rule of Experts: Egypt, Techno-Politics, Modernity*. Berkeley: University of California Press.

Mitrokhin, Nikolai. 2004. *Russkaia Pravoslavnaia Tserkov': Sovremennoe Sostoianie i Aktual'nye Problemy*. Moscow: Novoe Literaturnoe Obozrenie.

Miyazaki, Hirokazu. 2006. "Economy of Dreams: Hope in Global Capitalism and Its Critiques." *Cultural Anthropology* 21(2): 147–72.

———. 2003. "The Temporalities of the Market." *American Anthropologist* 105(2): 255–65.

Moscow Protestant Chaplaincy. 2009. "Report on Racial Violence and Harassment." Moscow: Task Force on Racial Violence and Harassment.

Mosse, David. 2004. *Cultivating Development: An Ethnography of Aid Policy and Practice*. London: Pluto Press.

Muehlebach, Andrea. 2012. *The Moral Neoliberal: Welfare and Citizenship in Italy*. Chicago: University of Chicago Press.

Parry, Jonathan. 1986. "The Gift, the Indian Gift, and the 'Indian Gift.'" *Man*, New Series, 21(3): 453–73.

Patico, Jennifer. 2008. *Consumption and Social Change in a Post-Soviet Middle Class*. Stanford, CA: Stanford University Press.

———. 2005. "To Be Happy in a Mercedes: Tropes of Value and Ambivalent Visions of Marketization." *American Ethnologist* 32(3): 479–96.

Petryna, Adriana. 2002. *Life Exposed: Biological Citizens after Chernobyl*. Princeton, NJ: Princeton University Press.

Phillips, Sarah D. 2008. *Women's Social Activism in the New Ukraine: Development and the Politics of Differentiation*. Bloomington: Indiana University Press.

Poppendieck, Janet. 1998. *Sweet Charity? Emergency Food and the End of Entitlement*. New York: Penguin Books.

Powell, Leslie. 2002. "Western and Russian Environmental NGOs: A Greener Russia?" In *The Power and Limits of NGOs: A Critical Look at Building Democracy in Eastern Europe and Eurasia*, ed. Sarah E. Mendelson and John K. Glenn, 126–51. New York: Columbia University Press.

Putnam, Robert D. 2000. *Bowling Alone: The Collapse and Revival of American Community*. New York: Simon and Schuster.

Quist-Adade, Charles. 2005. "From Paternalism to Ethnocentrism: Images of Africa in Gorbachev's Russia." *Race and Class* 46(4): 79–89.

Rakhuba, Sergey. 2006. "Christian Aid in the Wake of Beslan Terrorism." *East-West Church and Ministry Report* 14(3): 4–8.

Ransel, David L. 2015. "'They Are Taking That Air from Us': Sale of Commonly Enjoyed Properties to Private Developers." In *Everyday Life in Russia Past and Present*, ed. Choi Chatterjee, David L. Ransel, Mary Cavender, and Karen Petrone, 140–60. Bloomington: Indiana University Press.

Read, Rosie, and Tatjana Thelen. 2007. "Social Security and Care after Socialism: Reconfigurations of Public and Private." *Focaal* 50: 3–18.

Redfield, Peter. 2013. *Life in Crisis: The Ethical Journey of Doctors without Borders*. Berkeley: University of California Press.

———. 2005. "Doctors, Borders, and Life in Crisis." *Cultural Anthropology* 20(3): 328–61.

Redfield, Peter, and Erica Bornstein. 2010. "An Introduction to the Anthropology of Humanitarianism." In *Forces of Compassion: Humanitarianism between Ethics and Politics*, ed. Erica Bornstein and Peter Redfield, 3–30. Santa Fe, NM: School for Advanced Research Press.

Ries, Nancy. 2002. "'Honest Bandits' and 'Warped People': Russian Narratives about Money, Corruption, and Political Decay." In *Ethnography in Unstable Places: Everyday Lives in Contexts of Dramatic Political Change*, ed. Carol J. Greenhouse, Elizabeth Mertz, and Kay B. Warren. Durham, NC: Duke University Press.

———. 1997. *Russian Talk: Culture and Conversation during Perestroika*. Ithaca, NY: Cornell University Press.

Rivkin-Fish, Michele. 2005. *Women's Health in Post-Soviet Russia: The Politics of Intervention*. Bloomington: Indiana University Press.

Robbins, Joel. 2013. "Beyond the Suffering Subject: Toward an Anthropology of the Good." *Journal of the Royal Anthropological Institute* (N.S.) 19: 447–62.

Rogers, Douglas. 2008. "Old Belief between 'Society' and 'Culture': Remaking Moral Communities and Inequalities on a Former State Farm." In *Religion, Morality, and Community in Post-Soviet Societies*, ed. Catherine Wanner and Mark Steinberg, 115–47. Washington, DC: Woodrow Wilson Center Press.

Rudnyckyj, Daromir. 2010. *Spiritual Economies: Islam, Globalization, and the Afterlife of Development.* Ithaca, NY: Cornell University Press.

Salemink, Oscar. 2015. "The Purification, Sacralisation, and Instrumentalisation of Development." In *Religion and the Politics of Development,* ed. Philip Fountain, Robin Bush, and R. Michael Feener, 35–60. New York: Palgrave Macmillan.

Sampson, Steven. 1996. "The Social Life of Projects: Importing Civil Society to Albania." In *Civil Society: Challenging Western Models,* ed. Chris Hann and Elizabeth Dunn, 121–42. London: Routledge.

Sen, Amartya. 1995. *Inequality Reexamined.* Cambridge, MA: Harvard University Press.

Shevchenko, Olga. 2008. *Crisis and the Everyday in Postsocialist Moscow.* Bloomington: Indiana University Press.

Shlapentokh, Vladimir. 2006. "Trust in Public Institutions in Russia: The Lowest in the World." *Communist and Post-Communist Studies* 39(2): 153–74.

Shott, Susan. 1979. "Emotion and Social Life: A Symbolic Interactionist Analysis." *American Journal of Sociology* 84: 1217–1334.

Slocum, John W. 2009. "Philanthropic Foundations in Russia: Western Projection and Local Legitimacy." In *Globalization, Philanthropy, and Civil Society: Projecting Institutional Logics Abroad,* ed. David C. Hammack and Steven Heydemann, 137–59. Bloomington: Indiana University Press.

Smart, Alan. 2001. "Unruly Places: Urban Governance and the Persistence of Illegality in Hong Kong's Urban Squatter Areas." *American Anthropologist* 103(1): 30–44.

Song, Jesook. 2006. "Historicization of Homeless Spaces: The Seoul Train Station Square and the House of Freedom." *Anthropological Quarterly* 79(2): 193–223.

Steinberg, Mark D., and Catherine Wanner, eds. 2008. *Religion, Morality, and Community in Post-Soviet Societies.* Washington, DC: Woodrow Wilson Center Press; Bloomington: Indiana University Press.

Stephenson, Svetlana. 2006. *Crossing the Line: Vagrancy, Homelessness and Social Displacement in Russia.* Aldershot, UK: Ashgate.

Takaki Richardson, Carla. 2014. "The Long After: Disaster and Information Politics in Post-Quake Kobe, Japan." Unpublished PhD dissertation, University of California, Santa Cruz.

Taylor, Charles. 2007. *A Secular Age.* Cambridge, MA: Belknap Press of Harvard University Press.

Throop, C. Jason. 2010. *Suffering and Sentiment: Exploring the Vicissitudes of Experience and Pain in Yap.* Berkeley: University of California Press.

———. 2008. "On the Problem of Empathy: The Case of Yap Federated States of Micronesia." *Ethos* 36(4): 402–26.

Ticktin, Miriam. 2011. *Casualties of Care: Immigration and the Politics of Humanitarianism in France.* Berkeley: University of California Press.

Tocheva, Detelina. 2011. "Crafting Ethics: The Practices of Almsgiving in Russian Orthodox Churches." *Anthropological Quarterly* 84(4): 1011–34.

Tomalin, Emma. 2015. "Gender, Development, and the 'De-Privatisation' of Religion: Reframing Feminism and Religion in Asia." In *Religion and the Politics of Development,* ed. Philip Fountain, Robin Bush, and R. Michael Feener, 61–82. New York: Palgrave Macmillan.

Turner, Victor. 1969. *The Ritual Process.* Chicago: Aldine.

Urban, Michael. 2010. *Cultures of Power in Post-Communist Russia: An Analysis of Elite Political Discourse.* Cambridge: Cambridge University Press.

Verdery, Katherine. 2002. "Whither Postsocialism?" In *Postsocialism: Ideals, Ideologies and Practices in Eurasia,* ed. C. M. Hann, 15–21. London: Routledge.

———. 1996. *What Was Socialism and What Comes Next?* Princeton, NJ: Princeton University Press.

Wanner, Catherine. 2007. *Communities of the Converted: Ukrainians and Global Evangelism.* Ithaca, NY: Cornell University Press.

Wanner, Catherine, and Mark D. Steinberg. 2008. "Introduction: Reclaiming the Sacred after Communism." In *Religion, Morality, and Community in Post-Soviet Societies,* ed. Mark D. Steinberg and Catherine Wanner, 1–20. Washington, DC: Woodrow Wilson Center Press; Bloomington: Indiana University Press.

Watson, James L. 1988. "The Structure of Chinese Funerary Rites: Elementary Forms, Ritual Sequence, and the Primary of Performance." In *Death Ritual in Late Imperial and Modern China,* ed. James L. Watson and Evelyn S. Rawski, 3–19. Berkeley: University of California Press.

Weber, Max. 1946. "The Social Psychology of the World Religions." In *From Max Weber: Essays in Sociology.* Edited and translated by H. H. Gerth and C. W. Mills. New York: Oxford University Press.

Wedel, Janine R. 1998. *Collision and Collusion: The Strange Case of Western Aid to Eastern Europe 1989–1998.* New York: St. Martin's Press.

White, Anne. 1993. "Charity, Self-Help and Politics in Russia, 1985–91." *Europe-Asia Studies* 45(5): 788.

Wilkinson, Cal. 2014. "Putting 'Traditional Values' into Practice: The Rise and Contestation of Anti-Homopropaganda Laws in Russia." *Journal of Human Rights* 13(3): 363–79.

Zigon, Jarrett. 2010. *HIV Is God's Blessing: Rehabilitating Morality in Neoliberal Russia.* Berkeley: University of California Press.

———. 2008. "Aleksandra Vladimirovna: Moral Narratives of a Russian Orthodox Woman." In *Religion, Morality, and Community in Post-Soviet Societies,* ed. Catherine Wanner and Mark Steinberg, 85–113. Washington, DC: Woodrow Wilson Center Press.

———. 2007. "Moral Breakdowns and the Ethical Demand: A Theoretical Framework for an Anthropology of Moralities." *Anthropological Theory* 7: 131–50.

Index

www.ingramcontent.com/pod-product-compliance
Lightning Source LLC
Chambersburg PA
CBHW030349270326
41926CB00009B/1025